Teaching and Researching Motivation

APPLIED LINGUISTICS IN ACTION

General Editors:

Christopher N. Candlin and David R. Hall

Books published in this series include:

Teaching and Researching Motivation

Zoltán Dörnyei   2001

An imprint of **Pearson Education**

Harlow, England · London · New York · Reading, Massachusetts · San Francisco
Toronto · Don Mills, Ontario · Sydney · Tokyo · Singapore · Hong Kong · Seoul
Taipei · Cape Town · Madrid · Mexico City · Amsterdam · Munich · Paris · Milan

Pearson Education Limited
Edinburgh Gate
Harlow
Essex CM20 2JE
England

and Associated Companies throughout the world

Visit us on the World Wide Web at:
www.pearsoneduc.com

First published 2001

ISBN 0-582-38238-6 PPR

British Library Cataloguing-in-Publication Data
A catalogue record for this book is available from the British Library

Library of Congress Cataloging-in-Publication Data
Dörnyei, Zoltan.
    Teaching and researching motivation / Zoltan Dörnyei.
        p.   cm. — (Applied linguistics in action)
    Includes bibliographical references and index.
    ISBN 0–582–38238–6
        1. Language and languages—Study and teaching.   2. Motivation in education.   I. Title.
    II. Series.

P53.48.D67   2000
370.15′4—dc21   00–033121

Set by 35 in 11/13pt Janson
Produced by
Printed in Malaysia, LSP

Contents

General Editors' Preface

Applied Linguistics in Action, as its name suggests, is a Series which focuses on the issues and challenges to practitioners and researchers in a range of fields in Applied Linguistics and provides readers and users with the tools they need to carry out their own practice-related research.

The books in the Series provide readers with clear, up-to-date, accessible and authoritative accounts of their chosen field within Applied Linguistics. Using the metaphor of a map of the landscape of the field, each book provides information on its main ideas and concepts, its scope, its competing issues, solved and unsolved questions. Armed with this authoritative but critical account, readers can explore for themselves a range of exemplary practical applications of research into these issues and questions, before taking up the challenge of undertaking their own research, guided by the detailed and explicit research guides provided. Finally, each book has a section which is concurrently on the Series *web site* www.booksites.net/alia and which provides a rich array of chosen resources, information sources, further reading and commentary, as well as a key to the principal concepts of the field.

Questions that the books in this innovative Series ask are those familiar to all practitioners and researchers, whether very experienced, or new to the fields of Applied Linguistics.

- What does research tell us, what doesn't it tell us, and what should it tell us about the field? What is its geography? How is the field mapped and landscaped?

- How has research been carried out and applied and what interesting research possibilities does practice raise? What are the issues we need to explore and explain?

- What are the key researchable topics that practitioners can undertake? How can the research be turned into practical action?
- Where are the important resources that practitioners and researchers need? Who has the informaton? How can it be accessed?

Each book in the Series has been carefully designed to be as accessible as possible, with built-in features to enable readers to find what they want quickly and to home in on the key issues and themes that concern them. The structure is to move from practice to theory and research, and back to practice, in a cycle of development of understanding of the field in question. Books in the Series will be usable for the individual reader but also can serve as a basis for course design, or seminar discussion.

Each of the authors of books in the Series is an acknowledged authority, able to bring broad knowledge and experience to engage practitioners and researchers in following up their own ideas, working with them to build further on their own experience.

Applied Linguistics in Action is an **in action** Series. Its _web site_ will keep you updated and regularly re-informed about the topics, fields and themes in which you are involved.

We hope that you will like and find useful the design, the content, and, above all, the support the books will give to your own practice and research!

Christopher N. Candlin & David R. Hall
General Editors

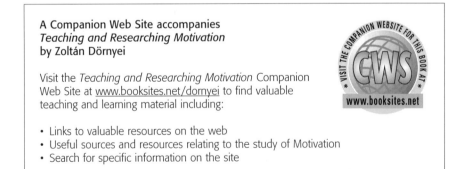

A Companion Web Site accompanies
Teaching and Researching Motivation
by Zoltán Dörnyei

Visit the *Teaching and Researching Motivation* Companion Web Site at www.booksites.net/dornyei to find valuable teaching and learning material including:

www.booksites.net

- Links to valuable resources on the web
- Useful sources and resources relating to the study of Motivation
- Search for specific information on the site

Author's Acknowledgements

Many friends and colleagues have had a strong impact on my thinking in the past. I am particularly grateful to:

- My wife, Sarah, who, besides being an invaluable source of feedback on my work for over a decade, has also taught me that one of the most motivating methods of learning English as a Second Language is to marry a native speaker!

- My PhD supervisor, Csaba Pléh, who introduced me to the topic of L2 motivation research on our second academic advisory session some 15 years ago, without knowing the extent of the influence this would have on the rest of my career.

- Marianne Celce-Murcia and Richard Clément who, throughout a decade of friendship and cooperation, have taught me much more than they may realise.

- Peter Skehan and all my other friends in the (ex-)Centre for Applied Linguistic Research at Thames Valley University, who have provided invaluable support during a difficult period of my life and who also demonstrated what an academic community can be at its best.

- Finally, Chris Candlin, who has been more than just an editor: he has launched me into the international publication scene in his *Methodology In Action* series with Prentice Hall (Dörnyei and Thurrell, 1992) and he – along with co-editor David Hall – promptly devised a new 'In Action' series, *Applied Linguistics in Action*, when I needed a forum for summarising my past work on L2 motivation! The thorough and insightful comments received have greatly enriched this book in terms of both its content and format.

Publisher's Acknowledgements

We are grateful to the following for permission to reproduce copyright material:

Figure 3.1.2 from 'A student's contributions to second language learning: Part II: Affective variables' by R C Gardner and P D MacIntyre in *Language Teaching* 26: 1–11 (1993), reproduced by permission of Cambridge University Press; Figure 3.7.1 from 'Effective motivational thinking: A cognitive theoretical approach to the study of language learning motivation' by E Ushioda, in Soler, E A and Espruz, V C (eds) *Current Issues in English Language Methodology*, 77–89 (1998), Universitat Jaume I, Castelló de la Plana, Spain, reproduced by permission of E Ushioda.

Introduction

We may not be aware of it, but <u>motivational issues</u> take up a <u>surprisingly</u> ✔ <u>large proportion of our everyday</u> talk.

- *In casual conversation*, when we <u>talk about likes</u> and <u>dislikes</u>, <u>interests</u> and <u>preferences</u>, <u>wishes</u> and <u>desires</u>, <u>goals</u> and <u>expectations</u>, we are in fact concerning ourselves with topics that researchers have long seen as being main motivational determinants of human behaviour.
- *At work*, when we complain about poor salaries, distressing colleagues, incompetent management, or, alternatively, when we are pleased by generous incentives, the recognition of our achievements and opportunities for promotion, we are addressing issues that are at the heart of the field of motivational psychology.
- The area of *second language education* is no exception in this respect. Here also we find that motivational concerns occupy much of our attention, for example, when we consider
  - how to encourage lazy students to work harder,
  - how to make language classes more inspiring,
  - how to supplement dull teaching materials,
  - what washback effects tests and exams have,
  - how different rewards and incentives work.

In short, the concept of motivation is very much part of our everyday personal and professional life and, indeed, few would ignore its importance in human affairs in general.

Given the vast relevance of motivation, we would expect it to be of primary concern for researchers interested in human achievement and learning. This is indeed the case: the study of motivation is a prominent area both in the fields of psychology and education. Given the long tradition of motivation research, we would also expect to find some well-established motivation models that have stood the test of time, along with some solid, theoretically sound educational recommendations to help to improve the effectiveness of our teaching. This, unfortunately, is *not* the case. In fact, the current state of motivation research could hardly be further from this expectation: contemporary motivational psychology is characterised by a confusing plethora of competing theories, with little consensus and much disagreement among researchers. In fact, we can say without much risk of exaggeration that 'motivation' is one of the most elusive concepts in the whole domain of the social sciences. This is, of course, no accident. Motivation theories attempt to explain nothing less than why people behave and think as they do, and human nature being as complex as it is, there are simply no cut and dried answers to be offered. In fact, the scope of theorising can be as broad as the differences among theoreticians in psychology.

Teaching and Researching Motivation is intended to achieve three purposes:

1. To provide a concise summary of the various theoretical positions and propositions in the field, outlining potential pitfalls and future directions.
2. To summarise the classroom applications and implications of the theoretical insights.
3. To describe the main approaches to conducting research on motivation to learn a second/foreign language (L2).

It is true that human behaviour is highly complex and therefore coming to grips with it is no easy task, but when we start understanding why and how we, and our L2 students, act as we do, this can be a most rewarding experience.

In accordance with the three main goals of the book, *Teaching and Researching Motivation* is made up of three main parts, accompanied by a fourth section which offers practical information and resources.

Section 1 sets the scene by providing the theoretical background and a summary of past research. It starts out by presenting six formidable challenges that have been the bane of many researchers' lives in the past. Following this, the section examines the most influential schools

> **Quote** Galloway, Rogers, Armstrong and Leo on the meaning of 'motivation'
>
> If motivation were a straightforward concept it would be uninteresting. The challenge is to find ways of conceptualising it which help teachers to understand children's progress and behaviour, thereby helping them to evaluate their classroom practice and teaching methods.
>
> Galloway et al. (1998: 42)

of motivational psychology and how they have responded to these challenges. After this general overview, the focus is narrowed down to the role of motivation in L2 learning and how our specific field has risen to the task of accounting for the role of motivation in second language acquisition. Fortunately, there is a lot to say in this section since L2 motivation research has traditionally been well developed and of high quality.

In Section II, instead of further pursuing the inquiries into the fundamental questions of human behaviour, the focus is on the practical knowledge that has been accumulated in past research. In an attempt to make the concept of motivation more education-friendly, the term 'motivation' is replaced more and more frequently by the form *motivating*, and abstract theories give way to concrete motivational strategies to be used in the classroom. This section is concluded by discussing two issues which, in spite of their great significance, have received very little attention either in mainstream psychology or L2 research:

- *Demotivation*, referring to those environmental stimuli and classroom events that cancel out even strong existing motivation in the students.
- *Teacher motivation*, that is, the nature of the teacher's own enthusiasm and commitment and the close links with student motivation.

Section III introduces a further angle, attempting to reshape the notion of motivation from an abstract and rather slippery concept into a concrete and *researchable* topic. This section will be particularly relevant to those who are planning their own motivation research projects. Motivation research can take various forms, ranging from small-scale classroom investigations to large-scale national surveys; it can aim at finding answers to practical questions, such as which tasks can generate more learner involvement, or it can seek to identify broad rules and tendencies with the intention of producing academic publications and dissertations. Different though they may be in their scope and purpose, all the various lines of enquiry share one thing in common: in order to find true answers to the questions posed, they need to observe certain research methodological guidelines. By summarising the main principles of research methodology that have been found particularly relevant to motivation research, I hope to help to maximise the validity of the answers arrived at in the various projects on L2 motivation.

Finally, Section IV is intended to serve as a practical reference section containing a collection of concrete resources and guidelines. It contains:

- a summary of the relevant areas of the social sciences which readers can turn to for further information and motivational insights;
- an overview of the place of motivation research within the field of applied linguistics and the ways in which it can be combined with linguistics-based approaches in an integrated manner;
- a list and brief description of the main journals and information databases that have been found useful in the past;
- a list of references to published motivation questionnaires and three sets of actual questionnaire items from studies in which the author has been involved.

What is motivation?

Chapter 1

Main challenges of motivation research

This chapter will...

- describe the complex meaning of the term 'motivation';
- discuss six main challenges of understanding human motivation.

The term 'motivation' presents a real mystery: people use it widely in a variety of everyday and professional contexts without the slightest hint of there being a problem with its meaning, and most of us would agree that it denotes something of high importance. Yet, when it comes to describing precisely what this important 'something' might be, opinions diversify at an alarming rate – researchers disagree strongly on virtually everything concerning the concept, and there are also some serious doubts whether 'motivation' is more than a rather obsolete umbrella term for a wide range of variables that have little to do with each other. In fact, according to Walker and Symons (1997), there was a point when the American Psychological Association considered replacing the word as a search term in the main psychological database, *Psychological Abstracts*, because, as a concept, it had too much meaning and therefore was not very useful. *interesting!*

What has prevented a consensus in motivation research in the past? In order to uncover the main currents which underlie and shape the field, let me present six main challenges that researchers have been confronted with. These are the challenges of

1. *consciousness vs unconsciousness* (i.e. distinguishing conscious vs unconscious influences on human behaviour);

oHP

> **Concept 1.1   The meaning of the term 'motivation'**
>
> Perhaps the only thing about motivation most researchers would <u>agree on</u> is that it, by definition, concerns the *direction* and *magnitude* of human behaviour, that is:
>
> - the *choice* of a particular action,
> - the *persistence* with it,
> - the *effort* expended on it.
>
> In other words, motivation is responsible for
>
> - *why* people decide to do something,
> - *how long* they are willing to sustain the activity,
> - *how hard* they are going to pursue it.

---

2. *cognition vs affect* (i.e. explaining in a unified framework both the cognitive and the affective/emotional influences on human behaviour);
3. *reduction vs comprehensiveness* (i.e. mapping the vast array of potential influences on human behaviour onto smaller, theoretically driven constructs);
4. *parallel multiplicity* (i.e. accounting for the interplay of multiple parallel influences on human behaviour);
5. *context* (i.e. explaining the interrelationship of the individual organism, the individual's immediate environment and the broader socio-cultural context);
6. *time* (i.e. accounting for the diachronic nature of motivation – that is, conceptualising a motivation construct with a prominent temporal axis).

Although an adequate theory of motivation ought to address all these issues, no psychological theory has even attempted to do so. There are, however, some important ongoing changes in this respect: as we will see in the next chapter, with the gradual decrease of the overpowering dominance of the cognitive approach in motivation research, a number of alternative perspectives have been put forward, and there is an increasing tendency to draw up more balanced and integrated constructs.

Quote 1.1 Dörnyei and Ottó's definition of L2 motivation   *def'd*

In a general sense, motivation can be defined as the dynamically changing cumulative arousal in a person that initiates, directs, coordinates, amplifies, terminates, and evaluates the cognitive and motor processes whereby initial wishes and desires are selected, prioritised, operationalised and (successfully or unsuccessfully) acted out.

Dörnyei and Ottó (1998: 65)

1.1 The challenge of consciousness vs unconsciousness

The first fundamental question about the nature of human motives we need to ask is *how conscious* – that is, being within the control of the individual – they are. Although most of the contemporary motivation literature takes it for granted that human behaviour can be explained by factors of which the individual is aware, it requires little justification that this is *not* always so. In fact, early theories of motivation were strongly influenced by Freud's (e.g. 1966) emphasis on deep, pervasive drives and instincts as being powerful directive influences on human behaviour. In a recent review of the conscious/unconscious issue, Sorrentino (1996) highlights the importance of non-conscious forces and argues that beha-viour *can* happen without reference to conscious thought, although conscious cognitions can inhibit or further instigate such behaviour and can also strengthen or weaken other competing action tendencies. We must add, furthermore, that humans do a lot of things as a matter of routine, and such relatively automated or habitual actions are often not under direct motivational control (e.g. most people do not make a conscious decision before, say, brushing their teeth in the morning).

On the other hand, it is also clear that many aspects of student beha-viour are quite logical and rational. This is particularly true if we consider learning behaviours in sustained learning processes, because, as Bandura (1991) concludes, most human behaviour is activated and regulated *over extended periods* by cognitive (anticipatory and self-reactive) mechanisms. Thus, along with other motivation researchers adopting a cognitive paradigm, I will take the view in this book that most of the significant   *D's view* thoughts and feelings that affect learning achievement in prolonged

Quote 1.2 Sorrentino on non-conscious motives

We have an incomplete picture of what determines information processing and performance if we do not look at both conscious and nonconscious forces as they interact with each other.... Evidence... leaves little room for those who believe that all behaviour must be preceded by conscious thought.... Clearly, much behaviour can occur without knowledge of the reasons for that behaviour. (p. 635)

Although nonconscious behaviour does indeed occur, conscious thought can also strengthen, weaken, or change the very nature of the behaviour. With that said, let me state clearly that conscious thought does not occur in a vacuum; it is often the product of nonconscious forces. It can also occur by association or by environmental cues. (p. 640)

Sorrentino (1996)

Quote 1.3 Weiner on consciousness

It is my belief that many (but not all) significant thoughts and feelings are conscious and are known by the actor... We may not be aware of psychological processes, or the 'how's' of psychology (how we learn, how we perceive, how we remember), but we often are aware of psycho-logical content, or the 'what's' of psychology (what we want, what we feel, for what reason we engage in an activity)... for the typical and preval-ent aspects of being – that is, considering how life is spent and what is reflected upon – direct access to the determinants of motivation and emotion is quite possible. For most of us at most times, a royal road to the unconscious is less valuable to the motivation researcher than the dirt road to consciousness.

Weiner (1986: 285)

educational situations are conscious and known by the learner. I do, however, acknowledge that this stance may 'suffer from a paucity of emotionality and a surfeit of rationality' (Berliner, 1989: 330).

1.2 The challenge of cognition vs affect

The current spirit in motivational psychology (and in psychology in general) is characterised by a *cognitive approach*. Motivation is no longer seen as a reflection of certain inner forces such as instincts, drives, emotional states, and psychical energy; nor is it viewed in strictly behavioural terms as a function of stimuli and reinforcement. Rather, current cognitive approaches place the focus on the individual's thoughts, beliefs, and interpretational processes that are transformed into action. At the same time, no researcher would question the fact that emotional experiences (e.g. anger, pride, gratitude, shame or anxiety) play a very important role in shaping human behaviour, and most comprehensive overviews of motivation recognise this influence. Yet, the two perspectives have been typically treated independently, separating emotional processes from cognitive or behaviouristic constructs, and the usual practice in textbooks on motivation has been to insert one chapter on emotions, often banished to the second half of the book.

Recently there have been several attempts to account for affect and cognition in unified frameworks (e.g. most notably in attribution theory; Weiner, 1986); indeed, as Ford (1992) summarises, the integration of emotional theories into the mainstream of motivational research is clearly one of the major priorities of motivational scholars. One interesting theory in this respect, put forward by John Schumann (1998), is directly related to language acquisition. In his recent book, *The Neurobiology of Affect in Language*, Schumann argues that second language acquisition is primarily emotionally driven and emotion underlies most, if not all, cognition (for more details, see 3.4). This view is in line with the main messages of two recent edited volumes on affect in second language learning by Arnold (1999) and Young (1999).

1.3   The challenge of reduction vs comprehensiveness

A striking feature of all mainstream motivation theories is their *lack of comprehensiveness*. They are typically anchored around a few selected motivational aspects (e.g. around a key concept or process), while largely ignoring research that follows different lines. This tendency is hardly surprising, given that the study of motivation concerns the immensely complex issue of human behaviour: because the number of potential determinants of human action is very extensive, a great deal of effort in motivation research has focused on drawing up *reductionist models*.

Concept 1.2   **Reductionist models of motivation**

Reductionist models of motivation reduce the multitude of potential determinants of human behaviour by identifying a relatively small number
of key variables to explain a significant proportion of the variance in
people's action. Thus, rather than being merely descriptive by listing
all the relevant motives, such constructs are theory-driven. With regard
to the specific behavioural domain they concern, reductionist models are
able to achieve increased precision in explaining the interrelationship
of the constituents, and the components can also be operationalised to
allow for the empirical testing of the model.

From this perspective, the main difference between various competing
theories lies in the selection of the principal factors to anchor the theory
around. This can be compared to lifting a large, loosely knitted net
(which symbolises human behaviour). If we lift it up by holding different
knots, very different shapes will emerge, even though the actual net
is exactly the same. The question, then, for motivational psychologists
has been to decide which knots to grab (i.e. which factors to assign a key
role in their theories) and how to lift the net up in order to obtain a
shape that makes most sense (i.e. what kind of relationships to specify
between the selected factors). Various motivation theories have proposed
different key 'knots' to be lifted, claiming that the selected central components subsume or mediate all the other main motives.

The other side of the coin is, however, that while the practice of mapping the multitude of motivational influences onto reductionist constructs
may be appropriate from a theory-building perspective, the only way to
do this effectively is by narrowing down the scope of behavioural events
the theory is concerned with to a fairly homogeneous set, which may be
insufficient to address complex, real-world problems effectively. So, while
a specific theory may be perfectly adequate to explain the motivational
basis of a certain, well-defined set of behaviours, it may be inappropriate
to account for the intricate motivational life of actual classrooms. To enable
us to describe student motivation with a precision that can be used as a
basis for practical measures, we need a detailed and most likely eclectic
model that represents multiple perspectives. Although some key motives
do stand out in terms of their general impact on learning behaviours,
there are many more motivational influences that are also fundamental in
the sense that their absence can cancel or significantly weaken any other
factors, whereas their active presence can boost student achievement.

> **Quote 1.4** Weiner on the complexity of student motivation
>
> A theory of student motivation ... will have to include many concepts and their interrelationships. Any theory based on a single concept, whether that concept is reinforcement, self-worth, optimal motivation, or something else, will be insufficient to deal with the complexity of classroom activities.
>
> Weiner (1984: 18)

1.4 The challenge of 'parallel multiplicity'

Even when a particular motivation theory is successful in explaining and predicting a specific course of action, the typical implication is that the actional process in question occurs in relative isolation, without any interference from other ongoing behaviours in which the actor is engaged. Regrettably, real life is in discordance with such neat theories because this assumption of isolated action is rarely valid in the strict sense. Although it is true that people pursue only a limited number of actions at a time, various action episodes can be simultaneously active. For example, a new action may be initiated while the success of the previous action is still being evaluated. This is particularly valid for classroom contexts where student motivation and achievement are the product of a complex set of interacting goals and intentions. Therefore, a central issue in analysing student motivation (and motivation in general) is to account for the interplay of the learners' *simultaneous focus on a number of different but interacting goals and activities*. I will refer to this issue as the challenge of 'parallel multiplicity'.

> **Quote 1.5** Ushioda on the interdependence of motivation to learn foreign languages and other subject matters
>
> Traditionally, researchers have tended to focus on language learning motivation in isolation. The literature has emphasised the distinctiveness of the motivation to learn a language by identifying the unique behavioural and psychological implications of acquiring a new set of habits, and of allowing 'elements of another culture into one's own lifespace'.
>
> Gardner (1979: 193)

But what has perhaps been overlooked in the process is the reality that the flesh-and-blood language student is often at the same time a student of mathematics or science or history, or has been a student of other disciplines in the past. As attested by the subjects in this introspective study, the language learner, unlike the researcher, seems unlikely to perceive the motivation for language learning to be wholly independent of the motivation (or lack of motivation) for other areas of learning. This relative perspective may be instrumental in helping to define or modify the developing goal structure of students' language learning motivation, as they weigh the potential pros and cons of making particular choices and pursuing different vocational directions.

Ushioda (1998: 83)

The main problem with the 'parallel multiplicity' perspective is that it further complicates the motivation field that has already been struggling with considerable challenges. Hardly any research has been done to examine how people deal with multiple actions and goals, how they prioritise between them and how the hierarchies of superordinate and subordinate goals are structured. Recently, Boekaerts has proposed a pioneering action hierarchy framework for studying the complexity of student motivation, but, as she concludes (1998: 21), such research is still in a rather preliminary stage.

Quote 1.6 Boekaerts on multiple goals in educational settings

Interdependent learning situations . . . require students to balance many goals and tasks simultaneously. In these social settings students may feel that they have to satisfy incongruent or even mutually exclusive goals, such as acquiring a new cognitive skill (mastery goal), coping with the threat of losing face (well-being goal), pleasing one's friends and pleasing the teacher (social goals). It should be noted that these two social goals may or may not be congruent. We know very little about how students determine goal priority and how they change their learning strategies and goal commitment in function of perceived goal conflict. We also know next to nothing about students' capacity to regulate divergent goals in terms of top-down and bottom-up goal processes (movement in their goal hierarchy) and about the tradeoffs that students make in terms of investing resources. Future research should address these issues.

Boekaerts (1998: 21)

1.5 The challenge of context

Motivational psychology has traditionally adopted an *individualistic* ✓ *perspective* (see Concept 1.3) in that it has typically concentrated on the individual in order to explain why the particular person behaves as he or she does. This makes intuitive sense since it is individuals who initiate actions and the immediate cause of human behaviour is indeed individual motivation. The problem with this position is that it is incomplete. Humans are social beings and human action is always embedded in a number of physical and psychological contexts, which considerably affect a person's cognition, behaviour and achievement (for a review, see Dörnyei, 2000).

Concept 1.3   **Two perspectives of the social world: individualistic and societal**

Psychologists looking at the relationship between the individual and the surrounding social world have typically adopted one of two perspectives: an *individualistic* or a *societal*.

1. In the *individualistic perspective*, the complexity of the social environment is only important inasmuch as it is reflected in the individual's mental processes and the resulting attitudes, beliefs and values; that is, this perspective views the social world through the individual's eyes. The individualistic perspective is most fully exploited in *social cognition theory*, which concerns how individuals process and store information about other people and how these mental processes affect their interaction with them.   *dy'd*

2. The *societal perspective* focuses on broad social processes and macro-contextual factors, such as sociocultural norms, intergroup relations, acculturation/assimilation processes and interethnic conflicts; from this perspective, the individual is usually seen as a reactive 'pawn' whose behaviour is determined by the more powerful forces at large. The most influential paradigm in this vein is *social identity theory* (cf. 3.6.1).

The tension between the two perspectives has been one of the most basic dilemmas in social psychology, dividing researchers into two starkly separated camps. (For a recent overview of the interrelationship of the two perspectives, see Abrams and Hogg, 1999.)

The individualistic perspective of motivational psychology does not lend itself easily to account for the contextual influences stemming from the sociocultural environment – hence the 'challenge of context'. Meeting this challenge requires more than simply adding a few situational factors to existing theories; rather, it necessitates the *combination* of the individualistic and the societal perspectives. We need to introduce sufficiently dynamic concepts that can bridge the gap between the two perspectives, while simultaneously doing both aspects justice. Attempts at achieving such a synthesis are discussed in 2.2 (focusing on general theories) and in 3.6 (looking at L2 acquisition specifically).

1.6 The challenge of time

The final challenge motivation researchers must face concerns *time*. Although most theories imply that motivation is a relatively stable emotional or mental state (measurable by tapping into it at one point of time, e.g. by administering a questionnaire), time is relevant to motivation constructs in at least two crucial areas (see Dörnyei, in press):

1. Motivation to do something usually evolves gradually, through a complex mental process that involves initial planning and goal setting, intention formation, task generation, action implementation, action control and outcome evaluation. These different subphases of the motivation process may be associated with different motives. Ignoring 'time' can (and often does) result in a situation when two theories are equally valid and yet contradict – simply because they refer to different *phases* of the motivation process.

2. When we talk about sustained, long-term activities, such as the mastering of a L2, motivation does not remain constant during the course of months or years. Rather, it is characterised by regular (re)appraisal and balancing of the various internal and external influences to which the individual is exposed. Even within a single course, most learners experience fluctuation in their enthusiasm/commitment, sometimes on a day-to-day basis. To account for the 'daily ebb and flow' of motivation, we need to develop a motivation construct that has a prominent temporal dimension.

Quote 1.7 Heckhausen on the sequential development of motivation

A big problem in the psychology of motivation is the manifold meanings carried by the concept motivation. Phenomena as dissimilar as wishes, decision making, and action are all associated with the concept of motivation. One possible approach to restricting this manifoldness is to try to separate the sequence of events involved in being motivated into 'natural', i.e. discrete phases. Curiously, this has rarely been consistently done.... Heckhausen and Kuhl (1985) divided the sequential development from the first stirrings of a wish to the formation of an intention to act into many hypothesised, discrete steps...

Heckhausen (1991: 175)

The challenge of time has been recently addressed by an increasing body of research in psychology (see 2.3), and some preliminary steps have also been taken in L2 research (see 3.7 and 3.8).

Chapter 2

Theories of motivation in psychology

This chapter will...

- describe the most influential motivation theories in motivational and social psychology;
- analyse how contemporary theories have responded to the challenges of context and time.

Contemporary motivational psychology appears to be in an exciting state of flux, with various multiple perspectives being increasingly recognised and pursued. In the following, I will present a selection of the most influential contemporary theories in motivational and social psychology. These theories focus on different aspects of the complexity of human motivation and cover a varying number of components, some of which overlap with each other while others are unique to a particular model. However, as Walker and Symons (1997: 16–17) summarise, when the leading theories on human motivation are viewed as a whole, five themes emerge. Human motivation is at its highest when people

- are competent
- have sufficient autonomy
- set worthwhile goals
- get feedback
- are affirmed by others.

> **Quote 2.1** Eccles, Wigfield and Schiefele on the state of the art of motivation research
>
> The view of motivation has changed dramatically over the last half of the 20th century, going from a biologically based drive perspective to a behavioural-mechanistic perspective, and then to a cognitive-mediational/constructivist perspective. The conception of the individual as a purposeful, goal-directed actor who must coordinate multiple goals and desires across multiple contexts within both short- and long-range time frames currently is prominent. As we approach the 21st century, the role of affect and less conscious processes is reemerging as a central theme. Complementing this more complex view of the psychology of motivation, researchers interested in the contextual influences on motivation are also adopting more complex and multicontextual frameworks.
>
> Eccles et al. (1998: 1074)

Of the six challenges listed in the previous chapter, one, the *challenge of consciousness vs unconsciousness*, has not been addressed by any mainstream contemporary motivation theory, and two further challenges, those of *cognition vs affect* and *parallel multiplicity*, have also largely been ignored. The majority of past research has been concerned with the *challenge of reduction*, that is, trying to distil a relatively small number of motivational factors that would subsume or mediate numerous other factors, thereby producing a theoretical (rather than descriptive) framework (2.1). Two particularly important new directions in motivation research are:

- the inclusion of *social motives* in the various research paradigms (in response to the *challenge of context*) (2.2),
- the examination of the *temporal dimension* of motivation (in response to the *challenge of time* (2.3).

2.1 Leading motivation theories in psychology

There are two focal research traditions investigating the causes of human behaviour in psychology:

- *motivational psychology*, which links behaviour to *motives* stemming from human mental processes;

- *social psychology*, which looks at action in the light of a broader social and interpersonal context, as reflected primarily by the individual's *attitudes*.

In the following I will summarise the most important paradigms in both traditions; we should note, however, that during the last few years the gap between social psychological and motivational psychological approaches to the understanding of human behaviour has decreased as a growing number of motivational studies have tried to incorporate a social dimension (see 2.2).

2.1.1   Expectancy-value theories

In motivational psychology the most influential conceptualisations during the last four decades have tended to adopt an *expectancy-value* framework, beginning with Atkinson's classic achievement motivation theory (see Concept 2.2) and subsequently further developed in various guises by a number of researchers (for a review, see Pintrich and Schunk, 1996; Wigfield, 1994). Underlying expectancy-value theories – similarly to most cognitive theories – is the belief that humans are innately active learners with an inborn curiosity and an urge to get to know their environment and meet challenges, and therefore the main issue in these value theories is not *what* motivates learners but rather what directs and shapes their inherent motivation.

How do these differ?

Concept 2.1   **Expectancy-value frameworks**

According to the main principles of expectancy-value theories, motivation to perform various tasks is the product of two key factors:

- the individual's *expectancy of success* in a given task,
- the *value* the individual attaches to success on that task.

The greater the perceived likelihood of goal-attainment and the greater the incentive value of the goal, the higher the degree of the individual's positive motivation. Conversely, it is unlikely that effort will be invested in a task if either factor is missing, that is, if the individual is convinced that he or she cannot succeed no matter how hard he or she tries, or if the task does not lead to valued outcomes.

Concept 2.2   **Achievement motivation and need for achievement**

Atkinson's achievement motivation theory (cf. Atkinson and Raynor, 1974) was the first comprehensive model of achievement motivation and dominated the field for decades. Although it is now considered to be an 'early' theory, its influence is still considerable and some of its components (e.g. 'need for achievement' and 'fear of failure') have been adopted by several contemporary models. The theory was formulated within an expectancy-value framework since achievement behaviours were seen by Atkinson to be determined by *expectancies of success* and *incentive values*. To these he also added two further components in his model:

1. *Need for achievement*: Individuals with a high need for achievement are interested in excellence for its own sake (rather than for the extrinsic rewards it can bring), tend to initiate achievement activities, work with heightened intensity at these tasks, and persist in the face of failure. This need becomes part of an individual's personality and affects the person's behaviour in every facet of life, including education.

2. *Fear of failure*: This is the opposite of need for achievement in that here the main drive to do well comes from avoiding a negative outcome rather than approaching a positive one.

Achievement motivation, then, was taken to be the sum of need for achievement, the probability of success and the incentive value of successful task fulfilment, minus the sum of fear of failure, the incentive to avoid failure and the probability of failure. That is, achievement-oriented behaviour was seen as the resultant of a conflict between approach and avoidance tendencies.

Expectancy of success

The 'expectancy' dimension of various theories is associated with the question of *Can I do this task?* Researchers have emphasised a number of different factors that determine the expectancy of success, and from an educational point of view the most important aspects include:

- processing one's past experiences (*attribution theory*),
- judging one's own abilities and competence (*self-efficacy theory*),
- attempting to maintain one's self-esteem (*self-worth theory*).

Attributional processes form one of the most important influences on the formation of people's expectancies, and their investigation was the dominant model in research on student motivation in the 1980s.

Attribution theory, associated with the work of Bernard Weiner (e.g. 1992), is based on the assumptions that people try to understand the causal determinants of their past successes and failures and the different types of causal attributions affect behaviour differently.

Concept 2.3   The main principle of attribution theory

The main principle of attribution theory is that the causal attributions one makes of past successes and failures (i.e. inferences about why certain outcomes have occurred) have consequences on future achievement strivings. As Graham (1994) summarises, the most common attributions in school environments are those to

- ability
- effort
- task difficulty
- luck
- mood
- family background
- help or hindrance from others.

Among these, *ability* and *effort* have been identified as the most dominant perceived causes in the western culture. Past failure that is ascribed to stable and uncontrollable factors such as low ability (e.g. 'I failed because I am too stupid') hinders future achievement behaviour more than failure that is ascribed to unstable and controllable factors (i.e. ones that the learner can change, such as effort; e.g. 'I didn't pass the test because I hadn't prepared enough for it').

Self-efficacy theory refers to people's judgement of their capabilities to carry out certain specific tasks and, accordingly, their sense of efficacy will determine their choice of the activities attempted, along with the level of their aspirations, the amount of effort exerted and the persistence displayed. Bandura (1993) proposes that self-efficacy is determined by four factors:

- *previous performance*
- *vicarious learning* (i.e. learning through observing models)
- *verbal encouragement by others*
- *one's physiological reactions* (e.g. anxiety).

People with a low sense of self-efficacy in a given domain perceive difficult tasks as personal threats; they dwell on their own personal deficiencies and the obstacles they encounter rather than concentrate on how to perform the task successfully. Consequently, they easily lose faith in their capabilities and are likely to give up. In contrast, a strong sense of self-efficacy enhances people's achievement behaviour by helping them to approach threatening situations with confidence, to maintain a task- rather than self-diagnostic focus during task involvement, and to heighten and sustain effort in the face of failure. It is important to note that self-efficacy beliefs are only indirectly related to actual competence and abilities because they are the product of a complex process of self-persuasion that is based on cognitive processing of diverse sources (e.g. other people's opinions, feedback, evaluation, encouragement or reinforcement; past experiences and training; observing peers; information about appropriate task strategies).

> **Quote 2.2** Bandura on self-efficacy beliefs
>
> People make causal contributions to their own functioning through mechanisms of personal agency. Among the mechanisms of agency, none is more central or pervasive than people's beliefs about their capabilities to exercise control over their own level of functioning and over events that affect their lives. Efficacy beliefs influence how people feel, think, motivate themselves, and behave.
>
> Bandura (1993: 118)

According to Covington's (1992) *self-worth theory*, people are highly motivated to maintain a fundamental sense of personal value and worth, especially in the face of competition, failure and negative feedback. This basic need for self-worth generates a number of unique patterns of motivational beliefs and face-saving behaviours in school settings, particularly when potential poor performance imposes a threat to the student's self-esteem. In such situations students may actually stand to gain by not trying, that is, by deliberately withholding effort, because this would allow failure to be attributed to lack of effort rather than to low ability. An example of this is when a learner spends insufficient time preparing for a test so that in the case of failure he or she can use the lack of sufficient striving as a mitigating excuse for poor performance, rather than have to admit a lack of competence, which would be far more damaging for the student's self-concept.

> **Quote 2.3** Covington on the importance of self-worth in schools
>
> Self-worth theory assumes that the search for self-acceptance is the highest human priority, and that in schools self-acceptance comes to depend on one's ability to achieve competitively. In our society there is a pervasive tendency to equate accomplishment with human value, or put simply, individuals are thought to be only as worthy as their achievements. Because of this, it is understandable that students often confuse ability with worth. For those students who are already insecure, tying a sense of worth to ability is a risky step because schools can threaten their belief in their ability. This is true because schools typically provide insufficient rewards for all students to strive for success. Instead, too many children must struggle to avoid failure. . . . In essence, then, self-worth theory holds that school achievement is best understood in terms of attempts by students to maintain a positive self-image of competency, particularly when risking competitive failure.
>
> Covington (1992: 74)

Value

Although expectancy theories provide powerful explanations of individuals' performance in different achievement situations, they do not systematically address another motivational question: *Does the individual want to do the task?* This is where the second component of expectancy-value theories, *value* (also labelled as 'valence', 'incentive value', 'attainment value', 'task value' and 'achievement task value' by various researchers) enters the picture. As Eccles and Wigfield (1995) point out, until recently most theorists using the expectancy-value model have focused on the expectancy component, while paying little attention to defining or measuring the value component. In an attempt to fill this·hiatus, Eccles and Wigfield developed a comprehensive model of task values, defining them in terms of four components (see also Brophy, 1999, for a recent, education-specific discussion):

- *attainment value*, that is, the personal importance of mastering a skill and doing well on a task;
- *intrinsic value*, that is, interest in or aesthetic appreciation of the subject/skills in question, and enjoyment coming from performing the activity;

3 • *extrinsic utility value*, that is, awareness of how well a task relates to current and future goals and what role learning plays in improving the quality of one's life or making one a better person;

4 • *cost*, that is, the negative value component, including factors such as expended effort and time, other actions that the planned action would exclude, and various emotional costs such as anxiety and fear of failure.

The overall achievement value of a task is made up of the interplay of these four components, and this value is believed to determine the strength or intensity of the behaviour.

2.1.2   Goal theories

A great deal of early research on general human motivation focused on basic human *needs*, the most important such paradigm being humanistic psychologist Maslow's (1970) need hierarchy, which distinguished five classes of needs:

- physiological
- safety
- love
- esteem
- self-actualisation.

Q: How do 'needs' & 'goals' differ? Do they differ?

In current research the concept of a 'need' has been replaced by the more specific construct of a *goal*, which is seen as the 'engine' to fire the action and provide the direction in which to act. Accordingly, in goal theories the cognitive perceptions of goal properties are seen as the basis of motivational processes. During the past decade two goal theories have become particularly influential:

(1) • *goal-setting theory*,
(2) • *goal-orientation theory*.

Goal-setting theory

Locke and Latham's (1990) *goal-setting theory* asserts that human action is caused by purpose, and, for action to take place, goals have to be set and pursued by choice. There are three particularly important areas where goals may differ; that is, in the degree of their *specificity*, *difficulty* and *goal commitment*.

Goal-setting theory is compatible with expectancy-value theories (2.1.1) in that commitment is seen to be enhanced when people believe that achieving the goal is possible (cf. expectancy) and important (cf. task values). Locke (1996) summarises the main findings of past research under five points:

1. The more difficult the goal, the greater the achievement.

2. The more specific or explicit the goal, the more precisely performance is regulated.

3. Goals that are both specific and difficult lead to the highest performance.

4. Commitment to goals is most critical when goals are specific and difficult (i.e. when goals are easy or vague it is not hard to get commitment because it does not require much dedication to reach easy goals, and vague goals can be easily redefined to accommodate low performance).

5. High commitment to goals is attained when (a) the individual is convinced that the goal is important; and (b) the individual is convinced that the goal is attainable (or that, at least, progress can be made towards it).

Concept 2.4   **How do goals affect performance?**

There are four mechanisms by which goals affect performance:

1. They direct attention and effort towards goal-relevant activities at the expense of actions that are not relevant.

2. They regulate effort expenditure in that people adjust their effort to the difficulty level required by the task.

3. They encourage persistence until the goal is accomplished.

4. They promote the search for relevant action plans or task strategies.

It is also important to note that goals are not only outcomes to shoot for but also standards by which to evaluate one's performance providing a definition of success. Thus, in the case of long-lasting, continuous activities such as language learning where there is only a rather distal goal of task completion (i.e. mastering the L2), the setting of *proximal subgoals* (e.g. taking tests, passing exams, satisfying learning contracts) may have a powerful motivating function in that they mark progress and provide immediate incentive and feedback. Attainable subgoals can also serve as an important vehicle in the development of the students' self-efficacy.

Goal-orientation theory

Goal-orientation theory was specifically developed to explain children's learning and performance in school settings. Currently it is probably the most active area of research on student motivation in classrooms (Pintrich and Schunk, 1996). As Ames (1992) summarises, the theory highlights two contrasting achievement goal constructs, or orientations, that students can adopt towards their academic work:

- *mastery orientation*, involving the pursuit of 'mastery goals' (also labelled as 'task-involvement goals' or 'learning goals') with the focus on learning the content;
- *performance orientation*, involving the pursuit of 'performance goals' (or 'ego-involvement goals') with the focus on demonstrating ability, getting good grades, or outdoing other students.

Thus, mastery and performance goals represent different success criteria and different reasons for engaging in achievement activity. Central to a mastery goal is the belief that effort will lead to success and the emphasis is on one's own improvement and growth. In contrast, a performance orientation views learning merely as a way to achieve a goal and the accompanying public recognition. Ames argues that mastery goals are superior to performance goals in that they are associated with a preference for challenging work, an intrinsic interest in learning activities and positive attitudes towards learning.

2.1.3 Self-determination theory

One of the most general and well-known distinctions in motivation theories is that of *intrinsic* versus *extrinsic motivation* – as Vallerand (1997) reports, the paradigm has been explored in over 800 publications to date. The first type of motivation deals with behaviour performed for its own sake in order to experience pleasure and satisfaction, such as the joy of doing a particular activity or satisfying one's curiosity. The second involves performing a behaviour as a means to an end, that is, to receive some extrinsic reward (e.g. good grades) or to avoid punishment. The theory also mentions a third type of motivation, *amotivation*, which refers to the lack of any regulation, whether extrinsic or intrinsic, characterised by a 'there is no point . . .' feeling.

Although intrinsic motivation has typically been seen as a unidimensional construct, Vallerand and his colleagues (see Vallerand, 1997) have recently posited the existence of three subtypes of intrinsic motivation

- to *learn* (engaging in an activity for the pleasure and satisfaction of understanding something new, satisfying one's curiosity and exploring the world);

- *towards achievement* (engaging in an activity for the satisfaction of surpassing oneself, coping with challenges and accomplishing or creating something);

- to *experience stimulation* (engaging in an activity to experience pleasant sensations).

Extrinsic motivation has traditionally been seen as something that can undermine intrinsic motivation: several studies have confirmed that students will lose their natural intrinsic interest in an activity if they have to do it to meet some extrinsic requirement (as is often the case with compulsory reading at school). Other studies, however, did not find the expected negative relationship between the two types of regulation, which has led Deci and Ryan (1985) to replace the intrinsic/extrinsic dichotomy with a more elaborate construct following the main principles of what the authors called *self-determination theory*. According to this, various types of regulations exist and these can be placed on a continuum between self-determined (intrinsic) and controlled (extrinsic) forms of motivation, depending on how 'internalised' they are (i.e. how much the regulation has been transferred from outside to inside the individual). As Deci and Ryan argue, if they are sufficiently self-

---

Concept 2.5   **Four types of extrinsic motivation**

1. *External regulation* refers to the least self-determined form of extrinsic motivation, coming entirely from external sources such as rewards or threats (e.g. teacher's praise or parental confrontation).

2. *Introjected regulation* involves externally imposed rules that the student accepts as norms to be followed in order not to feel guilty (e.g. rules against playing truant).

3. *Identified regulation* occurs when the person engages in an activity because he or she highly values and identifies with the behaviour, and sees its usefulness (e.g. learning a language which is necessary to pursue one's hobbies or interests).

4. *Integrated regulation* is the most developmentally advanced form of extrinsic motivation, involving choiceful behaviour that is fully assimilated with the individual's other values, needs and identity (learning English because its proficiency is part of an educated cosmopolitan culture one has adopted).

determined and internalised, extrinsic rewards can be combined with, or can even lead to, intrinsic motivation.

Finally, Deci and Ryan (1985) report on consistent findings that people will be more self-determined in performing a particular behaviour to the extent they have the opportunity to experience

- *autonomy* (i.e. experiencing oneself as the origin of one's behaviour),
- *competence* (i.e. feeling efficacious and having a sense of accomplishment),
- *relatedness* (i.e. feeling close to and connected to other individuals).

Deci and Ryan see these as fundamental human needs that individuals seek to satisfy.

2.1.4   Social psychological theories

In social psychology a key tenet is the assumption that *attitudes* exert a *directive influence* on behaviour since someone's attitude towards a target influences the overall pattern of the person's responses to the target. Two theories in particular detailing how this process takes place have become well known.

1. *The theory of reasoned action* (Ajzen and Fishbein, 1980). The chief determinant of action is a person's *intention* to perform the particular behaviour, which is a function of two basic factors:
   - 'attitude towards the behaviour',
   - 'subjective norm' (referring to the person's perception of the social pressures put on him/her to perform the behaviour in question).

   If there is a conflict between the two determinants, the relative importance of attitudinal and normative considerations determine the final intention.

2. *The theory of planned behaviour* (Ajzen, 1988). This is an extension of the theory of reasoned action by the addition of a further modifying component, *perceived behavioural control*. This refers to the perceived ease or difficulty of performing the behaviour (e.g. perceptions of required resources and potential impediments or obstacles). Behavioural performance can then be predicted from people's intentions to perform the behaviour in question and from their perceptions of control over the behaviour. In situations where a person has complete control over behaviour, intention alone is sufficient to explain action, as described by the theory of reasoned action. (For a review of empirical studies testing these models, see Ajzen, 1996; for a good critique, see Eagly and Chaiken, 1993.)

2.2 Sociocultural and contextual influences on behaviour

Perhaps the most important new development in motivational psychology during the past decade has been an increasing emphasis placed on the study of motivation that stems from the sociocultural context rather than from the individual. Human action is always embedded in a number of physical and psychological settings of varying breadth and abstraction, and central to the current social shift in motivation research has been the growing recognition that all these environmental dimensions have a certain amount of influence on one's cognition, behaviour and achievement. Consequently, contemporary accounts of motivation and other related psychological constructs (such as identity, self-esteem, or self-efficacy) have increasingly abandoned the tacit assumption of environmental generalisability and included contextual factors as independent variables into the research paradigms; furthermore, there is a growing body of studies pursuing more situated approaches in which the focal issue is context per se (e.g. Hickey, 1997; Paris and Turner, 1994; Rueda and Dembo, 1995; for a review, see Dörnyei, 2000).

2.2.1 Social motivation

Weiner (1994) refers to the complex of motives that are directly linked to the individual's social environment as *social motivation*, emphasising the interpersonal nature of this type of motivation; examples offered by Urdan and Maehr (1995) include action associated with

- social welfare goals, such as becoming a productive member of society;
- social solidarity goals, such as trying to bring some degree of honour to one's family;
- social approval goals, such as doing well in school to gain the approval of peers or teachers.

Social motivation can be contrasted to *personal motivation*, which can be examined in the absence of significant others; it concerns issues such as

- fulfilling personal desires,
- gaining knowledge to satisfy one's curiosity or to become more educated,
- the impact of self-confidence and self-efficacy on one's achievement strivings.

Since most personal cognitions and emotions are – directly or indirectly – socially constructed, in many situations social and personal motivation are difficult to separate; yet, as Weiner argues, the contrast may be useful in highlighting two different priorities or aspects of interest in motivation research.

Quote 2.4 Weiner on 'social' versus 'personal' motivation

A fuzzy yet useful and conceptually reasonable distinction can be drawn between social and personal motivation. For example, how others react to the shy or the handicapped in school – with help, flight, aggression, etc. – illustrates what I mean by social motivation. On the other hand, how these stigmatised individuals react to and cope with their plights, exemplifies what I mean by personal motivation. Social motivation requires the psychological presence of another, and determines reactions to that person, dyad, or group.... personal motivation, by contrast, can be studied in the absence of significant others, as is usually the case in the analysis of achievement motivation.

Weiner (1994: 557)

How can we conceptualise social motivation and how can we incorporate it into the established constructs? One particularly fruitful approach to analysing the social dimension of motivation involves focusing on *social goals*. During the past decade, goal theoreticians such as Ford (1992) have been trying to integrate social components in their taxonomies by distinguishing

- *within-person goals* (concerning desired consequences within the individual, such as bodily sensations or understanding and knowledge),
- socially grounded *person-environment goals* (concerning desired consequences with respect to the relationship between people and their environments, such as power or responsibility).

Such conceptualisations suggest that social goals and corresponding social behaviours make an independent contribution to achievement outcomes, operating in tandem with task-related goals in a complementary manner (for reviews, see Urdan and Maehr, 1995; Wentzel, 1999).

Goal theory is not the only motivational framework that can accommodate social aspects. Several researchers working within an attribution theory paradigm (2.1.1) have also attempted to examine the social dimension of motivation by studying *social judgement* (i.e. when the perceiver is making causal inferences about others rather than about his or her own past successes and failures), thus involving an *inter*personal as opposed to the traditional *intra*personal attributional analysis (Weiner, 1994).

Finally, in a recent hierarchical model of extrinsic and intrinsic motivation, Vallerand (1997) has also included contextual and situational factors, affecting motivation through their impact on people's perceptions of competence, performance and relatedness. (For a summary of these basic human needs, see 2.1.3.) Social factors that facilitate such perceptions will lead individuals to re-engage in the activities in which these perceptions were experienced because such activities allow them to satisfy their psychological needs. Thus, these factors increase situational intrinsic motivation and self-determined forms of motivation.

2.2.2   Cultural aspects of motivation

In the foreword to a collection of studies focusing on the impact of cultural diversity and cross-cultural issues on motivation, Pintrich and Maehr (1995) point out that although early studies of motivation and achievement were concerned with sociocultural factors, throughout the years the research community's interest in the sociocultural origins of achievement has 'waxed and waned'. However, as they note, interest in this area has currently exhibited increased vigour, which is partly due to the fact that distinctive cultural and ethnolinguistic groups are increasingly present and constitute a salient feature in most societies.

The key tenet in motivation studies adopting a cross-cultural perspective is the widespread assumption, confirmed again and again in various milieux, that setting-specific sociocultural values mediate achievement cognition and behaviour. Sociocultural values can be conceived as normative beliefs about what is right or wrong in thought and action that are shared by most members of a given cultural or social group (Phalet and Lens, 1995). With regard to academic achievement, three particular aspects of such values have been found to be relevant (Chen and Stevenson, 1995):

- the value placed on education,
- cultural beliefs about learning,
- social support for academic pursuits from family and peers.

The best documented cross-cultural difference in value systems is the contrast between *individualism* and *collectivism* as cultural syndromes observed in western and oriental cultures respectively. This sociocultural contrast is manifested in every facet of achievement motivation and behaviour. Already the notion of 'achievement' carries a strikingly different meaning in the two types of culture: as Triandis (1995) summarises, achievement for individualists is individual achievement, and is often seen as a means for 'self-glory, fame, and immortality' (p. 20). For collectivists, achievement is group achievement, for the sake of the ingroup, or to show the superiority of the ingroup in relation to outgroups. Thus, goal attainment for individualists is associated with concepts such as pleasure, self-determination and self-fulfilment, whereas collectivists are motivated by their group (although see Littlewood, 1999, for a word of caution about the validity of such generalisations).

Quote 2.5 Triandis on achievement and motivation in collectivist and individualist cultures

Individualism and collectivism are cultural syndromes, that differentiate the main cultures of Europe and North America, north of the Rio Grande from the main cultures of Africa, Asia, and the Pacific Islands.... Individualists focus on the achievement of personal goals, by themselves, for the purpose of pleasure, autonomy, and self-realisation. Collectivists focus on the achievement of group goals, by the group, for the purpose of group well-being, relationships, togetherness, the common good, and collective utility.

Triandis (1995: 1)

2.2.3   Social motivation and the microcontext of learning

The macrocontextual influences discussed above work in combination with the effects of the learner's *microcontext* (i.e. the immediate learning environment). The study of student motivation is a particularly fertile ground for analysing social motivation, because for average school pupils, 'school' represents primarily a social arena and not the scene of academic work. They are there because they have to be there rather than because they want to perform tasks, and they are often more interested in issues such as love, personal image or social standing than the mastery of school subjects. Student motivation therefore lends itself to analysis from multiple perspectives with a strong social emphasis (for recent reviews, see Juvonen and Wentzel, 1996; Wentzel, 1999; Wigfield, Eccles and Rodriguez, 1998), and this social relevance was well demonstrated in one of the largest-scale empirical research projects on the sociocultural component of student motivation to date, conducted by McInerney and his colleagues (see McInerney et al., 1997), involving over 2,800 participants in five different cultural groups. The researchers administered a detailed questionnaire, and by using a variety of statistical procedures they distilled a final set of ten motivational factors representing a very good fit; it is remarkable that half of the emerging factors were socially determined:

- *competition* with peers;
- *power*, relating to positions of authority like group leadership;
- *affiliation* – that is, cooperation with peers;
- *social concern* – that is, caring for each other;
- *recognition* – that is, the desire to please the teacher and receive praise from friends, teachers and parents.

In the following, I will examine the four most important factors in the learning environment: the students' *parents, teachers, peer group* and *school*.

Parental influences

It may be easy to forget that the students' motivation to learn in school contexts is strongly affected by certain people who are *not* directly involved in the school scene: the students' *parents*. Educational psychologists have long recognised that various family characteristics and practices are linked with school achievement, and one of the central mediators between family and school is generally thought to be motivation (Gottfried et al., 1994). As Eccles et al. (1998) summarise, four parenting factors have been traditionally identified as significantly shaping student motivation:

- developmentally appropriate timing of achievement demands/pressure;
- high confidence in one's children's abilities;
- a supportive affective family climate;
- highly motivated role models.

In an attempt to separate parenting practices from their antecedents and their socialising consequences, recent psychological research has produced a more complex picture of parental influences. Eccles et al. (1998) present a summary construct of all the variables and associations that have been tested by past research, comprising six main components:

- parent, family and neighbourhood characteristics;
- child and sib characteristics;
- parents' general beliefs and behaviour;
- parents' child-specific beliefs;
- parent-specific behaviours;
- child outcomes.

Each of these components is broken down to further constituents, resulting in an intricate multivariate model with many established and assumed links.

The teachers' motivational influence

The teachers' role in shaping student motivation is just as complex as that of the parents. This is so because teachers also act as key figures, or authorities, who affect the motivational quality of the learning process by providing mentoring, guidance, nurturance, support and limit setting. The focus in research on the motivational impact of teachers has traditionally been on trying to distil the unique characteristics or traits that distinguished successful practitioners from unsuccessful ones. These 'trait approaches' have by and large proved inconclusive because motivational effectiveness appears to be determined by an interplay of several broad factors (related to the teacher's personality, enthusiasm, professional knowledge/skills and classroom managerial style), whose various combinations can be equally effective. However, one thing with which everybody would agree is that teachers are powerful *motivational socialisers*. Being the officially designated leaders within the classroom, they embody group conscience, symbolise the group's unity and identity, and serve as a model or a reference/standard. They also function as an 'emotional amplifier of the group whose appeals and example are critical for mobilising the group' (Jesuíno, 1996: 115). Simply speaking, to lead means to direct and energise, that is, to motivate.

A useful way of organising the multiple influences teachers have on student motivation is by separating four interrelated dimensions (for practical examples, see Chapter 5):

1. *The personal characteristics* of teachers (e.g. level of motivation/commitment, warmth, empathy, trustworthiness, competence, etc.), determining the rapport between teachers and students and largely responsible for the *affiliative motive*, which refers to the students' need to do well in school in order to please the teacher or other

superordinate figures (including their parents) (Ausubel et al., 1978). The impact of teacher characteristics on students' motivation will be discussed in 5.2.1 and 7.2.2 in detail.

2. *Teacher immediacy*, which is one aspect of teachers' classroom behaviour that has been found by instructional communication researchers to have a considerable effect on student motivation (for a review, see Christophel, 1990). *Immediacy* refers to the perceived physical and/or psychological closeness between people, and cumulative results from several studies indicate that teachers' verbal and non-verbal immediacy behaviours that reduce the distance between teacher and students (e.g. addressing students by name, using humour, moving around in class, including personal topics and examples) may impact levels of learning by modifying student classroom motivation.

[margin handwritten notes: dfy'd ; culturally bound?]*

3. *Active motivational socialising behaviour*, by which teachers can exert a direct and systematic motivational influence by means of *actively socialising* the learners' motivation through appropriate

   - *modelling* (setting an example both in terms of effort expenditure and orientations of interest in the subject);

   - *task presentations* (calling students' attention to the purpose of the activity they are going to do, its interest potential and practical value and the strategies that may be useful in achieving the task, thus raising students' interest, metacognitive awareness and expectation of success);

   - *feedback/reward system* (which communicates a clear message about their priorities, value preferences and attributional beliefs).

   Through these channels, teachers communicate their beliefs, expectations and attitudes, thereby pressing their students to adopt similar beliefs, attitudes, expectations and associated behaviours. (For reviews, see Brophy and Kher, 1986; Juvonen and Nishina, 1997; Pintrich and Schunk, 1996.)

4. *Classroom management*: Teachers are in almost total control of the running of the classroom, including setting and enforcing rules, establishing procedures and organising grouping activities. These in turn greatly influence the students' motivation – therefore, the teachers' *classroom management practices* constitute a fourth central motivational domain. It requires little justification that smoothly running and efficient classroom procedures enhance the learners' general well-being and sense of achievement and thus promote student motivation. It was found already over 60 years ago in Lewin

et al.'s (1939) classic study on leadership styles that a lack of order (associated with laissez-faire leadership) generates a great deal of stress and undermines student achievement. Two aspects of the managerial role are particularly important:

- *Setting and maintaining group norms.* As argued under 'group motivation' below, group norms are central determinants of student behaviour in classroom settings. Through their position as designated leaders, teachers have a special responsibility in setting up and maintaining these rules (for practical strategies, see 5.2.1 and 5.2.2). If the teacher does not pay enough attention to enforcement of the established norms, learners immediately receive a clear message that those rules are not really important, which will result in the rules rapidly being discounted and disobeyed.

- *The teacher's type of authority.* Providing order in itself may not be sufficient to generate motivation because student motivation is also a function of the teacher's *authority type*, that is, whether the teacher is *autonomy supporting* or *controlling*. Sharing responsibility with students, offering them options and choices, letting them have a say in establishing priorities, and involving them in the decision-making process enhance student self-determination and intrinsic motivation (Deci et al., 1991). I will come back to the issue of how to balance learner autonomy and classroom structure when discussing group motivation below. The differences between cooperatively, competitively and individualistically organised classrooms will also be treated there.

seems culturally bound?

Group motivation

A long-standing truism of educational psychology is that learners are individuals and must be treated as such if we expect to optimise their motivation and learning. As an abstract proposition, this statement is compelling but not entirely true. Swezey et al. (1994) argue convincingly that although most theories of motivation attempt to explain motivational processes at the individual level, action conducted within groups might show motivational characteristics which stem from the group as a social unit rather than from the individual members. For example, in many classrooms, a student's lack of motivation can be traced to a real or imagined fear of being isolated or rejected by peers and being labelled a 'brain', a 'nerd', a 'creep' or a 'swot'.

> **Quote 2.6** McCaslin and Good on group motivation in the classroom
>
> Student motivation and learning are typically conceptualised as individual variables; assessments locate their presence or absence within students. The inherently social nature of classroom learning challenges this notion of individualism, however. The need for student 'belongingness' or 'affiliation' has been articulated by educators for some time. The power of social identity construct in understanding both individual students and the types of relationships among them (e.g. norms and status perceptions that support complementary dominant/submissive relationships), however, is just beginning to be realised in classroom research and theoretical developments.
>
> McCaslin and Good (1996: 642)

In response to this recognition, a growing number of studies in social and educational psychology have recently looked into group-specific cognitive constructs, such as *group efficacy* and *group goals* (e.g. Little and Madigan, 1997; Silver and Bufanio, 1996; Stroebe et al., 1996; Weldon and Weingart, 1993). Other studies have looked at the impact of interpersonal processes on student behaviour within learner groups, typically emphasising the importance of the socionormative influences of *peer pressure*. In a comprehensive overview of the role of group dynamics in education, Ehrman and Dörnyei (1998) demonstrate that the motivational impact of peer relationships can be studied more meaningfully within a broader framework of group influences that incorporate the intricate interplay of three main factors:

- the group's *structure* (made up of four components: intermember relations, group norms, group roles and the status hierarchy within the group),
- the group's *developmental level* (i.e. the group's degree of maturity in terms of cohesiveness, independence/self-reliance and productivity),
- the teacher's *leadership style and behaviour*.

Although group-related motives have received increasing attention in the psychological literature, this line of research is still far from being exhausted. One particular area that lends itself to much further research is linking the vast literature of *group norms* (i.e. the overt and covert rules and social standards that govern behaviour in any community;

Concept 2.6   **Hersey and Blanchard's 'situational leadership' theory**

The complex relationship between social motives stemming from the microcontext on the one hand and educationally relevant outcomes on the other is well illustrated by Hersey and Blanchard's (1988) *situational leadership theory*. This states that effective leaders should adapt flexibly to different follower needs at different developmental stages of the group. When a group forms, immature members are most productive with a lot of external organisational input (e.g. coordinating actions, setting subtasks, proposing solutions, allocating resources). However, after the group has achieved more maturity and can work smoothly, the leader can gradually delegate more and more power to the students, thereby promoting autonomy and further group development. Thus, from this point of view, teacher control needs to be exerted according to the chronological, cognitive, emotional and subject-matter maturity of the learners, following a general progress in leadership style from *telling* to *selling*, *participating* and finally *delegating*.

see Dörnyei and Malderez, 1997, 1999; Webb and Palincsar, 1996) to the *individual member's motivation*, as both concepts denote directive influences on behaviour. In fact, norms can be seen as the group-level equivalents of individual-level motives.

Quote 2.7   **Ehrman and Dörnyei on group norms**

Norms are the rules that govern behaviour within any community, whether at the national culture level or within a small task group. They are sometimes overt (e.g. dress codes, rules of conduct), but more often they are implicit and covert (for example, expectations that newcomers discover only by violating them because group members take them for granted, such as avoiding certain taboo subjects). . . . Norms are a constant of classroom life. They specify acceptable behaviour in the class group and contribute to conditions assumed by the group and/or its leadership to be optimal for effective learning. Norms are the standards by which group members regulate their own behaviour to make task accomplishment possible. . . . Most important from an educational perspective, group norms – many of them implicit – regarding learning effort, efficiency and quality substantially enhance or decrease the students' academic goal striving, work morale and learning achievement.

Ehrman and Dörnyei (1998: 130–1)

It is also unclear at this stage how *group goals* relate to individual goals. Finally, *group cohesiveness* (i.e. the strength of intermember relations, or the 'magnetism' or 'glue' that holds the group together and maintains it as a system) has been well documented to lead to increased group productivity (cf. the meta-analyses by Evans and Dion, 1991; Gully et al., 1995; Mullen and Copper, 1994), but the motivational mediators responsible for this effect have not yet been specified in detail.

Concept 2.7   **Cooperative learning and motivation**

A prominent aspect of group motivation concerns the unique motivational setup of *cooperative learning*, which is a generic name for a number of related methods of organising classroom instruction in order to achieve common learning goals via cooperation. In a cooperatively organised classroom, students work in small groups in which each member shares responsibility for the outcome and is equally rewarded (which can be contrasted to a 'competitive' structure in which students work against each other and only the best ones are rewarded). In many ways, cooperative learning can also be seen as a philosophy that *maximises student collaboration*, and investigations have almost invariably proved that this approach is superior to most traditional forms of instruction in terms of producing learning gains and student achievement. Cooperative learning has been shown to generate a powerful *motivational system* to energise learning; for example, Sharan and Shaulov (1990) found in a large-scale study that more than half of the variance in student achievement in three academic subjects was caused by the 'motivation to learn' variable, which is a substantial impact rarely demonstrated in motivation studies in general. This strong motivational effect is the result of a number of different motives coming into force in cooperatively organised classrooms (see Dörnyei, 1997; Slavin, 1996), and it provides unambiguous evidence that if a number of individuals form a social unit by joining in a group, under certain conditions the motivational level associated with this collection of people can significantly exceed the motivational level the individuals would have demonstrated if they had remained independent.

School motivation

A recent development in the study of social motivation is the re-cognition that there is an additional psychological environmental level between the learners' microcontext (class group) and macrocontext (sociocultural milieu): the *school as a whole*. In a pioneering article,

Maehr and Midgley (1991) have argued that schools vary in their general climate and policies, for example in terms of:

- school-wide stress on accomplishment,
- general expectations regarding student potential,
- school-level authority and management structures,
- the teachers' sense of efficacy,
- grouping practices,
- evaluation practices,
- promoting ability tracking.

This variation influences the motivation of both teachers and students in a fundamental way. Anderman and Maehr (1994) report on a study which demonstrated that school effects seem to increase with grade level: whereas in the 4th grade these explained 7% of the variance in motivation, the figure grew to 21% when students reached the 10th grade.

Quote 2.8 Pintrich and Schunk on school motivation

A focus on schools as the unit of analysis has not been adopted by many psychologists interested in motivation, but there are a few exceptions (see Maehr and Midgley, 1991 ...). Psychologists, given their disciplinary traditions, have tended to focus on individuals and have been concerned with how individuals' motivational beliefs, perceptions, needs, goals, and so on can influence motivation and behaviour. . . . At the same time, as will become clear in this chapter, many of the psychological ideas regarding individual motivation are relevant to a school-level analysis. Nevertheless, a move to a discussion of school influences involves a shift from a more psychological perspective to a more sociological and cultural perspective.

Pintrich and Schunk (1996: 370)

2.3 The temporal dimension of motivation

It was argued in 1.6 that motivation is not a relatively constant state but rather a more dynamic entity that changes over time, with the level of effort invested in the pursuit of a particular goal oscillating between regular ups and downs. Therefore, an adequate theory of motivation needs to include a featured temporal dimension that accounts for systematic patterns of transformation and evolution in time (Dörnyei, in press). Although few researchers would question this claim, hardly any of the existing motivation theories contain temporal aspects and even the few constructs which do include certain time elements typically focus on broad issues such as past attributions or future goals, rather than detailing sequences or patterns of motivational events and components (cf. Husman and Lens, 1999; Karniol and Ross, 1996; Raynor and Roeder, 1987). One valuable exception to this generalisation has been offered by German psychologists Heinz Heckhausen and Julius Kuhl (e.g. Heckhausen, 1991; Heckhausen and Kuhl, 1985). Their theory of motivational processes, often referred to as *Action Control Theory*, introduces a 'temporal perspective that begins with the awakening of a person's wishes prior to goal setting and continues through the evaluative thoughts entertained after goal striving has ended' (Gollwitzer, 1990: 55).

Although Heckhausen and Kuhl's work touches upon a number of different aspects of motivational processing and do not add up to a fully-fledged process-oriented model, a central feature of the two scholars' approach is the distinction of separate, *temporally ordered phases* within the motivational process. The most important distinction is between the intention-formation process of the '*predecisional phase*' and the implementation process of the '*postdecisional phase*':

- *Predecisional phase*. This decision-making stage (or 'choice motivation') has been the main focus of most mainstream psychological theories of motivation in the past, with the analyses centring around complex *planning* and *goal-setting* processes during which initial wishes and desires are articulated and evaluated in terms of their desirability and chance of fulfilment.

- *Postdecisional phase*. This implementational/volitional stage (or 'executive motivation') involves motivational *maintenance* and *control* during the enactment of the intention. The key issues to be examined here are the phenomena of action initiation, perseverance, and overcoming various internal obstacles to action.

Building on the above principles, Kuhl (1987) developed a more detailed theory of action control. The key component of Kuhl's action control model is *intention*, which is defined as an 'activated plan to which the actor has committed herself or himself' (p. 282). In order for action to take place, two memory systems need to be activated at the same time:

> **Quote 2.9** Heckhausen on the distinction between the formation and implementation of intentions
>
> Research on motivation can be divided into two main camps. One of these studies how intentions are formed, the other how they are implemented. Why one wants to do something and that one wants to do it is one thing, but its actual implementation and successful completion is another. The first involves contemplating the reasons for doing something, i.e. considering various incentive-laden consequences of possible action or inaction. This is 'motivation' in the narrow sense. The second is a matter of concrete implementation of actions appropriate to the attainment of a goal chosen in the motivation phase. This is 'action', or because the intended is willed, it can also be called 'volition'.... Curiously, research in motivation in its various epochs has rarely addressed both problems at the same time.
>
> Heckhausen (1991: 163)

- *motivation memory*, which is content-independent, that is, when it is activated, it serves as a continuous source of activation supporting any structure that is currently dominant in other memory systems;
- *action memory*, which contains behavioural programmes for the performance of the particular act.

An activated plan with support from the motivation memory system becomes what Kuhl (1987: 284) calls a 'dynamic plan', which means that the executional process has been initiated. From this point on the motivation system carries out a new, chiefly *maintenance* or *action control* role: it keeps sustaining (i.e. energising) the pursuit of the intention and also protecting it against the detrimental effects of competing plans. Once the plan has been completed, the motivation system is turned off. If the execution of the plan is unsuccessful, an attempt is made to abandon the plan.

An important facet of Action Control Theory is the summary of main mechanisms that can be employed for the purpose of action maintenance, that is, *action control strategies* available to protect ongoing behavioural intentions (see Concept 2.9). Being the first of its kind, this taxonomy has been very influential in shaping subsequent research into the self-regulatory mechanisms related to motivation and affect, particularly in educational settings.

Quote 2.10 Kuhl on 'action control'

We know from everyday experience that we do not always carry out our intentions. Choice of a goal and persistence in striving for it do not guarantee that goal-related intentions will be actually performed. In many cases, a certain amount of effort is needed to enact an intention. It takes effort to maintain an intention, to shield it from the press resulting from competing action tendencies, and to strengthen it if necessary until it has been carried into effect. I assume that this kind of self-regulatory effort is required not only for enacting 'difficult' intentions (e.g. to quit smoking) but also for enacting seemingly easy intentions (e.g. to make a phone call). Since 'effort' is a phenomenal summary term that probably refers to a variety of mechanisms, our task is to investigate the specific mechanisms that mediate the enactment of intentions. I have proposed the term 'action control' to refer to these self-regulatory mechanisms.

Kuhl (1986: 424)

Concept 2.8   Kuhl's concept of 'action' versus 'state orientation'

In an attempt to explain why people often fail to do things without any 'rational' explanation (i.e. when the motivational content of the intention would appear to justify action), Kuhl (1987) introduced the constructs of *action versus state orientation*.

- In the *action orientation mode*, the focus of individuals is on a fully-developed and realistic action plan; they are inclined to visualise themselves taking action and are disposed to act their intentions out.

- In the *state orientation mode*, however, 'attention focuses on the present state (*status quo*), a past state (especially: a failure) or a future state (especially: unrealistic goals)' (p. 289); this mode (which is similar in many ways to 'learned helplessness') is therefore seen as a counter-productive disposition. State-oriented people tend to be hindered by 'intrusive thoughts about bugs, slips in strategy, and failure' (Boekaerts, 1994: 434); they often procrastinate and are prone to ruminate on acting rather than getting down to it.

Kuhl assumes that the two orientations are, to some extent, established individual difference factors; that is, some people are more inclined towards one orientation than the other.

Concept 2.9   Kuhl's taxonomy of action control strategies

1. *Selective attention*, that is, intentionally ignoring attractive alternatives or irrelevant aspects.

2. *Encoding control*, that is, selectively encoding only those features of a stimulus that are related to the current intention.

3. *Emotion control*, that is, the active inhibition of emotional states that may undermine the enacting and protection of the intention, as well as the conscious generation of emotions that are conducive to the implementation of the intention.

4. *Motivation control*, which is an active process of changing the hierarchy of tendency strengths when a more powerful alternative arises, for example, by focusing on what would happen if the original intention failed and by keeping in mind favourable expectancies or positive incentives.

5. *Environment control*, that is, manipulating the environment in a way that the resulting environmental (or social) pressure or control makes the abandoning of the intention more difficult (e.g. by making a social commitment or asking people not to allow one to do something), or by creating safeguards against undesirable environmental temptations (e.g. by removing objects that invite unwanted activities).

6. *Parsimony of information processing*, which essentially refers to a 'let's not think about it any more but get down to doing it' strategy, particularly if further processing may reveal information that undermines the motivational power of the current intention.

Further reading

Process-oriented approaches to motivation

For a general overview, see Dörnyei (in press). Heckhausen's major summary of motivation has been translated into English (Heckhausen, 1991). Heckhausen and Kuhl's (1985) co-authored study is a most creative and inspiring article, though admittedly no easy reading. Much of Kuhl's work has been published in English (e.g. Kuhl, 1985, 1986, 1987, 1992), and a summary of his more recent research (primarily focusing on action and state orientations) can be found in a volume edited by Kuhl and Beckmann (1994). Work in educational psychology that follows Heckhausen and Kuhl's process-oriented conception by highlighting 'volitional' aspects of motivation includes Boekaerts (1994), Corno (1993, 1994), Corno and Kanfer (1993), Kanfer (1996), Snow and Jackson (1994), Snow et al. (1996) and Wolters (1998).

Chapter 3

Motivation to learn a foreign/second language

This chapter will...

- describe the main theories of L2 motivation;
- analyse how L2 theories have responded to the challenges of context and time.

Although 'motivation to learn' is already an intricate, multifaceted construct, when the target of the learning process is the mastery of a L2, the picture becomes even more complex. On the one hand, a L2 is a 'learnable' school subject in that discrete elements of the communication code can be taught explicitly. Thus, the results of studies on academic achievement motivation are of direct relevance when talking about the mastery of a L2. On the other hand, language is also socially and culturally bound, and serves as the primary channel of social organisation in society. This means that the mastery of a L2 is not merely an educational issue, comparable to that of the mastery of other subject matters, but it is also a deeply social event that requires the incorporation of a wide range of elements of the L2 culture.

In view of this inherent complexity, it should not come as a surprise that there has been a considerable diversity of theories and approaches in the study of the motivational determinants of second language acquisition and use. Depending on their research priorities, scholars have highlighted different aspects of L2 motivation and, just like in the arena of mainstream motivational psychology, few attempts have been made to synthesise the various lines of enquiry. The most influential motivation

> **Quote 3.1** Gardner on the social nature of second language acquisition
>
> The learning of a second (or foreign) language in the school situation is often viewed as an educational phenomenon, and 'second languages' as a curriculum topic is considered in much the same light as any other school subject. The thesis proposed here is that such a perspective is categorically wrong, and that 'second languages', unlike virtually any other curriculum topic, must be viewed as a central social psychological phenomenon. The rationale underlying this view is that most school subjects involve learning elements of the student's own cultural heritage.... Such is not the case with second languages, however. In the acquisition of a second language, the student is faced with the task of not simply learning new information (vocabulary, grammar, pronunciation, etc.) which is part of his *own* culture but rather of *acquiring* symbolic elements of a *different* ethnolinguistic community.... Furthermore, the student is not being asked to learn about them; he is being asked to acquire them, to make them part of his own language reservoir. This involves imposing elements of another culture into one's own lifespace. As a result, the student's harmony with his own cultural community and his willingness or ability to identify with other cultural communities become important considerations in the process of second language acquisition.
>
> Gardner (1979: 193–4)

theory in the L2 field has been proposed by Robert Gardner, who, together with his colleagues and associates in Canada, literally founded the field; therefore the following overview of the L2 motivation scene will start with a summary of his work. Following this, a number of alternative constructs will be presented, with special sections devoted to describing how L2 researchers have responded to the challenges of context and time (1.5–1.6). Some of the most important developments in L2 motivation research have been associated with an increased educational focus, and these approaches will be described in Chapter 4.

3.1 Gardner's motivation theory

It is no accident that L2 motivation research was initiated in Canada and that it was dominated by a social psychological emphasis there. The understanding of the unique Canadian situation with the coexistence of the Anglophone and Francophone communities speaking two of the world's most vital languages has been an ongoing challenge for researchers in the social sciences, and the Canadian government has always actively promoted (and sponsored) research in this vein. Gardner and Lambert (1972) saw second languages as mediating factors between different ethnolinguistic communities in multicultural settings and, accordingly, considered the motivation to learn the language of the other community to be a primary force responsible for enhancing or hindering intercultural communication and affiliation. A key tenet of this approach is that the individual's attitudes towards the L2 and the L2 community, as well as his or her ethnocentric orientation in general, exert a directive influence on one's L2 learning behaviour, which makes intuitive sense (since people are unlikely to be successful in learning a language whose speakers they despise) and which is also in line with the traditional stance in social psychology mentioned earlier that someone's attitude towards a target influences the overall pattern of that person's responses to the target.

> **Quote 3.2** Lambert on the genesis of L2 motivation research
>
> The need for a social psychology of language learning became apparent to me when O. H. Mowrer in the 50s began to examine the emotions involved in the interaction between talking birds and their trainers, and the effects such interaction had on the birds' skill at talk development. At about the same time Susan Ervin started her work on the role of emotions and attitudes on the child's first- and second-language development, and Robert Gardner and I began to look at bilingual skill development from the same perspective.
>
> Lambert (1980: 416)

orientation = goal

A key issue in Gardner's (1985) motivation theory is the relationship between *motivation* and *orientation* (which is Gardner's term for a 'goal'). Various psychological approaches differ greatly in terms of the assumed role of goals in them: in goal theories, obviously, goals constitute the motivational foci, whereas in self-determination theory, for example, goals do not appear in the core motivation concept at all. Although Gardner's motivation theory falls into the latter category (i.e. orientations are strictly speaking *not* part of 'motivation' but function merely as motivational antecedents), ironically it is two orientations labelled as *integrative* and *instrumental* that have become the most widely known concepts associated with Gardner's work in the L2 field.

Concept 3.1   **Integrative and instrumental orientation**

- *Integrative orientation* concerns a positive disposition toward the L2 group and the desire to interact with and even become similar to valued members of that community; it was defined in Gardner and Lambert's (1959: 271) pioneering study as the 'willingness to be like valued members of the language community'.

- *Instrumental orientation* is the utilitarian counterpart of integrative orientation in Gardner's theory, pertaining to the potential pragmatic gains of L2 proficiency, such as getting a better job or a higher salary.

According to Gardner (1985), motivation proper subsumes three components:

- *motivational intensity*
- *desire to learn the language*
- *attitudes towards learning the language*.

Thus, in his view, 'motivation' refers to a kind of central mental 'engine' or 'energy-centre' that subsumes effort, want/will (cognition) and task-enjoyment (affect). Gardner argues that these three components belong together because the truly motivated individual displays all three. The role of orientations, then, is to help to arouse motivation and direct it towards a set of goals, either with a strong interpersonal quality (integrative) or a strong practical quality (instrumental).

Gardner's motivation theory has four distinct areas:

- the construct of the *integrative motive*;
- a general learning model, labelled the *socio-educational model*, which integrates motivation as a cornerstone;
- the *Attitude/Motivation Test Battery* (AMTB), which, apart from being a frequently used standardised instrument with well-documented psychometric properties, also offers a list of various influential motivational factors (including classroom-specific variables such as the appraisal of the teacher and the course);
- a recent *extended L2 motivation construct* developed together with Paul Tremblay (Tremblay and Gardner, 1995).

3.1.1   The integrative motive

Perhaps the most elaborate and researched aspect of Gardner's motivation theory has been the concept of the *integrative motive*, which is defined

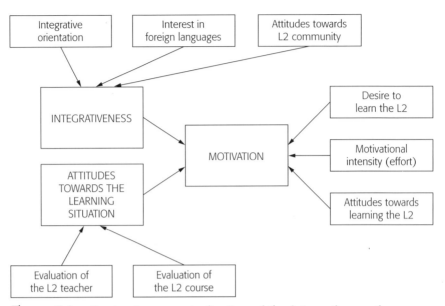

Figure 3.1   Gardner's conceptualisation of the integrative motive

as a 'motivation to learn a second language because of positive feelings toward the community that speaks that language' (Gardner, 1985: 82–3). The integrative motive is a composite construct made up of three main components (see Figure 3.1 for a schematic representation):

1. *Integrativeness*, which subsumes integrative orientation, interest in foreign languages, and attitudes towards the L2 community, reflecting the 'individual's willingness and interest in social interaction with members of other groups' (Gardner and MacIntyre, 1993a: 159).

2. *Attitudes towards the learning situation*, which comprises attitudes towards the language teacher and the L2 course.

3. *Motivation*, that is, effort, desire, and attitude towards learning.

Factor analytical studies examining data from samples in various parts of the world have again and again produced a factor made up of all, or many of, the above components, attesting to the fact that L2 motivation is generally associated with a positive outlook towards the L2 group and the values the L2 is linked with, regardless of the nature of the actual learning context. For example, in a large-scale nationwide study in Hungary, a language-learning environment that is strikingly different from Canada in that it is largely monolingual and monocultural, and foreign languages are taught primarily as a school subject with very

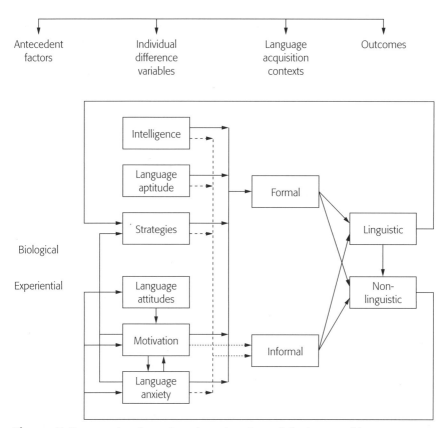

Figure 3.2   Gardner's socio-educational model of second language acquisition (Gardner and MacIntyre, 1993: 8)

limited direct contact with L2 speakers, Dörnyei and Clément (2000) found integrativeness to be the most powerful general component of the participants' generalised language-related affective disposition, determining language choice and the general level of effort the students intended to invest in the learning process.

3.1.2   The socio-educational model

The *socio-educational model* (see Gardner and MacIntyre, 1993a, and Figure 3.2, for a schematic representation) is concerned with the role of various individual difference characteristics of the student in the learning of a L2. Its main importance lies in its clear separation of four distinct aspects of the second language acquisition process:

- antecedent factors (which can be biological or experiential such as gender, age or learning history)
- individual difference (i.e. learner) variables
- language acquisition contexts
- learning outcomes.

The main learner variables covered by the model are intelligence, language aptitude, language learning strategies, language attitudes, motivation, and language anxiety. These, in turn, affect L2 attainment in formal and informal learning contexts, resulting in both linguistic and non-linguistic learning outcomes.

Quote 3.3   Gardner on the socio-educational model

It must be emphasised that there is no intention here to convince others that the model is the true or final one. I personally don't believe it is. I do feel, however, that it contains many elements which must be considered in future developments. A true test of any theoretical formulation is not only its ability to explain and account for phenomena which have been demonstrated, but also its ability to provide suggestions for further investigations, to raise new questions, to promote further developments and open new horizons. This model has those capabilities and, hopefully as a result of the account given here, they will be realised.

Gardner (1985: 166)

3.1.3   The Attitude/Motivation Test Battery

The Attitude/Motivation Test Battery (AMTB, see Gardner, 1985: Appendix) is a multicomponent motivation test made up of over 130 items (see the list of constituent scales below) which has been shown to have very good psychometric properties, including construct and predictive validity (Gardner and MacIntyre, 1993b). It operationalises the main constituents of Gardner's theory and it also includes language anxiety measures (L2 class anxiety and L2 use anxiety) as well as an index of parental encouragement. Adaptations of the test have been used in several data-based studies of L2 motivation all over the world (including Clément et al., 1994; Kraemer, 1993; for a review, see Gardner and MacIntyre, 1993a), and at the moment it is still the only published standardised test of L2 motivation.

Constituent scales of the Attitude/Motivation Test Battery

- Attitudes towards French Canadians (10 Likert scale items)
- Interest in foreign languages (10 Likert scale items)
- Attitudes towards European French people (10 Likert scale items)
- Attitudes towards learning French (10 Likert scale items)
- Integrative orientation (4 Likert scale items)
- Instrumental orientation (4 Likert scale items)
- French class anxiety (5 Likert scale items)
- Parental encouragement (10 Likert scale items)
- Motivational intensity (10 multiple choice items)
- Desire to learn French (10 multiple choice items)
- Orientation index (1 multiple choice item)
- Evaluation of the French teacher (25 semantic differential scale items)
- Evaluation of the French course (25 semantic differential scale items)

3.1.4   Tremblay and Gardner's revised model

In response to calls for the 'adoption of a wider vision of motivation' (Tremblay and Gardner, 1995: 505) in the 1990s, Tremblay and Gardner extended Gardner's social psychological construct of L2 motivation by incorporating into it new elements from expectancy-value (2.1.1) and goal theories (2.1.2). Figure 3.3 presents their proposed extended model, which is fairly straightforward in suggesting a *language attitudes* → *motivational behaviour* → *achievement* sequence. The novel element is the inclusion of three mediating variables between attitudes and behaviour:

- *Goal salience*, referring to the specificity of the learner's goals and the frequency of goal-setting strategies used.
- *Valence*, subsuming the traditional scales of the 'desire to learn the L2' and 'attitudes towards learning the L2', thus denoting a L2-learning-related value component.
- *Self-efficacy*, comprising anxiety and 'performance expectancy' (the latter referring to the expectancy to be able to perform various language activities by the end of the course).

Thus, the model offers a synthesis of Gardner's earlier, socially grounded construct and recent cognitive motivational theories, and

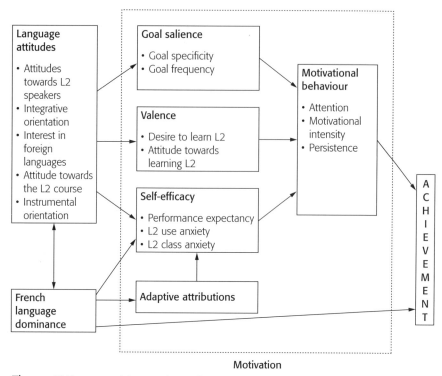

Motivation

Figure 3.3   **Tremblay and Gardner's (1995) model of L2 motivation**

demonstrates that additional variables can be incorporated into Gardner's socio-educational model of L2 learning without damaging its integrity. In line with Gardner's past data-based approach, the new model has also been empirically tested, and in a sample of 75 Canadian students learning French a statistically adequate goodness of fit index was demonstrated.

Further reading

Aspects of Gardner's motivation theory

For more detailed analyses of the integrative/instrumental dichotomy and the integrative motive, see Dörnyei (1994a, 1994b), Gardner (1996), Gardner and MacIntyre (1991), Gardner and Tremblay (1994a, 1994b). For a recent study investigating an extended version of the socio-educational model (also including variables such as learning strategy use and field independence), see Gardner et al. (1997; see 10.4.3, for more details) and Gardner (1996). For an interesting study adapting the socio-educational model to the study of statistics, see Lalonde and Gardner (1993).

3.2 Expectancy-value theories in L2 motivation research

Although no real expectancy-value model has been proposed in L2 motivation research, several components associated with the expectancy-value framework have been incorporated into various L2 research paradigms. To start with, Gardner's (1985) motivation theory concerned several value aspects:

- *intrinsic value*, measured by the 'desire to learn the L2' and 'attitudes towards learning the L2' scales, which have been subsumed under 'valence' in Tremblay and Gardner's (1995) extended model (3.1.4);
- *extrinsic utility value*, measured primarily by the integrative and instrumental orientation scales.

However, the labelling of the scales and their theoretical integration into the integrative motive did not follow expectancy-value principles in Gardner's original theory. Tremblay and Gardner's (1995) revised model can be seen as a definite move towards adopting an expectancy-value framework, as reflected by the prominent 'valence' component as well as the 'self-efficacy' cluster, which includes a 'performance expectancy' variable.

The most explicit treatment of value-expectancy-related components in the L2 field has been offered by

- Clément's (1980) investigation of *linguistic self-confidence*,
- the research on *attributions* in L2 learning.

3.2.1   Clément's concept of linguistic self-confidence

Over the last two decades, Richard Clément and his colleagues have conducted a series of empirical studies examining the interrelationship between social contextual variables (including ethnolinguistic vitality; cf. 3.6.1), attitudinal/motivational factors, self-confidence and L2 acquisition/acculturation processes (for reviews, see Clément et al., 1994; Noels and Clément, 1996; see also 3.5.3 and 3.6.3). These are particularly important in our present context in that their inner-conceptualised *linguistic self-confidence* construct bears many similarities to self-efficacy theory discussed above (2.1.1).

Self-confidence in general refers to the belief that a person has the ability to produce results, accomplish goals or perform tasks competently. It appears to be akin to self-efficacy, but is used in a more general sense: self-efficacy is always specific to a concrete task whereas self-confidence is usually used to refer to a generalised perception of one's coping potentials, relevant to a range of tasks and subject domains. Linguistic self-confidence was first introduced in the L2 literature by Clément et al. (1977) to describe a powerful mediating process in multi-ethnic settings that affects a person's motivation to learn and use the language of the other speech community. Clément and his associates provided evidence that in contexts where different language communities live together, the quality and quantity of the *contact* between the members will be a major motivational factor in learning the other community's language, determining future desire for intercultural communication and the extent of identification with the L2 group. Thus, linguistic self-confidence in Clément's view is primarily a socially defined construct (in contrast to the cognitive nature of 'self-efficacy' in the motivational psychological literature), although self-confidence also has a cognitive component, the 'perceived L2 proficiency'. Recently, Clément et al. (1994) have extended the applicability of the self-confidence construct by showing that it is also a significant motivational subsystem in foreign language learning situations, in which there is little direct contact with members of the L2 community but considerable indirect contact with the L2 culture through the media, for example, as is the case with world languages such as English.

Quote 3.4 Clément, Dörnyei and Noels on the relationship between interethnic contact and self-confidence in second language acquisition

In a multiethnic context, positive attitudes would orient the individual to seek contact with members of the L2 community. To the extent that this contact is relatively frequent and pleasant, self-confidence in using the L2, operationally defined in terms of low anxious affect and high perceptions of L2 competence would develop. This being the case, the availability of extracurricular contact provides the conditions for the development of a motivational process which is relatively independent of the attitudinal process delineated in previous research and theorising.

Clément et al. (1994: 422–3)

Further reading

Linguistic self-confidence and its role in L2 acquisition

Clément (1980, 1986), Clément et al. (1994, 1977), Clément and Kruidenier (1985), Labrie and Clément (1986), Noels and Clément (1996), Noels et al. (1996). See also 3.6.3.

3.2.2   Attributions of L2 learning successes and failures

In spite of a great number of people spending a considerable amount of time studying foreign languages, only relatively few are likely to ever reach a level of L2 proficiency that will satisfy them without any reservations. Accordingly, language learning in most people's minds is inevitably associated with perceptions of some degree of *learning failure*. For this reason, *attribution theory* (2.1.1), that is, the analysis of how people process past experiences of failure (and success), and what consequences these will have on future achievement strivings, is a particularly relevant research area in the L2 field.

> **Quote 3.5** Skehan's call for more research on attributions
>
> It would be desirable if more attribution theory research were carried out in the language learning field. Such research might even synthesise many of the IDs [individual difference variables] discussed in this book into a more coherent account of language learning.
>
> Skehan (1989: 52)

Given the theoretical significance of attributions in L2 motivation, and given the fact that this significance has been repeatedly voiced in the literature (e.g. Dörnyei, 1990; Julkunen, 1989; Schmidt et al., 1996; Skehan, 1989; Tremblay and Gardner, 1995), it is surprising how little actual research has been conducted in the area. One reason for this may be related to the traditionally *quantitative nature* of L2 motivation research (cf. 9.1.1): the effects of causal attributions are complex, varying as a function of the type of attributions made and the attributional style and biases of the learners, and questionnaire-based studies focusing on linear relationships of broad categories have not been adequate to do this intricate process justice. This claim is underscored by the fact that two recent, relatively small-scale, qualitative studies by Williams and Burden (1999) and Ushioda (1996b, 1998) have provided a rich source of insights into the causal attributional processes of L2 learners (see Concept 3.2).

Concept 3.2   **Attributional findings in two qualitative studies**

1. In a two-stage interview study of Irish learners of French, Ushioda (1996b, 1998) found that maintaining a positive self-concept and a belief in personal potential in the face of negative experiences hinged on two *attributional patterns*:

   - attributing positive L2 outcomes to personal ability or other internal factors (e.g. effort, perfectionist approach);
   - attributing negative L2 outcomes or lack of success to temporary (i.e. unstable) shortcomings that might be overcome (e.g. lack of effort, lack of opportunity to spend time in the L2 environment).

   These two patterns coincide almost exactly with the recommendations made in educational psychology concerning the promotion of motivation-enhancing attributions (cf. 5.2.4).

2. Williams and Burden (1999; included as a sample study in 10.6.2) were concerned with the developmental aspects of learner attributions in L2 studies. Their interview study revealed clear differences between the different age groups studied in terms of the learners' construction of success and in the range of attributions provided for success and failure:

   - 10–12 year olds saw the main reasons for success as listening and concentrating;
   - older children provided a wider range of attributions, including ability, level of work, circumstances and the influence of others.

   A noteworthy finding was that there was hardly any mention of the application of appropriate learning strategies when explaining successes, indicating a lack of awareness of the importance of strategy use.

3.3   Self-determination theory and L2 motivation

Because of the widespread influence of Deci and Ryan's (1985) theory of intrinsic/extrinsic motivation and self-determination in mainstream psychology (2.1.3), several attempts have been made in L2 research to incorporate some of the elements of the theory in L2-specific models. Douglas Brown (1981, 1990, 1994) has been one of the main proponents of emphasising the importance of *intrinsic motivation* in the L2 classroom, and he has also offered a number of strategies on how to achieve such an optimal state (discussed in Chapter 5).

Quote 3.6 Brown on the importance of intrinsic motivation in the L2 classroom

Traditionally, elementary and secondary schools are fraught with extrinsic-ally motivated behaviour ... schools all too often teach students to play the 'game' of pleasing teachers and authorities rather than developing an internalised thirst for knowledge and experience. ... Over the long haul, such dependency focuses students too exclusively on the material or monetary rewards of an education rather than instilling an appreciation for creativity and for satisfying some of the more basic drives for knowledge and exploration. ... The notion here is that an intrinsically oriented school can begin to transfer itself into a more positive, affirming environment ... The result: an appreciation of love, intimacy, and respect for the wisdom of age.

Brown (1994: 39–41)

Another aspect of self-determination theory that has been applied to the L2 field has been the emphasis on fostering *learner autonomy* in L2 classrooms in order to increase student motivation. This emphasis is relatively new; however, a number of recent reviews and discussions (e.g. Benson, 2000; Dickinson, 1995; Ehrman and Dörnyei, 1998; Ushioda, 1996a, 1998) provide evidence that L2 motivation and learner autonomy go hand in hand, and, as Ushioda (1996a) explicitly states in a monograph on motivation and learner autonomy, 'Autonomous language learners are by definition motivated learners' (p. 2).

Quote 3.7 Dickinson on autonomy and motivation

This review of a selection of the literature on motivation seeks a justification for the promotion of learner autonomy among language learners. It has been shown that there is substantial evidence from cognitive motivational studies that learning success and enhanced motivation is conditional on learners taking responsibility for their own learning, being able to control their own learning and perceiving that their learning successes and failures are to be attributed to their own efforts and strategies rather than to factors outside their control. Each of these conditions is a characteristic of learner autonomy as it is described in applied linguistics.

Dickinson (1995: 173–4)

3.3.1   Noels and her colleagues' work on self-determination in L2 studies

The most explicit treatment of self-determination theory in L2 contexts has been offered recently by Kim Noels and her colleagues (Noels et al., 1999, 2000). Noels et al. (2000) set out to develop a new L2-specific instrument for assessing L2 learners' orientations from a self-determination perspective (i.e. a questionnaire that measures various types of intrinsic and extrinsic orientations in L2 learning), and to relate the obtained measures to

- various antecedent and consequence measures (perceptions of competence, freedom of choice, anxiety, and the intention to continue L2 studies – all assessed by scales well established in educational psychology) to serve as criterion measures;
- Clément and Kruidenier's (1983) influential system of four types of orientations: instrumental, knowledge, travel, friendship.

The researchers found that instrumental orientation corresponded closely to *external extrinsic regulation* (for the taxonomy of different types of extrinsic motive, see 2.1.3), whereas the other three orientations were associated with more self-determined and intrinsic types of motive. Although this line of research is still inconclusive (because, for example, the important question of how *integrative orientation* relates to extrinsic/intrinsic regulation is still to be answered), it has far-reaching

---

Quote 3.8   Noels, Pelletier, Clément and Vallerand on an unexpected finding concerning 'identified regulation' (which was the most self-determined extrinsic form of motivation they measured)

With regards to the correlations between the subscales and the criterion variables, although several of the predicted relations were evident, contrary to expectations, the identified regulation subscale has a stronger relation with the criterion variables than the IM [intrinsic motivation] subscales. . . . this finding might suggest that those who naturally enjoy the feeling of learning a L2 may not necessarily feel personally involved in the learning process – they may view language learning as puzzle or a language game that has few repercussions in everyday life. In order to foster sustained learning, it may not be sufficient to convince students that language learning is interesting and enjoyable, but that it is also personally important for them.

Noels et al. (2000)

potentials in the study of L2 motivation. Language-learning goals (or 'orientations' in Gardner's term) are a central issue in motivation research, but the great number of diverse goals L2 learners may pursue (cf. Coleman, 1995; Oxford and Shearin, 1996) has made it difficult to establish a theoretical framework for these. Applying the intrinsic/extrinsic continuum and the scale developed by Noels her colleagues can be helpful in going beyond a merely descriptive level and organising goals systematically. Furthermore, this paradigm is particularly useful for analysing the classroom climate and the L2 teacher in terms of how controlling or autonomy supporting they are, which has immediate practical implications for educating autonomous, self-regulated L2 learners (Noels et al., 1999; cf. 3.6.5).

3.4   Schumann's neurobiological model

During the past decade, John Schumann and his colleagues at UCLA have pursued a novel line of research by examining second language acquisition from a neurobiological perspective. Several articles have reported on various phases of this programme and a recent monograph by Schumann (1998), *The Neurobiology of Affect in Language*, offers a summary of the author's theory. As suggested by the title, *affect* (i.e. issues related to feelings and emotions) in this book is seen as central to the understanding of L2 attainment. This is because, as the author argues, second language acquisition is emotionally driven and emotion underlies most, if not all cognition.

The key constituent of Schumann's neurobiological theory is *stimulus appraisal.* According to the model, the brain evaluates the environmental stimuli it receives and this leads to an emotional, and consequently to a behavioural, response. Schumann postulates five dimensions along which stimulus appraisals are made:

- *novelty* (degree of unexpectedness/familiarity)
- *pleasantness* (attractiveness)
- *goal/need significance* (whether the stimulus is instrumental in satisfying needs or achieving goals)
- *coping potential* (whether the individual expects to be able to cope with the event)
- *self and social image* (whether the event is compatible with social norms and the individual's self-concept).

Under different labels, these dimensions have been discussed extensively by motivational psychologists in the past, and Schumann's theory constitutes, in effect, an attempt at formulating a neurobiologically validated theory of human motivation and action (with a special emphasis on L2 learning behaviours). This theory is still in a progress of continuous development: recently, Schumann (2000) has related stimulus appraisals to biological notions of value, and discussed how such appraisals become part of the person's value system through a special 'memory for value'. He has also outlined a conception of learning as a form of 'mental foraging' (i.e. foraging for knowledge), which engages the same neural systems as organisms use when foraging to feed or mate, and which is generated by an incentive motive and potentiated by the stimulus appraisal system.

Motivational psychology has been struggling with the abundance of diverse approaches and the often incompatible terminology introduced by the various theories (cf. 1.3), and the same situation characterises the field of second language acquisition, in which many research traditions coexist in an interdisciplinary fashion. The main attraction of Schumann's neurobiological approach from this perspective lies in the fact that it offers a completely new type of validity for motivation theories by connecting abstract theoretical constructs to concrete biological mechanisms detected in the brain.

3.5 Constructs emerging from empirical studies

From the very beginnings of L2 motivation research, there has been an emphasis on testing the various theoretical constructs in data-based studies, thereby establishing a 'research tradition that has continually focused attention on the reliability and validity of measures which define variables' (Gardner, 1985: 165). In fact, various elements of Gardner's motivation theory (3.1) actually emerged from statistical analyses of field data, and in this respect Gardner's work has been superior to many of the influential motivational approaches in mainstream psychology, which have often been speculative in nature. With the advance of research in the L2 field, a number of extended motivation questionnaires were developed and administered in diverse sociocultural contexts, and the subsequent multivariate statistical analyses have produced several new L2 motivation constructs (for two examples, see Examples 3.1 and 3.2).

Example 3.1 Work by Schmidt, Boraie and Kassabgy (1996) in Egypt

One particularly important empirical contribution has been offered by Schmidt et al. (1996), who present the analysis of a detailed motivation questionnaire administered to over 1,500 Egyptian learners of English (for more details about this study, see 10.2.3). By factor analysing the data, a matrix of nine main factors emerged, and the validity of this construct has been analysed by the authors by comparing it with two other empirical studies (Dörnyei, 1990, and Julkunen, 1989) that had been conducted in similar, foreign language learning contexts. Schmidt et al. labelled the nine factors as follows:

- *determination* (indicating a commitment to learn English)
- *anxiety* (about using English in class)
- *instrumental orientation*
- *sociability* (referring to the importance of getting along with fellow students and the teacher)
- *attitude to foreign culture* (also including the attitudes to L2 speakers)
- *foreign residence* (indicating a desire to spend an extended period in an English speaking country)
- *intrinsic motivation* (involving the enjoyment gained from learning the L2)
- *beliefs about failure* (referring to attributions to external causes)
- *enjoyment* (a single-item factor, similar to 'intrinsic motivation').

Although the results of different factor analytic studies are difficult to compare because the factor matrices are a function of the selection of the items submitted to the analysis (i.e. a factor cannot emerge if no items in the questionnaire tap into it; cf. 10.2.2), Schmidt et al.'s results show remarkable similarities with those of Dörnyei (1990) and Julkunen (1989). Both Schmidt et al. and Dörnyei identified similar factors related to instrumental orientation, foreign residence, foreign culture/people, and intrinsic motivation. This latter factor also emerged in Julkunen's study, as did anxiety. Finally, all three studies produced factors associated with attributions.

Schmidt et al. (1996) also processed their data using a different statistical procedure, *multidimensional scaling*, which produced a more parsimonious construct of three components that were labelled as

- *affect* (with a strong emphasis on intrinsic motivation)
- *goal-orientedness*
- *expectancy*.

The authors suggest that these basic dimensions are probably universal and neurobiologically based. The resemblance of the three construct constituents to key components of major psychological models (cf. 2.1.1–2.1.3) is certainly striking, although we must note that in multidimensional scaling the labelling of the scales is far more ambiguous than the labelling of factors in factor analysis (cf. 9.2.6).

Example 3.2 Work by Clément, Dörnyei and Noels (1994) in Hungary

In order to examine motivation in an environment in which the social dimension might be less featured, Clément et al. (1994) examined Hungarian language learners who studied English in a school context without any substantial contact with members of the L2 community. The analysis of the data pointed to the existence of a tripartite motivation construct amongst these learners, consisting of

- *integrativeness*
- *linguistic self-confidence*
- *appraisal of the classroom environment*.

The emergence of the first two components was not unexpected and confirmed the validity of earlier research findings (cf. 3.1.1 and 3.2.1). The third, classroom-specific component – which included the evaluation of the *L2 teacher* and the *course* (in a similar way to the AMTB; 3.1.3) as well as a novel element, the evaluation of the learner group in terms of its *cohesiveness* – corresponded to the 'attitudes towards the learning situation factor' in Gardner's (1985) integrative motive construct, and also provided empirical support for the validity of the 'pedagogical shift' in motivation research discussed in Chapter 4.

The various empirically based constructs are often specific to the investigated samples and learning situations and are therefore not always generalisable in a straightforward manner; furthermore, they are often theoretically eclectic in the sense that the computer analyses indicate certain associations between variables for which no theoretical explanations are readily available. On the other hand, the factors and links detected in idiosyncratic situations appear to share many similarities, attesting to the existence of some broad, generalisable factors/dimensions that make up the motivational disposition of L2 learners. In an attempt to identify these common dimensions, I have carried out a synthesis *How done?* of thirteen different constructs (cf. Dörnyei, 1998a) by tabulating the main motivational domains underlying them. I found that almost all the motivational constituents of the selected models/frameworks could be classified into seven broad dimensions:

1. *Affective/integrative dimension*, referring to a general affective 'core' of the L2 motivation complex, including variables such as integrative motivation, affective motive, language attitudes, intrinsic motivation, attitudes towards L2 learning, enjoyment and interest.
2. *Instrumental/pragmatic dimension*, referring to extrinsic, largely utilitarian factors.
3. *Macrocontext-related dimension*, referring to broad, societal and sociocultural factors such as multicultural, intergroup and ethnolinguistic relations.
4. *Self-concept-related dimension*, referring to learner-specific variables such as self-confidence, anxiety and need for achievement.
5. *Goal-related dimension*, involving various goal characteristics.
6. *Educational context-related dimension*, referring to the characteristics and appraisal of the immediate learning environment (i.e. classroom) and the school context.
7. *Significant others-related dimension*, referring to the motivational influence of parents, family and friends.

The different L2 motivation constructs varied in the extent of emphasis they placed on each of the seven dimensions and in the way they linked the different factors to each other and to the process of second language acquisition.

3.6 L2 motivation and the social context

I have argued earlier that human motivation is to a large extent socially shaped and this contextual dependence is particularly prominent when the target behaviour is the learning of a L2, due to the multifaceted nature and role of language itself. Because of the human species' 'unusual capacities for language and thought', human environments are to a large extent 'symbolic in nature, and these symbols are not only cognitive in structure and content, they are also emotionally, socially, and motivationally loaded' (Bronfenbrenner, 1993: 6). Acquiring a L2 successfully, then, involves taking on a host of behavioural and cognitive attributes of another sociocultural community. This means that, as mentioned in the introduction of this chapter, unlike several other school subjects, a foreign language is not a socially neutral field. We also need to remember that most nations in the world are multicultural and the majority of people in the world speak at least one L2, and this underscores the importance of the social dimension of L2 motivation.

> **Quote 3.9** Williams on the social nature of L2 studies
>
> There is no question that learning a foreign language is different to learning other subjects. This is mainly because of the social nature of such a venture. Language, after all, belongs to a person's whole social being: it is part of one's identity, and is used to convey this identity to other people. The learning of a foreign language involves far more than simply learning skills, or a system of rules, or a grammar; it involves an alteration in self-image, the adoption of new social and cultural behaviours and ways of being, and therefore has a significant impact on the social nature of the learner.
>
> Williams (1994: 77)

In providing a state-of-the-art description of the L2 field in the light of constructivist challenges, McGroarty (1998) argues that a key issue to be studied by researchers is the analysis of the degree to which the wider social environment supports or hinders the acquisition of L2 competence. When it comes to motivational issues, McGroarty's claim is particularly valid. Foreign/second languages are learned in such diverse contexts that a lack of accounting for the contextual differences might render any motivation theory useless. Studying English, for example, will have considerably different motivational overtones in, say, a post-colonial environment such as Hong Kong, in a second language acquisition context such as Canada, or in a monolingual and monocultural foreign language-learning context such as Hungary. Furthermore, in many learning situations the students in a L2 class do not form a homogeneous sample but consist of various ethnolinguistic groups. In such contexts, therefore, a central factor to consider is the interplay of the students' diverse language identities and how this interaction impacts on the study of the target language.

> **Quote 3.10** McGroarty on the importance of socially grounded research in applied linguistics
>
> Research both within applied linguistics and across a range of related social sciences suggests that, until linguists develop better means of describing the interrelationships between the individual and group psychosocial, cognitive, and linguistic aspects of language acquisition and teaching and the opportunities and constraints of the social contexts surrounding language acquisition and development, they cannot hope to address the most intellectually challenging and practically significant aspects of language learning and teaching.
>
> McGroarty (1998: 4)

In many ways, Gardner's social psychological theory of L2 motivation, described earlier (3.1), belongs to this section. Because this theory has been so influential in the L2 field, it made sense to start Chapter 3 with it; however, there was another reason for treating it separately, which touches upon a core issue in conceptualising social motivation. Despite the fact that social attitudes play a crucial part in Gardner's theory, McNamara (1997) has recently characterised it as existing 'in an intergroup vacuum', and similar appraisals of attitude–behaviour studies in general have also been made in the social psychological literature (e.g. Terry et al., 1999). This issue concerns one of the most basic dilemmas in social psychology (discussed in 1.5), the discord between

> **Quote 3.11** Terry, Hogg and Duck on the individualistic perspective of attitude–behaviour studies in social psychology
>
> Attitude researchers have focused much of their attention on attitude–behaviour relations and attitude change.... Despite the fact that such issues are embedded centrally in the realm of social psychology, the role of social influence in attitude–behaviour relations ... has received less attention. For the most part, an individualistic perspective has been taken – attitudes are regarded as part of people's personal belief structures – and, as a consequence, most research on attitude–behaviour relations and attitude change has been conducted at this same level of abstraction.
>
> Terry et al. (1999: 280)

two interrelated and yet starkly separated perspectives that one can adopt when analysing the social world:

- a *macro-perspective*, focusing on broad societal processes and contexts (e.g. social identity theory; 1.5 and 3.6.1);
- a *micro-perspective*, focusing on the individual's idiosyncratic perception of the social world through the individual's eyes (e.g. social cognition theory; 1.5).

Ideally, the two perspectives should be combined; however, the question of how to generate a synthesis of a social and a personal identity as parallel contributors to and results of individual (learning) behaviours has not been satisfactorily answered yet, particularly if we take into account that 'identities are multiple and situationally anchored, shaped by the contexts in which they are relevant' (McGroarty, 1998: 597).

Quote 3.12 Operario and Fiske on the need to combine the individualistic and societal perspectives

Social cognition and social identity still have much to learn from one another. Social cognition researchers must continue to remember the significance of society, and its implications for internal processes; social identity must continue to remember the significance of the self, and the internal states that moderate reactions to one's context.

Operario and Fiske (1999: 48)

On the individualistic–societal continuum, Gardner's theory would be placed more towards the individualistic end: Although it was partly inspired by an interest in the interrelationship of the Anglophone and Francophone communities in Canada, Gardner's actual motivation theory does *not* address the complexities of this relationship and neither does it concern the varying social influences that can be found in different parts of Canada due to varying proportions of the two communities living together. Instead – in line with the traditional individualistic approach both in motivational psychology and in attitude–behaviour studies within social psychology – societal issues are reflected in the theory only through the individual's attitudes towards members of the other community.

There are four approaches to the understanding of environmental influences on second language acquisition that are significant in that they attempt to integrate the micro and the macro, that is, the individual with the social structural context:

- the *intergroup model* by Howard Giles and his colleagues;
- the *acculturation theory* in second language acquisition by John Schumann;
- the study of *situated language identity* by Richard Clément, Kim Noels and their associates;
- the conceptualisation of *motivational investment* by Bonny Norton.

Although these are not motivational theories in the strict sense (and only the last one makes explicit references to motivation), they are relevant to the understanding of the social aspects of L2 motivation because of the fundamental effect various sociocultural factors (analysed by these theories) have on linguistic practices and behaviours (2.2). In the following, I will first provide a brief overview of the four approaches and then summarise the existing L2 research on the motivational impact of the microcontext of learning (i.e. the parents', teacher's, the group's and the school's motivational influence).

3.6.1   The intergroup model

The *intergroup model* (Giles and Byrne, 1982) offers a situated social psychological framework for examining the conditions under which the members of minority ethnic groups in a multicultural setting successfully acquire and use the dominant language. The central concept underlying the model is the individual's self-concept, and the major motivating force is one of developing or maintaining a positive self-image. Giles and Byrne adopted social identification theory as their guiding framework, going back to Tajfel's conceptualisation of the *social identity* of an individual as 'consisting of those aspects of his self-image, positively or negatively valued, which derive from his membership of various social groups to which he belongs' (Tajfel, 1978: 443). The relevance of social identity to the understanding of cross-linguistic practices is underscored by Rampton's (1995: 7) observation that social identity in certain multicultural contexts is increasingly determined by ethnic identification: 'With the late industrial crisis in the political representation of the working-class movement, people in subordinate material and economic positions are increasingly invited to conceptualise their political situation in terms of their ethnicity.'

Because social identity has an important bearing on one's personal attitudes, values and aspirations, as well as on one's ethnolinguistic behaviours (e.g. interaction with members of the target language community), Giles and Byrne proposed that it was also associated with a number of important linguistic processes and practices with regard to L2 attainment. That is, they related the learners' motivation to acquire native-like linguistic competence in the L2 to their sense of identification with the linguistic ingroup and their perception of the relationships between linguistic in- and outgroups (Kelly et al., 1993).

In order to specify more precisely some of the personal and situational factors that enhance the salience of ethnic identification for individuals, that is, to situate the sociolinguistic and social psychological processes underlying interethnic behaviour within their proper sociostructural contexts, Giles and Byrne included into their paradigm the concepts of perceived 'ethnolinguistic vitality', perceived 'group boundaries' and 'multiple group membership':

- *Ethnolinguistic vitality* refers to a complex of three sociostructural factors that determine a particular ethnic group's distinctiveness as a collective entity:
  - *status factors* (economic, political, social, sociohistorical, and language)
  - *demographic factors* (relating to the size and distribution of the group)
  - *institutional support factors* (representation of the ethnic group in the media, education, government, church).
- *Group boundaries* determine the degree of ease or difficulty of individual mobility in and out of group membership.
- *Multiple group membership* is important in that most individuals are members of a number of other social categories besides the ethnic one (e.g. professional bodies/organisations), and the resulting multiple influences on one's self-concept have an impact on the salience of one's personal identification with the ethnic category.

Although the intergroup model is very useful in explaining a range of macrolinguistic phenomena in multicultural settings (e.g. why certain ethnic groups, and not others, remain distinctive ethnic collectivities that maintain their language while embedded in dominant groups), the theory has also generated considerable criticism. Husband and Saifullah Khan (1982), for example, have questioned the theoretical underpinning of the definition of ethnolinguistic vitality, claiming that the theory fails to account for the interrelationship of the various components

Concept 3.3   **Conditions under which minority group members will be most likely to acquire nativelike proficiency in the dominant group's language (Giles and Byrne, 1982)**

1. Ingroup identification is weak and/or the L1 is not a salient dimension of the individual's ethnic group membership (i.e. the individual does not define himself or herself strongly as a member of a community with a prominent linguistic marker).

2. Quiescent interethnic comparisons exist (i.e. the individual does not suffer from an ethnic 'inferiority complex').

3. Perceived ingroup vitality is low (i.e. the ethnic group is not seen as having a high social status, is not too numerous, and has not obtained a high institutional profile).

4. Perceived ingroup boundaries are soft and open (i.e. the ethnic group is seen as culturally and linguistically related to the dominant group, and mobility between the ingroup and the outgroup is easy).

5. Strong identification exists with many other social categories, each of which provides adequate group identities and a satisfactory intragroup status (i.e. alternative group membership – professional, political, or religious – can compensate for the weakening of the ethnic belonging).

but rather provides an 'uncritical naming of parts' (p. 195), thereby promoting a '*clear* but dangerously simplified analysis of types of ethnolinguistic groups' (p. 194). In their response, Johnson et al. (1983) have agreed that 'there is as yet no grand theory for the study of language, ethnicity and intergroup relations' (p. 258), but they consider the notion of vitality an appropriate 'starting point from which to explore the difficult link between sociological (collective) and social-psychological (individual) accounts of language, ethnicity and intergroup relations' (p. 258).

Johnson et al.'s (1983) response indicates that the debate is rooted in the basic conflict between the individualistic and societal perspectives mentioned earlier. The intergroup theory can be placed towards the societal end of the continuum as it shows only limited sensitiveness to situated cases: apart from the recognition of the significance of multiple group memberships, it does not elaborate on the interplay of the complex and often contradictory identity perceptions across a range of category memberships. Thus, as Williams (1992) summarises, the theory does not specify how the individual's quest for a positive identity is related to the group members' collective upward social mobility. In other words, the theory fails to specify how personal characteristics and dispositions mediate the general processes proposed. Several attempts have been made to integrate the two perspectives, most notably by:

- Bourhis et al. (1981), who have devised a 'Subjective Vitality Questionnaire' to assess the individuals' own representations of vitality that mediates ethnolinguistic behaviour.
- Allard and Landry (for a review, see 1994), who have developed the 'Beliefs on Ethnolinguistic Vitality Questionnaire', which reflects a broader conceptualisation of subjective ethnolinguistic vitality in terms of a system of beliefs that is more compatible with a theory of human behaviour (e.g. it includes goal beliefs concerning language use that are very similar to behavioural intentions).
- Harwood et al. (1994), who have set up a heuristic framework that articulates some of the important determinants and consequences of vitality assessment, also incorporating Allard and Landry's theory. The model consists of three broad constituents:
  - elements of the situation (including objective vitality, interethnic contact dimensions, ethnolinguistic identity)
  - elements of vitality cognitions (e.g. salience of vitality concerns, degree of intergroup difference)
  - communicative manifestations (e.g. inter/intragroup language behaviour) and attitudinal and cognitive outcomes (e.g. stereotypes and relational strategies towards outgroup speakers).

3.6.2   Acculturation theory

Schumann's (1978, 1986) *acculturation theory* examines the same kind of interethnic context as the intergroup model (i.e. multiethnic settings from a minority group perspective), and some of the propositions of the two frameworks overlap. However, the two key concepts Schumann uses to explain the minority group's propensity (or the lack of it) to acquire the dominant ethnolinguistic group's language – *social distance* and *psychological distance* – are rooted in a research tradition different from social identity theory. His primary concern is the process of *acculturation,* that is, the 'social and psychological integration of the learner with the target language group' (p. 29); the main tenet of the theory is that *social* and *psychological distance* between the language learner and the target language speakers is detrimental to the attainment of the target language, inasmuch as the learner will acquire the L2 only to the degree that he or she establishes social and psychological contact with the dominant group. Thus, Schumann's focus on 'distance' can be seen as another attempt at introducing sufficiently dynamic concepts that can bridge the gap between the individualistic and societal perspectives in the study of L2 practices.

Concept 3.4   **Factors determining social and psychological distance in Schumann's acculturation theory**

Social variables

1. *Social dominance patterns*. If the two groups are too distant on the superior–inferior continuum, this will undermine L2 attainment – this factor appears to be similar to (but not the same as) Giles and Byrne's (1982) 'interethnic comparison' factor.

2. *Integration strategy type*:
   - 'assimilation' (i.e. giving up own lifestyle and values in favour of those of the target language group) maximises contact;
   - 'preservation' (i.e. maintaining own lifestyle and values and rejecting those of the target language group) creates social distance;
   - 'adaptation' (i.e. adapting to the lifestyle and values of the target language group, while maintaining own lifestyle and values for intragroup use) yields varying degrees of contact.

3. *Enclosure*. The extent to which the learner's group shares the same social facilities (e.g. churches, schools, recreational facilities, professions) as the target language group determines the amount of intergroup contact.

4. *Cohesiveness*. A cohesive ethnic ingroup keeps the learner separated from the target language group – this factor bears resemblance with Giles and Byrne's (1982) 'ingroup identification' factor.

5. *Size*. If the L2 group is large, intragroup contact will be more frequent than intergroup contact.

6. *Cultural congruence*, or similarity between own group and the target language group. This affects the degree of contact between the two groups → a factor that is similar in some aspects to Giles and Byrne's (1982) 'ingroup boundaries' factor.

7. Attitudes towards the target language group. These are assumed to affect interethnic contact.

Individual variables

8. *Intended length of residence* in the target language area. This determines the learner's eagerness to develop more extensive contacts with the target language group.

9. *Language shock.* The extent of fear that one will appear comic by not being able to do oneself justice in the target language.

10. *Culture shock.* The anxiety and disorientation experienced upon entering a new culture due to the recognition that established mechanisms to cope with routine activities do not work in the new environment, which creates psychological distance.

11. *Motivation.* The learner's reasons for attempting to acquire the target language is a central determinant of psychological distance.

12. *Ego-permeability.* The extent of the individual's established ego rigidity in terms of the fluidity of mental categories (e.g. general and language identity) determines the receptivity to outside influences such as new languages and culture, thus affecting learning inhibition and tolerance of ambiguity.

As Gardner (1985: 137) points out, acculturation theory is essentially a model of 'language non-acquisition' in that it describes a number of factors that can inhibit language acquisition. Schumann's (1978, 1986) framework clearly extends the intergroup typology by adding to it important motivational conditions related to the learner's social cognition and social situation. However, the downside of this wish to combine various perspectives is the reduced theoretical cohesiveness of the model in terms of the level of abstraction of his categories.

3.6.3   Situated language identity

The most situated, socio-contextual approach to understanding language behaviours in multicultural settings has been pursued by Richard Clément, Kim Noels and their associates in Canada (e.g. Clément and Noels, 1992; Côté and Clément, 1994; Noels and Clément, 1996; Noels et al., 1996). Their objective was to create the foundations of a 'situated identity theory', which can be seen as a follow-up to the work of Giles and his colleagues on ethnic identity and ethnolinguistic vitality. Although the Canadian scholars' work is particularly forward-pointing with regard to the basic individual-collective dilemma in social psychology (described earlier), their ongoing research effort has not as yet yielded a comprehensive model.

Clément and Noels (1992) accept the basic assumption of social identity theory that individuals seek to view themselves positively and that a positive image is determined socially. In settings where the language serves as an important dimension of group identity, the desire to maintain a positive social identity is strongly linked to the motivation of pursuing various linguistic practices. This means, in practical terms, that the individual is likely to identify with the group with the greatest ethnolinguistic vitality, and this identification may lead to linguistic *assimilation* into the majority group or *integration* with the minority group.

> **Quote 3.13** Clément and Noels on the situational character of social identification
>
> The link between vitality and identification is...co-determined by a number of additional factors. Among others, it is entirely possible that situational factors may override the effects of social factors and promote, if only momentarily, membership in groups defined along dimensions other than language.... ethnolinguistic identity may thus best be seen as situationally bound, such that individuals slip in and out of particular group memberships as required by immediate contextual demands.
>
> Clément and Noels (1992: 205)

Clément, Noels and their colleagues do not offer a comprehensive taxonomy of all the major situational variables that can modify the macro-processes at the societal level (i.e. linguistic assimilation/integration) but they offer firm empirical evidence of the impact of a number of such factors, highlighting at the same time the complex interrelationship patterns among these. It is noteworthy that in a study which included both micro-social and macro-social characteristics of concrete task-situations, Côté and Clément (1994) found only few significant relationships at the macro-level (represented by relative ethnolinguistic vitality); the researchers explained this by arguing that such macro-variables need to be aroused by specific situational contingencies, for example the perception of *ethnic threat*. Other influential situational factors investigated include:

- the relative minority/majority status of the speaker in the immediate surroundings;
- the private/public facet of language use;

- the existence of strong normative pressures within the ethnic group;
- the quality and quantity of contact with members of another ethnic group.

Clément and his colleagues also posit that the acquired communicative competence in the target language will have a 'washback' effect on the learners' identity, thereby creating an interactive process (i.e. perceptions of identity affect second language acquisition and the achieved level of L2 proficiency affects perceptions of identity). For minority group members, for example, the development of L2 skills and a second ethnic identity may undermine or alter the original ethnic identity because increased L2 competence results in the individual's identifying with the L2 community (Noels et al., 1996).

3.6.4 Motivational investment

Doing research on immigrant women in Canada, Bonny Norton (2000; Norton Pierce, 1995) was confronted with the inadequacy of existing L2 theories to describe the pattern of actual motivational influences relevant to her specific sample. These women came from various socio-cultural backgrounds (e.g. escaping East European communism or Peruvian terrorism), had different levels of education, and varied considerably in the extent of their family responsibilities while trying to establish their existence in Canada. As Norton found, the 'baggage' of social history and personal identity (in terms of their gender and ethnic background) they brought to the L2 learning process was so loaded – resulting in a very complex relationship between power, identity and language learning – that the concept of 'motivation' as described by various theoretical approaches in the past failed in her view to capture the dynamic processes involved. Therefore, instead of using the term 'motivation', Norton introduced the concept of *investment* to describe the 'socially and historically constructed relationship of learners to the target language, and their often ambivalent desire to learn and practice it' (Norton, 2000). Using metaphors borrowed from economics, she explained the concept of investment as a process aimed at acquiring a wider range of symbolic and material resources, which will in turn increase the value of the *cultural capital* of the learners. The main drive behind learning is the expectation or hope to have a good return on that investment, thereby giving learners access to hitherto unattainable resources.

> **Quote 3.14** Norton on the distinction between investment and instrumental motivation
>
> The conception of instrumental motivation presupposes a unitary, fixed, and ahistorical language learner who desires access to material resources that are the privilege of target language speakers. The notion of investment, on the other hand, conceives of the language learner as having a complex social history and multiple desires. The notion presupposes that when language learners speak, they are not only exchanging information with target language speakers, but they are constantly organising and reorganising a sense of who they are and how they relate to the social world. Thus, an investment in the target language is also an investment in a learner's own identity, an identity which is constantly changing across time and space.
>
> Norton (2000)

Although the motivational aspects of investment are not elaborated by Norton (2000) and therefore we cannot speak about a fully fledged motivation theory in her case, the concept is very important in the sense that it highlights the necessity to introduce motivational constructs that can describe relations with the L2 that are 'complex, contradictory, and in a state of flux'. In this, Norton's approach is very close to that of motivational psychologists Maehr and Braskamp (1986), whose book *The Motivation Factor: A Theory of Personal Investment* also introduces a similar construct, *personal investment*, that is intended to 'capture the underlying meaning of the disparate behavioural patterns commonly associated with motivation' (p. 6). Interestingly, although drawing on different sources, these authors also believe that in order to describe behavioural patterns that are at the heart of social motivation, it may be useful to apply economic metaphors. Thus, they argue that motivational problems are problems of resource distribution in that 'Motivation can be properly thought of as a process whereby people take certain available resources – their time, talent, and energy – and distribute them as they choose' (p. 7).

The dynamic character of the concept of 'investment' becomes particularly important in the light of the six challenges of motivation research outlined in Chapter 1: the metaphor is readily usable when addressing three of the challenges, those of *time*, *context* and *parallel multiplicity*.

> **Quote 3.15** Maehr and Braskamp on the dynamic character of the notion of 'investment'
>
> It is important to remember that motivation is a *dynamic* process. Personal investment occurs as part of a continuous stream of ever-changing events. ...personal investment is both a product and a producer of dynamic interaction with a variety of persons, situations, and events. The effects of one's personal investment feed back to affect the continuing investment of oneself. We can take a picture of the variables in motivation at any given moment, but such a static portrayal seldom does justice to what in reality is a very dynamic and continuous flow of events.
>
> Maehr and Braskamp (1986: 10–12)

3.6.5 The motivational influences of the immediate learning situation (microcontext)

Because of the prominent social dimension of second language acquisition, the study of the broad sociocultural context (macrocontext) of L2 learning has been an important research direction for over two decades, and some of this research – e.g. the approaches covered in 3.6.1–3.6.4 – has direct motivational relevance. However, far less attention has been paid to analysing the microcontext of L2 learning, that is, the role the classroom milieu and the school environment play in the learning process. In 2.2.3, I argued that parents, teachers, the learner's peer group and the school play a significant role in shaping student motivation in general; let us now examine briefly the findings that research in the L2 field has produced concerning these issues.

Parents

Parental influence on L2 motivation was considered a major component by Gardner (1985) in his social psychological theory because parents were seen to 'act as the major intermediary between the cultural milieu and the student' (p. 109). Accordingly, he devoted a chapter to the issue in his 1985 book, and the standardised motivation test he and his colleagues have developed (the AMTB; 3.1.3) also contains a whole scale measuring 'parental encouragement'.

Gardner (1985) has identified two main dimensions of the role that parents play in their children's learning process:

- an *active role*, which involves encouragement, support and monitoring, and
- a *passive role*, which involves indirect modelling and communicating attitudes related to L2 learning and the L2 community.

He presents empirical evidence for both types of influence and concludes that although in many cases the two are in harmony, when they are not, the passive role becomes more effective. This implies that even educationally appropriate support practices (e.g. encouraging children to prepare their homework) can be overruled by latent negative language attitudes harboured by the parents.

In order to test Gardner's dual influence hypothesis, Colletta et al. (1983) conducted an empirical survey to examine 'community and parental influence' with regard to Anglophone students enrolled in a French immersion programme in bilingual Ottawa. Their results by and large confirmed Gardner's theory, and they also found that active parental influence had a considerable impact on the students' linguistic self-confidence, thus identifying a further L2-specific mediating variable between parental influence and student motivation (the first being the children's language attitudes shaped after their parents'). In a recent study, Gardner et al. (1999) provide further confirmation that parental encouragement is associated with the development of attitudes towards the learning situation and with the language-learning efforts of the children.

Teachers

As we have seen in 2.2.3, the motivational influence of the teachers is manifold, ranging from the effects of their personality and competence to their active socialising practices. Indeed, Clark and Trafford (1995) found that teachers and students both regard the teacher–pupil relationship as the most significant variable affecting pupils' attitudes towards L2 learning. In their position of group leaders, teachers are also largely responsible for the development of group characteristics in the class, which in turn affect student motivation. Yet, in spite of this central role, teachers have been a rather overlooked factor in research on L2 motivation, and even when teacher-related variables were included in research paradigms, these tended to be global appraisals, typically using versions of the teacher appraisal scale in Gardner's (1985) Attitude/Motivation Test Battery (e.g. Clément et al., 1994; Djigunović, 1994; Mihaljević, 1992). This scale contains 25 items in the semantic differential format (i.e. presenting bipolar adjectives as two extremes of a continuum on which respondents are asked to evaluate their language teacher, such as efficient–inefficient or boring–interesting; 9.2.1), divided into four clusters:

- general evaluation
- rapport
- competence
- inspiration.

As Gardner and MacIntyre (1993a) explain, the rationale for using such a broad approach was to ensure generalisability across different learning situations and studies.

Dörnyei's (1994a) model of L2 motivation (4.2.3) offers a more elaborate conceptualisation of teacher-specific motivational components, by including three main constituents (for definitions, see 2.2.3 and 4.2.3):

- *affiliative motive*
- *authority type* (autonomy supporting or controlling)
- *direct socialisation of motivation* (modelling, task presentation and feedback).

However, this framework was largely conceptual in nature with little empirical testing of the subcomponents.

Recently, Noels et al. (1999) have conducted a pioneering study in which they examined the motivational impact of the teacher's communicative style, particularly the extent to which it is perceived to support students' autonomy and to provide useful feedback about students' learning process. In accordance with the findings in educational psychology (e.g. Deci and Ryan, 1985), Noels and colleagues found that the degree of the teachers' support of student autonomy and the amount of informative feedback they provided was in a significant positive relationship with the students' sense of self-determination and enjoyment (which is also in line with theoretical considerations regarding learner autonomy; Benson, 2000). Interestingly, this directive influence did not reach significance with students who pursued learning primarily for extrinsic reasons. This is a good example of the fact that the teacher–motivation relationship is rather complex and therefore broad appraisals of the teacher (such as the scale in the AMTB) can capture only a limited amount of the variance in the teacher's motivational impact.

Learner group

As discussed in 2.2.3, group-related issues are very much at the heart of the affective dimension of classroom learning and the available evidence supports this with regard to the study of foreign languages as well. In a classroom investigation, Clément et al. (1994) found that perceived group cohesiveness substantially contributed to the learners' overall motivation construct and correlated significantly with various language criterion measures. This finding formed the empirical basis for including a set of group-specific motivational components (consisting of *goal-orientedness*, the *norm and reward system*, *group cohesion* and *classroom goal structures*) in Dörnyei's (1994) construct of L2 motivation (see 4.2.3, for more details). Further support for the influence of group characteristics on the learners' motivational basis was provided by:

- Hotho-Jackson (1995), who examined the role of the group context in the learners' tendency to give up their language studies.
- Dörnyei (1995b), who found that the conscious creation and maintenance of effective group norms concerning the preparation of written home assignments resulted in a homework completion rate of more than 96% among voluntary young adult language learners, in contrast to rates as low as 60% in the same institution without teacher efforts to emphasise such norms.
- Dörnyei (1997), who analysed the motivational basis of cooperative learning (i.e. collaborative learning in small groups) and Julkunen (1989), who obtained empirical confirmation about the superiority of cooperative language learning over competitive or individualistic goal structures.
- Dörnyei and Kormos (2000), who identified a positive relationship between L2 learners' willingness to engage in communicative tasks and (a) the speakers' social status and (b) the quality of the social relationship between the speaker and the interlocutor.

School

Given that the study of whole-school effects on student motivation has been a relatively recent development in educational psychology, it should not be surprising that this line of research is absent in the L2 field. On the other hand, indications that such research would be fruitful are numerous. By examining school characteristics we could understand, for example, why, in certain language-learning contexts, state schools are rather unsuccessful in developing the students' L2 competence, whereas private institutions (e.g. language schools or further education colleges) achieve considerable success even if neither the teachers nor the teaching materials differ substantially.

3.7 The temporal dimension of L2 motivation

Earlier (in 1.6 and 2.3) I argued that a major challenge for motivation theories is to describe the temporal organisation of motivation, that is, to portray motivational processes as they happen in time. This is of particular importance when the target of our interest is a sustained learning process, such as the mastery of a L2, that can take several years to be successfully accomplished. Although most practitioners with sufficient classroom experience are aware of the fact that during the course of such a lengthy process student motivation does not remain constant, hardly any research has been done on analysing the dynamics of L2 motivational change and identifying typical sequential patterns and developmental aspects. Exceptions include work by Williams and Burden, Ushioda, and Dörnyei and Ottó (the latter to be discussed in 3.8).

3.7.1 Focus on time by Williams and Burden

Because of its educational relevance, Marion Williams and Bob Burden's (1997) motivation theory will be described in the next chapter (4.2.4) in detail, but the temporal focus of their model will be summarised here. The time element is represented in the work of Williams and Burden by their separation of three stages of the motivational process along a continuum:

Reasns for doing something
→ Deciding to do something
→ Sustaining the effort, or persisting.

As the authors argue, the first two stages may be seen as more concerned with *initiating motivation* while the last stage involves *sustaining motivation*, and Williams and Burden emphasise that these two aspects of motivation should be clearly differentiated. This conceptualisation bears a close resemblance to Heckhausen's (1991) motivational dichotomy of 'intention formation' (or choice motivation) and 'intention implementation' (or executive motivation) discussed in 2.3, and is also in accordance with the approach of Dörnyei and Ottó's (1998) process model (3.8).

> **Quote 3.16** Williams and Burden on the need to separate the generation and maintenance of motivation
>
> It is important to emphasise here that motivation is more than simply arousing interest. It also involves sustaining interest and investing time and energy into putting the necessary effort to achieve certain goals. We make this point because so often, from a teacher's point of view, motivation is seen as simply sparking an initial interest, for example, presenting an interesting language activity. However, motivating learners entails far more than this.
>
> Williams and Burden (1997: 121)

3.7.2   Focus on time by Ushioda

Ema Ushioda (1994, 1996b) has been arguing for some time in favour of qualitative research approaches that would be more sensitive to the representation of the dynamic nature of the L2 motivation construct. In a longitudinal interview study with motivated Irish learners of French (for a review, see 1998), 16 of the 20 participants defined their L2 motivation principally in terms of the impact of a positive learning history. With respect to the learners' future goal-orientation, her data suggest that this is 'more appropriately conceived as a potentially *evolving* dimension of language learning motivation, rather than its necessary rationale' (Ushioda, 1998: 81–2). As she concludes,

> **Quote 3.17** Ushioda on the need for new research approaches to explore the dynamic nature of L2 motivation
>
> Within the context of institutionalised learning especially, the common experience would seem to be motivational flux rather than stability. . . . Yet, the potential for developing a dynamic theory of L2 motivation would seem to extend beyond the phenomenon of motivational loss or growth alone. In this respect, a more introspective type of research approach is needed to explore qualitative developments in motivational experience over time, as well as to identify the contextual factors perceived to be in dynamic interplay with motivation.
>
> Ushioda (1996b: 240–1)

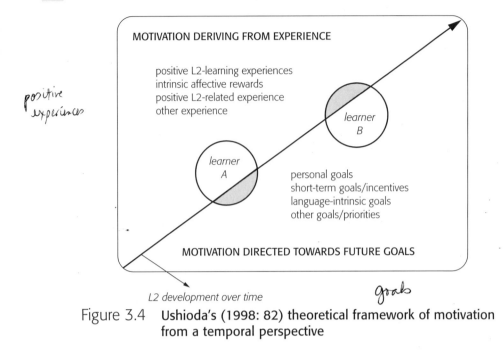

positive experience (handwritten margin note)

Figure 3.4   Ushioda's (1998: 82) theoretical framework of motivation
from a temporal perspective

definitive goal structures may take considerable time to crystallise; in
the meantime, the motivational mainspring sustaining the engagement
in L2 learning may well be the learners' L2-related and L2-learning-
related experience. That is, 'they may feel motivated to pursue language study because they perceive that this is what they are good at or
what they enjoy most, and where therefore their future potential must
lie' (p. 82).

Figure 3.4 offers a schematic representation of Ushioda's conception
of L2 motivation from a temporal perspective. Learner A in the figure
is motivated by positive experiences, with goal-directed patterns playing
only a minor role. In contrast, Learner B's motivational thought structure is predominantly goal-directed. As Ushioda (1998) emphasises, the
motivational pattern of Learner B can represent a potential later stage
in the evolution of Learner A's motivational thinking, as future goals
assume greater importance. 'In this respect, the notion of a temporal
frame of reference shaping motivational thinking integrates the phenomenon of evolution over time, which seems central to the learner's
experience of and thus conception of language learning motivation'
(pp. 82–3).

and vice versa? (handwritten margin note)

3.8   Dörnyei and Ottó's process model of L2 motivation

To conclude this chapter on various models of and theoretical approaches to L2 motivation, I will describe a recent L2 motivation theory that I have developed together with István Ottó in response to the challenge of describing motivational processes over time (Dörnyei and Ottó, 1998). This model organises the motivational influences of L2 learning along a sequence of discrete actional events within the chain of initiating and enacting motivated behaviour. Our primary objective was to introduce a process-oriented perspective of motivation; a secondary goal was to synthesise a number of different lines of research in a unified framework, thereby construing a non-reductionist, comprehensive model.

Figure 3.5 presents the schematic representation of our proposed process model of L2 motivation, which contains two main dimensions:

- *Action Sequence*
- *Motivational Influences.*

The first dimension represents the behavioural process whereby initial wishes, hopes and desires are first transformed into *goals*, then into *intentions*, leading eventually to *action* and, hopefully, to the *accomplishment of the goals*, after which the process is submitted to final *evaluation*. The second dimension of the model, Motivational Influences, includes the *energy sources* and *motivational forces* that underlie and fuel the behavioural process.

3.8.1   Action Sequence

Following Heckhausen and Kuhl's Action Control Theory (2.3), the motivated behavioural process in our model has been divided into three main phases:

- *preactional phase*, corresponding roughly to 'choice motivation' that precedes the launching of action;

- *actional phase*, corresponding to 'executive motivation' that energises action while it is being carried out;

- *postactional phase*, involving critical retrospection after action has been completed or terminated.

MOTIVATIONAL INFLUENCES   ACTION SEQUENCE

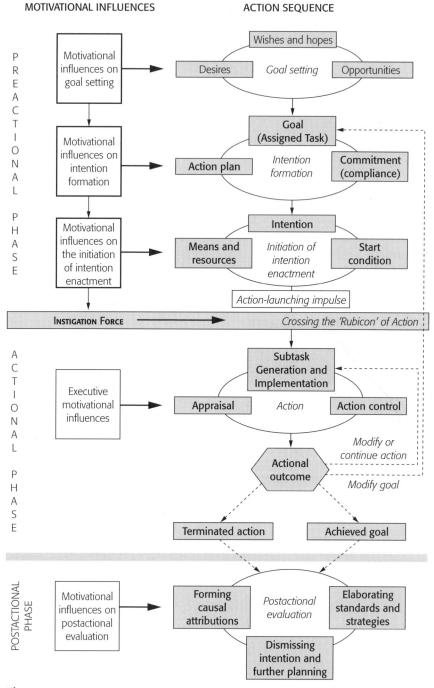

Figure 3.5   Dörnyei and Ottó's (1998: 48) process model of L2 motivation

Preactional phase

The *preactional phase* concerns the process of choosing a course of action to be carried out. Within this phase we can distinguish three subprocesses:

- *goal setting*
- *intention formation*
- *the initiation of intention enactment.*

In some cases these follow on from each other very rapidly, almost simultaneously, but often there is a serious time lapse between them and the sequence can also terminate before reaching action. The antecedents of *goal setting* in our model are broad *wishes/hopes, desires* and *opportunities* (this last component is included because on occasions the starting point of the motivated behavioural process is not the individual's fantasy land but rather an emerging opportunity). However, it is assumed that every individual entertains a great number of wishes, hopes and desires, and comes across several action opportunities that, for some reason or another, will not be further pursued. Therefore, the first key component of the action sequence in our model is when the goal-setting process reaches a concrete outcome, an actual *goal* – it is at this point that the motivated behavioural process begins in earnest.

Because it represents the first concrete decision the learner has taken, the goal is an important element in the motivated action sequence but it does *not* directly initiate action. The immediate antecedent of action in our model is the *intention*, which we see as being qualitatively different from a 'goal' in that it already involves *commitment*. This is an important distinction and it has been made in order to account for the huge difference which exists between the multiple goals and long-term plans the individual may harbour at a given point of time, and the far fewer concrete intentions the individual will hope to carry out. Commitment making can be a highly responsible personal decision, staking personal prestige and even material resources on the goal, and it may also involve forgoing other possible goals or pastimes, along with the rewards that might have attended them (Baumeister, 1996).

Adding commitment to a goal is a crucial step in the motivational process but it is not sufficient in itself to energise action if the goal is not translated into the concrete steps the individual needs to take. Thus, a final necessary step in generating a fully operational intention is to develop a manageable *action plan* which contains the necessary technical details regarding the planned action, namely the

- *action schemata* (i.e. concrete guidelines such as subtasks to implement, and a number of relevant strategies to follow) and
- *the time frame* (i.e. temporal specifications regulating the actual timing of the onset of action, e.g. a concrete time – 'I'll get down to it tomorrow' – or a condition – 'I'll do it when I have finished this').

what about spontaneity?

Although a plan of action does not have to be fully completed before initiating an act – it may be (and usually is) finalised while acting – there must be at least a general action plan before one is able to act at all.

An intention is the immediate antecedent of action, but it is important to realise that action does not follow automatically from it. The right opportunity for starting the action may never materialise, or the means and resources may not be made available, leaving the intention unfulfilled. Thus, our model suggests that there are two necessary conditions for issuing an 'action-launching impulse' (Heckhausen and Kuhl, 1985: 137):

- the availability of the necessary *means and resources*, and
- the *start condition*.

Actional phase

The onset of action results in significant qualitative changes in one's motivation. Following Heckhausen (1991), we believe that it can be compared to crossing a metaphorical 'Rubicon': by actually embarking on the task (e.g. enrolling in a language course) the individual has been committed to action and now the emphasis shifts from deliberation and decision making to the implementation of action. In other words, 'choice motivation' is replaced by 'executive motivation'.

Concept 3.5   On the 'Rubicon' of action

The *Rubicon* was a small stream at the northern border of Italy in the era of the Roman Empire. In order to protect Roman democracy from military coups, a specific law forbade a general to lead an army out of the province to which he was assigned. In 49 BC, after a great deal of internal political turmoil, Julius Caesar's forces crossed the river Rubicon, thereby violating the law and declaring war against the Roman Senate (starting a three-year civil war that left Caesar ruler of the Roman Empire). 'Crossing the Rubicon' has since then become a phrase to describe a step that definitely commits a person to a given course of action. Heckhausen (1991) named his motivation theory the 'Rubicon Model of Action Phases' based on this analogy.

During the *actional phase* three basic processes come into effect:

1. *Subtask generation and implementation*. This refers to learning proper. Action initiation starts with implementing the subtasks that were specified by the action plan; however, as mentioned earlier, action plans are rarely complete (particularly not with sustained activities such as the pursuit of L2 learning) and during the course of action, one continuously generates (or is assigned) subtasks/subgoals.

2. A complex ongoing *appraisal* process. One continuously evaluates the multitude of stimuli coming from the environment and the progress one has made towards the action outcome, comparing actual events with predicted ones or with ones that an alternative action sequence would offer.

3. The application of a variety of *action control* mechanisms. These mechanisms, closely linked with the appraisal process, refer to 'knowledge and strategies used to manage cognitive and noncognitive resources for goal attainment' (Corno and Kanfer, 1993: 304). That is, action control processes involve self-regulatory mechanisms that are called into force in order to enhance, scaffold or protect learning-specific action; active use of such mechanisms may 'save' the action when ongoing monitoring reveals that progress is slowing, halting or

---

Concept 3.6   **On the notion of 'action control' and its relevance to school learning**

Although the term 'action control' may sound novel, similar processes have been the subject of an increasing amount of research in educational psychology for the past decade under the umbrella term of 'self-regulatory strategies' (a subclass of which are 'learning strategies', which have been discussed in the L2 field in detail; e.g. Oxford, 1990). Action control strategies are particularly important from an educational point of view. As Wong and Csikszentmihalyi (1991) have found, studying and schoolwork in general are considered among adolescents to be the least rewarding activities. When in class or doing homework, students report 'low intrinsic motivation and negative experience. They generally feel sad, passive, constrained, bored, detached, and lonely' (p. 544). Schneider et al. (1995) further report a strong negative relationship between being in an academic class and feeling motivated, which they explain by the fact that students tend to find most academic classroom activities unenjoyable and uninteresting. All this creates fertile ground for distractions that need to be controlled for the sake of learning effectiveness.

> **Quote 3.18** Corno on the importance of action control strategies in academic learning
>
> The world is replete with enchanting distractions for even the most eager of students. Schools are complex social networks as well as places of work. Homes provide children with television, computer games, and compact discs. After-school clubs engulf what little spare time children have. To succeed academically, students must learn to cope with the competition between their social and intellectual goals and to manage and control the range of other distractions that arise. Volitional [i.e. action control] strategies have a promising role to play in achieving these goals.
>
> Corno (1994: 248)

backsliding. For the purpose of our model, we will distinguish between three types of self-regulatory strategy:

- *motivation maintenance strategies*
- *language learning strategies*
- *goal-setting strategies.*

On the basis of the interplay of the appraisal and control processes, the ongoing action will lead to some kind of *actional outcome*: the optimal scenario is that the actor achieves his or her goal, whereas the other extreme is terminating the action completely. However, arriving at a dead end during the actional phase does not necessarily lead to action abandonment:

- If the motivational foundation of the initial wish or desire was sufficiently powerful, the individual may mentally step back to the preactional phase, revise the concrete goal to be pursued and form a new intention (e.g. by lowering the level of aspiration).
- Alternatively, by maintaining the original intention, the individual may fine-tune or modify the strategies and subtasks applied in the pursuit of the goal during the actional phase.
- Finally, in case of a temporary interruption, action can be continued at a later time.

Postactional phase

The postactional stage begins after either the goal has been achieved or the action has been terminated; alternatively, it can also take place when action is interrupted for a longer period (e.g. a holiday). The main processes during this phase entail evaluating the accomplished action outcome and contemplating possible inferences to be drawn for future actions. During this phase, the learner compares initial expectancies and plans of action to how they turned out in reality and forms *causal attributions* about the extent to which the intended goal has been reached. This critical retrospection contributes significantly to accumulated experience, and allows the learner to elaborate his or her *internal standards* and the repertoire of *action-specific strategies*. It is through such evaluation that an individual can develop a stable identity as a successful learner (Boekaerts, 1988).

The formation of adequate standards to compare actual and potential performance, and the extension of the repertoire of personalised action-control strategies already serve to prepare the ground for the future, but before further action can be taken, the initial intention has to be *dismissed* to give way to new wishes, goals and intentions. An accomplished intention may clear the way for a subsequent intention leading to a more distant superordinate goal – in this case the postactional motivation process evolves into a preactional phase and the cycle begins anew.

3.8.2 Motivational influences on the different action phases of the model

The action sequence dimension described above outlines the sequential pattern of the motivational process but it is incomplete without a second, complementary dimension of motivation which is made up of the various *motivational influences* that fuel the actional sequence. These energy sources can be enhancing or inhibiting, depending on whether they contribute to the successful implementation of the goal or dampen the actor's endeavour.

As indicated in Figure 3.5, motivational influences form five clusters, according to the five specific phases of the motivated action sequence they affect:

1. Motivational influences on goal setting.
2. Motivational influences on intention formation.
3. Motivational influences on the initiation of intention enactment.
4. Executive motivational influences.
5. Motivational influences on postactional evaluation.

Concept 3.7   **On the interrelationship of the five sets of motivational influences**

The first three clusters of motivational influences (associated with the *preactional phase*) in Figure 3.5 are linked with arrows to each other, indicating that the preactional motivational system works like a series of interlinked filters:

1. Only the wishes that receive sufficient support from the first set of motivational influences qualify for becoming *goals*.

2. These goals are then submitted to a second motivational phase, intention formation, where new energy sources are added to the resultant motivational force, and if this exceeds the necessary threshold for stepping further, the goal becomes a fully-fledged *intention*.

3. Finally, an *action-launching impulse* will be issued if the sum of the influences that have fuelled the intention so far and the new factors that come into force in the third, action initiation phase reaches a certain level of strength.

4. The overall resultant motivational force associated with the preactional phase is labelled in the figure as the *instigation force*, which determines the intensity of action initiation.

Moving further 'down' Figure 3.5, however, the executive motivational influences associated with the *actional phase* are *not* directly related to the motives affecting the earlier stages of the process. This is in line with Heckhausen and Kuhl's 'Action Control Theory' (2.3), which emphasises that 'executive motives' are largely different from the motives making up 'choice motivation'. Only by assuming such a division of motives related to the preactional and the actional phases can we explain, for example, the frequent phenomenon of

- someone deciding to enrol in a language course (motivated by 'choice motivation'),
- then soon dropping out (because the 'executive motives' fail to sustain the instigation force),
- and then again re-enrolling in the course (since after the action engagement has been terminated, the preactional forces become activated again).

The reason why such cycles do not go on ad infinitum is that after the termination (or completion) of action, a third set of motivational influences – associated with the *postactional phase* – come into force, and the explanations one arrives at during this phase about the previous sequence (e.g. 'I simply don't have the time/energy/aptitude for L2 learning') significantly affect subsequent action tendencies.

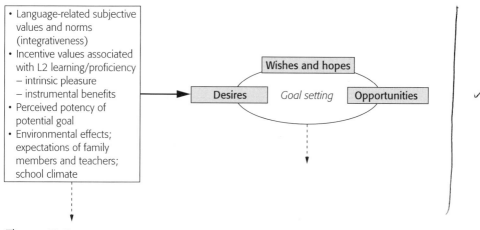

Figure 3.6   **Motivational influences on goal setting**

Goal setting

Why do learners select certain goals and not others? In our model we have distinguished four main motivational factors that underlie the goal-setting process (Figure 3.6).

- First and foremost are the individual's *subjective values and norms* that have developed during the past, as a reaction to past experiences. From a L2 learning perspective, these involve basic beliefs and feelings about the significance of being internationally open, knowing foreign languages and participating in cross-cultural communication. A great deal of this factor has been well captured by Gardner's (1985) concept of 'integrativeness' (3.1.1).

- The general values and norms interplay with the specific *incentive values* (2.1.1 and 3.2) associated with L2 learning. Such values can be the *intrinsic pleasure* one gains from learning languages (3.3), and the *instrumental benefits* the knowledge of the L2 can bring about such as a good job or increased travel opportunities (i.e. 'instrumental motivation'; 3.1).

- The value preferences already screen out many 'unsuitable' wishes and desires, and they also help to determine the general *potency of the goals* (i.e. a subjective feeling, or expectancy, about the general probability of achieving the respective goal; 2.1.1).

- Finally, the *external environment* (such as the expectations of family members and teachers, and the role of the school environment; 2.2, 3.6) also exerts a considerable influence on our choice of potential goals.

Intention formation

Arriving at a goal means that the individual has formulated an 'I want to' type of internal statement. However, the fact is that not every goal will be realised. Simply having the incentive to strive for a goal does not guarantee that the person will actually undertake the effort that is required. There are a great number of factors that determine whether the goal will be further processed into an *intention*, and therefore *intention formation* involves a process of weighing the feasibility and desirability of the available options, and visualising the possible consequences of one's potential actions (Figure 3.7).

Important factors determining the intention formation process are:

- the learner's perceived *expectancy of success* (2.1.1);
- the perceived *relevance* of the goal (i.e. how important L2 learning is in relation to their current life concerns);

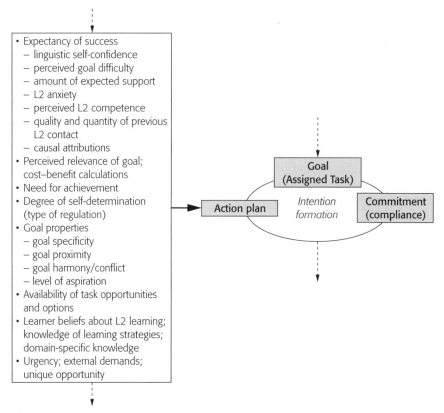

Figure 3.7   **Motivational influences on intention formation**

- the accompanying *cost–benefit calculations* (i.e. the comparison of positive and negative values; cf. 2.1.1) the individual makes.

Furthermore, in accordance with the principles of achievement motivation theory (2.1.1), self-determination theory (2.1.3) and goal-setting theory (2.1.2), intention formation is also assumed to be influenced by

- *need for achievement* and *fear of failure*;
- *self-determination* (or learner autonomy);
- various *goal properties* (such as goal specificity, e.g. setting concrete sub-goals such as learning 50 words every evening; goal proximity, e.g. preparing for a forthcoming language exam; goal harmony/conflict, e.g. the afternoon language course clashes with the karate training; and the level of aspiration, e.g. some people only want to acquire a working knowledge of a language whereas others strive for near-native proficiency).

As was said earlier, the development of an action plan is an imperative to forming a fully operational intention. This is why the *availability of task opportunities and options* is an important, though not indispensable, motivational condition. Further, equally important, determinants of the quality of the action plan one develops are the

- *learner's beliefs about L2 learning*
- *knowledge of learning strategies*
- sufficient *domain-specific knowledge*.

These factors form influential predispositions in the learners about the learning process, stemming from the learners' families, peer groups, and prior learning experiences. For example, if someone thinks of the study of a language only as tedious and hard work characterised by endless memorisation of bilingual word lists, this will obviously reduce his or her initial enthusiasm, whereas an informed, 'made to measure' action plan (e.g. a computer devotee deciding to learn through specially designed computer games) might give the necessary incentive to engage in the learning process.

Finally, in certain cases commitment does not happen even if many of the above-mentioned motivational influences are in place. At such times what we need is a final 'push', such as

- some sort of *urgency*;
- powerful *external demands* (e.g. you need to pass a language exam to qualify for a job or scholarship);
- a *unique opportunity* (e.g. to travel abroad).

The initiation of intention enactment: crossing the 'Rubicon' of action

It is not always the case that intentions are implemented immediately after their formation; quite frequently there is some delay before action takes place, and, as mentioned earlier, in certain cases even fully operationalised intentions never reach the actional phase. This indicates that there is a separate processing phase between intention formation and action: the *initiation of intention enactment*. This is not to be confused with 'intention formation', which concerned the actual decision whether to do a certain thing; here the main question is finding the right point in time for actualising the intention to act, particularly with respect to seeking and utilising suitable opportunities and the preparation of appropriate steps for implementation.

Figure 3.8 presents the main motivational influences that affect the action initiation phase:

- First and foremost among these is Kuhl's concepts of *action vs state orientation* (2.3.1).

- A second variable affecting the enactment of an intention is the person's *perceived behavioural control*, referring to the perceived ease or difficulty of performing the behaviour (2.1.4). Simply stated, one must believe that one has sufficient control over the outcome to exert effort towards achieving it.

- There are also some negative forces working against intention enactment. These may be caused by various *distracting influences and obstacles*, which obviously stand in the way of action implementation, particularly if powerful *competing action tendencies* are available.

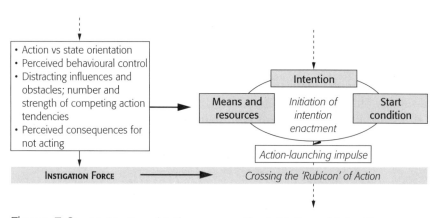

Figure 3.8   Motivational influences on the initiation of intention enactment

- Finally, should one be inclined to abandon the enactment of an intention due to some of the above difficulties, there is one more powerful factor that comes into force, potentially making the person think again: the *perceived consequences for not acting*.

Actional processes

Once an initial wish has 'obtained' sufficient motivational support to pass all the hurdles, the individual is ready to embark on a course of action. The intensity of the 'action-launching impulse' (Heckhausen and Kuhl, 1985: 137) will depend on the cumulative or resultant force of all the motivational influences active in the preactional phase (i.e. *instigation force*). As discussed earlier (2.3), the impact of this force is soon affected by a new set of motivational influences (see Figure 3.9) that come into force only once action has started. Not surprisingly, the biggest group of such executive motives concerns the appraisal system and the outcome of the appraisal process. The rest of the components concern the effectiveness of the action control processes, the impact of external influences such as the teacher's role, and factors inherent to the action itself.

Probably the most important influence on ongoing learning is the perceived *quality of the learning experience*. The five stimulus appraisal dimensions in Schumann's theory (i.e. novelty, pleasantness, goal/need significance, coping potential, and self and social image; see 3.4) capture well the various situation-specific appraisals proposed in the L2 literature (e.g. Crookes and Schmidt's, 1991, system made up of interest, relevance, expectancy and satisfaction, also adopted by Dörnyei, 1994a; see 4.2.1 and 4.2.3), as well as covering several of the most important current issues in the educational psychological literature (e.g. the concern about self-esteem/self-worth, self-efficacy, intrinsic interest, well-being).

Because learning is a goal-oriented activity, *the perceived contingent relationship between action and outcome* and the *perceived progress* the learner has made on this contingent path deserves explicit treatment. Students constantly evaluate how well they are doing in terms of approaching the desired outcome, and if they feel that their action is conducive to reaching that outcome they experience a feeling of *success*, which then provides further motivation. A further powerful factor regarding learning experiences that was already mentioned with respect to the intention formation stage is the learner's *sense of self-determination/autonomy* (2.1.3, 3.3). Besides the learner, there are certain other key figures affecting the motivational quality of the learning process, namely the

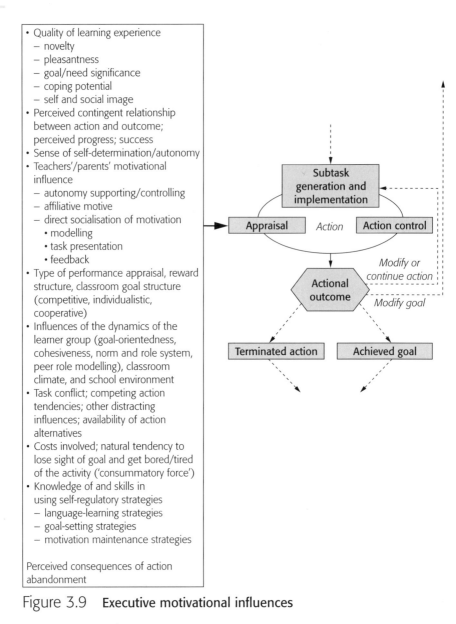

Figure 3.9   **Executive motivational influences**

teacher and the *parents* (2.2.3, 3.6.5). Particularly featured aspects of how teachers structure classroom life are the type of *performance appraisal* and *reward structure* (5.2.4), and the more general *classroom goal structure* (indicating whether learning in the classroom is individualistically, competitively or cooperatively structured; 2.2.3). Parents and teachers are not the only external sources of situation-specific motivation. An increasing body of research has highlighted the influence of the *learner group* and the *classroom climate* (2.2.3, 3.6.5).

It probably requires little justification that *task conflict, competing action tendencies, other distracting influences* and the *availability of action alternatives* have a weakening effect on the resultant motivational force associated with the particular course of action. In such cases, unless effective action control strategies are activated, the behavioural process may be interrupted and in some cases terminated. This is why *knowledge of and skills in using self-regulatory strategies* such as learning strategies, goal-setting strategies and motivation maintenance strategies (detailed in Chapter 5) constitute an important source of scaffolding and enhancing motivation. Further negative influences are provided by the *costs* involved in pursuing the activity – a factor already mentioned at the intention formation phase. Finally, just as in the preactional phase, the last motivational factor to be listed here is the *perceived consequences of action abandonment*. It is sometimes only when everything else fails and one is about to quit, that one thinks over what action abandonment would really entail, and the perceived possible negative consequences may activate enough energy to keep going.

Postactional evaluation

Postactional evaluation has an important role in determining the learners' sense of success, achievement and satisfaction, which will then influence how they approach subsequent learning tasks. In our model we distinguished four major motivational influences that are active in the postactional phase: *attributional factors, self-concept beliefs*, the quality and quantity of *evaluational/attributional cues and feedback* and *action versus state orientation* (Figure 3.10). *see 2.1.1*

I have already summarised the main principles of attribution theory in 2.1.1 (i.e. that the different ways people explain their past successes and failures affect their future achievement behaviour). What is particularly important here is that there are considerable individual differences in how people form attributions. These are referred to as *attributional styles* (i.e. habitual ways of explaining events) and *attributional biases* (i.e. incorrect inference rules that are used to make attributions, e.g. basic attribution errors such as the tendency to attribute something to personal factors while ignoring relevant, or even crucial, situational factors, and vice versa).

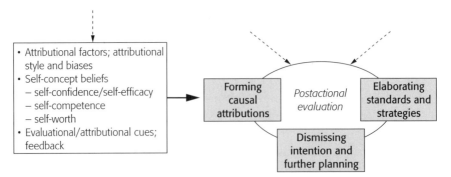

Figure 3.10   Motivational influences on postactional evaluation

Self-concept beliefs, including one's established level of *self-confidence/ self-efficacy*, *self-competence* and *self-worth* in different domains, also influence the result of postactional evaluation. Learners with relatively high self-perceptions handle occasional failures much better than learners with low self-worth beliefs in that they tend to heighten and sustain effort in the face of failure, while mobilising new strategies to tackle the task.

The evaluational process is also a function of external *evaluational/ attributional cues*. Of all the attributional cues in classroom contexts, the most featured one from the learners' point of view is the *feedback* from the teacher (2.2.3 and 5.2.4). Finally, although one might think that nothing could be simpler than abandoning an action, this is not always the case. People are known to get stuck in unfruitful activities, unable to 'cut their losses', and this is why Kuhl has extended the concepts of *action vs state orientation* (2.3) to apply to the 'disengagement from an intention and the initiation of a new course of action in situations in which the intention has become unattainable or in which changing conditions require a change in the goal hierarchy' (Kuhl and Goschke, 1994: 95) (2.3.1).

II Motivation and language teaching

Chapter 4

'Education-friendly' approaches in motivation research

This chapter will . . .

- describe the 'reform movement' in L2 motivation research, whose explicit objective was to make motivation theory more appropriate for classroom application;
- present the L2 motivational frameworks that have been developed with educational relevance in mind.

The main focus in Section II is how the findings of past motivation research can benefit language teachers in their day-by-day classroom practice. Although no one would doubt that an increasing understanding of student motivation can have significant practical implications, it is questionable whether motivation research in general has reached a level of sophistication that would allow scholars to translate research results into straightforward educational recommendations. The crux of the problem is that although there are many effective motivational principles and guidelines that can help practitioners, these principles do not add up to a coherent theory. Furthermore, most of the available practical recommendations are subject to situational constraints; that is, they lack universal generalisability and cannot therefore be prescribed 'blindly', without adapting them to the particular learning situation in which they are to be used. For these reasons, the most educational researchers can do at present is to raise teachers' 'motivational awareness' by providing them with a menu of potentially useful insights and suggestions from which they can select according to their actual priorities and concerns, and the characteristics and composition of their students.

> **Quote 4.1** Graham and Weiner on the practical relevance of motivation theories in the *Handbook of Educational Psychology*
>
> The laws of physics aided the construction of the Golden Gate Bridge and the laws of biology helped eradicate smallpox. In a similar vein, theories of motivation may assist in the creation of rules to enhance human performance. We acknowledge at the outset that this motivational goal is presently more a dream than a reality and will not reach fruition in the reader's lifetime. Thus, those beginning this chapter with the anticipation that after reading the final paragraph they can go back into the classroom and soon have all the students working with intensity and positive affect will be disappointed.
>
> Graham and Weiner (1996: 63)

A good starting point for summarising the education-specific aspects of L2 motivation research is to describe a major shift in thinking which took place at the beginning of the 1990s and which has resulted in researchers paying increasing attention to motivational processes underlying classroom learning, thereby making motivation research more 'education-friendly'.

4.1 The educational shift in L2 motivation research

Robert Gardner's motivation theory (3.1) involved an influential, socially grounded approach and most studies examining the affective domain of L2 learning before the 1990s adopted this paradigm. However, by the 1990s mainstream motivation psychology had developed a number of cognitive constructs which had proved to be highly successful in investigating pedagogical issues in general educational contexts but had not been properly utilised in the study of L2 learning/teaching. Consequently, a growing number of researchers (e.g. Brown 1990, 1994; Crookes and Schmidt, 1991; Dörnyei, 1994a, 1994b; Julkunen, 1989, 1993; Oxford and Shearin 1994, 1996; Schmidt et al., 1996; Skehan, 1989, 1991; Ushioda, 1994, 1996a; Williams, 1994) voiced their feelings that there was an increasing gap between general and L2 motivational theories, and the desire for increased convergence engendered a flourish of both empirical research and theorising on motivation. Over a hundred papers have been published on the subject during the past decade (for a review,

Concept 4.1   **The educational orientation in L2 motivation research**

The common theme underlying the new emerging educational orientation in the first half of the 1990s was the belief that motivational sources closely related to the learners' immediate classroom environment have a stronger impact on the overall L2 motivation complex than had been expected. Thus, there was a growing perception of the need to elaborate and extend motivation constructs not only to account for these situation-specific motives but also to render them more suitable for immediate classroom application. In order to achieve this, scholars typically deviated from the traditional social psychological approach both in their goals and emphases, yet the significance of the broad sociocultural orientations and language attitudes advocated by Gardner and his Canadian associates was never questioned.

see Dörnyei, 1998a) and the number of new motivation theories and constructs proposed has already reached double figures.

The emerging educational shift in thought cannot be specifically tied to any particular school or scholars because, as the above list shows, a number of researchers in different parts of the world appeared to project similar ideas at almost the same time. The educational orientation was in the air. The most influential pioneering article in this vein is usually considered to be Crookes and Schmidt (1991) and a good summary of the various positions is provided by the 'Modern Language Journal debate' (Dörnyei, 1994a, 1994b; Gardner and Tremblay, 1994a, 1994b; Oxford, 1994; Oxford and Shearin, 1994).

Quote 4.2   Crookes and Schmidt's call for education-friendly motivation research

Discussion of the topic of motivation in second-language (SL) learning contexts has been limited by the understanding the field of applied linguistics has attached to it. In that view, primary emphasis is placed on attitudes and other social psychological aspects of SL learning. This does not do full justice to the way SL teachers have used the term motivation. Their use is more congruent with definitions common outside social psychology, specifically in education. (p. 469)

In brief, we seek to encourage a program of research that will develop from, and be congruent with the concept of motivation that teachers are convinced is critical for SL success. (p. 502)

Crookes and Schmidt (1991)

Oxford (1996) has characterised the educational shift as a 'revolution in our thinking'. However, this very peaceful revolution differed from 'real' revolutions in at least two significant ways:

- It never involved the wish to 'wipe the slate clean' and discard the previously dominant theory (i.e. Gardner's social psychological theory), only the intention to *expand* it by incorporating additional factors that would offer increased explanatory power with regard to specific language-learning tasks and behaviours in classroom settings.

- Instead of being 'beheaded' (as is done in a proper revolution), the authorities of the old 'regime' took an active part in revitalising the field and contributing to what Gardner and Tremblay (1994b) referred to as the emerging 'motivational renaissance'. For example, Tremblay and Gardner's (1995) motivation model (3.1.4) was – ironically – far less 'Gardnerian' than Dörnyei's (1994a) (4.2.3) or Dörnyei and Ottó's (1998) (3.8) in the sense that it did *not* acknowledge the existence of the integrative motive at all whereas the latter two constructs did.

Quote 4.3 Stipek on the importance of classroom-specific motives

Study after study demonstrates that although students bring some motivational baggage – beliefs, expectations, and habits – to class, the immediate instructional context strongly affects their motivation. Decisions about the nature of the tasks, how performance is evaluated, how rewards are used, how much autonomy students have, and myriad other variables under a teacher's control largely determine student motivation.

Stipek (1996: 85)

Gardner was not unaware of the importance of the learning situation in shaping student motivation. To the contrary: one of the three main constituents of the integrative motive (3.1) was the *attitudes towards the learning situation*, comprising attitudes towards the teacher and the course, and the Attitude/Motivation Test Battery contain two elaborate scales (with a total of 50 items) measuring these. However, as argued in 3.1, the main emphasis in Gardner's socio-educational model had not been on elaborating on the range of possible motivational antecedents (many of which would be related to the classroom environment) but on determining whether motivation has been aroused and specifying the learning consequences of this arousal in relation to the impact of other non-motivational factors (such as intelligence).

> **Quote 4.4** Oxford and Shearin's reaction to Gardner's conclusion that the source of motivation is relatively unimportant provided motivation is aroused
>
> While this conclusion might be true for researchers, quite possibly the source of motivation is very important in a practical sense to teachers who want to stimulate students' motivation. Without knowing where the roots of motivation lie, how can teachers water those roots?
>
> Oxford and Shearin (1994: 15)

The educational shift had a liberating effect on L2 motivation research, leading to an unprecedented boom in the field. Within a period of 5–6 years the complete research scene had been reshaped and classroom issues had been put firmly on the research agenda; as a result, our knowledge about the motivational foundation of instructed L2 learning has increased considerably. At the same time, we must also note that there appears to be a worrisome tendency for the new, educationally relevant constructs and approaches (and I hasten to add that some of my own work also falls into this 'danger zone') to become increasingly conceptual, without having sufficient research grounding; for example, none of the four pedagogically motivated constructs to be presented in 4.2 has considerable empirical support within L2 contexts. Pertinent data-based research will also need to account for the impact of the sociocultural and political macrocontext on the classroom-based processes (thereby addressing the 'challenge of context'; 1.5).

> **Quote 4.5** Gardner and Tremblay on the need for research-based motivation models
>
> We also advocate the exploration of other motivational theories as a way of expanding the motivation construct but recognise that such endeavour is of no value in the absence of pertinent empirical research. We are very much aware that such demands make the agenda and the expansion more challenging. However, on with the challenge!
>
> Gardner and Tremblay (1994a: 366)

4.2   Educationally motivated constructs

Psychological models – even the best ones – cannot offer more than a hugely simplified reflection of the actual reality they concern, and the value of any model, therefore, lies in the degree of its usefulness in interpreting real-world processes. L2 motivation constructs can be evaluated according to two criteria:

unclear how these diff

- how conducive they are to the advancement of the field;
- how much practical utility value they possess.

The models presented in the previous chapter were selected because of their merits with respect to the first criterion. I will now describe four constructs – developed by Crookes and Schmidt (1991), Oxford and Shearin (1994, 1996), Dörnyei (1994a) and Williams and Burden (1997) – which have been developed with the purpose of educational utility in mind. They are not models proper as they do not go beyond listing and clustering certain key variables without specifying their exact interrelationship; instead, they can be seen as organisational frameworks designed to help to get orientated among the plethora of motivational influences relevant in the language classroom.

Quote 4.6 Uguroglu and Walberg on the applicability of psychological constructs of motivation to education

One problem in applying psychological constructs of motivation to education is the surplus rather than the shortage of theories. Educators are confronted with a number of rival positions, each of which seems to have some degree of plausibility. Moreover, empirical results such as coefficients of predictive validity are insufficient criteria for adjudicating between rival constructs, because empirical research often remains unrelated to theory. Many theories lack empirical testing in the natural settings of the classroom, and few studies compare rival theoretical positions in classroom settings.

as needed

Uguroglu and Walberg (1986: 1)

4.2.1   Crookes and Schmidt's theory

Although there had been calls for adopting a broader research agenda in the study of L2 motivation (e.g. Brown, 1990; Julkunen, 1989; Skehan, 1989), Graham Crookes and Richard Schmidt's (1991) article in the journal *Language Learning* has been usually regarded as the most influential one in initiating the 'educational shift'. This is partly due to the excellent timing of the paper – the authors formulated a view that had been brewing in the profession but had not been articulated in explicit terms and detail – and partly due to the multiple roles the paper fulfilled:

- It was first and foremost a 'position paper', as also marked in the title ('Motivation: Reopening the research agenda'), with a clearcut and strongly stated stance, thereby setting the tone for a number of further studies.

- It contained a well-researched review of both the L2 and the mainstream psychological literature of motivation with over 140 references, introducing the work of several prominent motivational psychologists for the first time in the L2 field.

- It rose to the challenge of addressing the necessarily eclectic and multifaceted nature of L2 motivation by distinguishing between various levels of motivation and motivated learning (micro, classroom, syllabus/curriculum, and extracurricular levels), and thus highlighted several paths along which subsequent research could proceed.

- Drawing on Keller's (1983) comprehensive education-oriented theory of motivation, the authors presented a parsimonious motivation framework made up of four components – interest, relevance, expectancy and satisfaction/outcomes – that provided a ready-to-use alternative to Gardner's (1985) integrative-instrumental dichotomy.

- Finally, it outlined an explicit and detailed research agenda by formulating a series of key questions organised according to a theoretical sequence.

Concept 4.2   **The four levels of motivation and motivated learning in Crookes and Schmidt's theory**

- *The micro level*, which deals with the motivation/attention interface, that is, with motivational effects on the cognitive processing of L2 stimuli.
- *The classroom level*, which deals with techniques and activities in motivational terms, drawing on Keller's conceptualisation.
- *The syllabus/curriculum level*, at which content decisions based on needs analysis come into play.
- *Extracurricular level (long-term learning)*, which concerns informal, out-of-class and long-term factors, and 'continuing motivation'.

Concept 4.3   **Keller's motivation system adopted by Crookes and Schmidt**

Keller's (1983) four-component system that was adopted by Crookes and Schmidt is a prime example of a successful educational construct. It draws together some of the most important lines of research in motivational psychology and synthesises them in a way that the outcome is relevant to and accessible for classroom application. The framework has four components:

1. *Interest* is related to intrinsic motivation and is centred around the individual's inherent curiosity and desire to know more about himself or herself and his or her environment.

2. *Relevance* refers to the extent to which the student feels that the instruction is connected to important personal needs, values, or goals. At a macro level, this component coincides with instrumentality; at the level of the learning situation, it refers to the extent to which the classroom instruction and course content are seen to be conducive to achieving the goal, that is, to mastering the L2.

3. *Expectancy* refers to the perceived likelihood of success and is related to the learner's self-confidence and self-efficacy at a general level; at the level of the learning situation, it concerns perceived task difficulty, the amount of effort required, the amount of available assistance and guidance, the teacher's presentation of the task, and familiarity with the task type.

4. *Satisfaction* concerns the outcome of an activity, referring to the combination of extrinsic rewards such as praise or good marks and to intrinsic rewards such as enjoyment and pride.

4.2.2   Oxford and Shearin's approach

Rebecca Oxford and Jill Shearin's article was the first of an emerging debate in three issues in the 1994 volume of the *Modern Language Journal* (with the other contributors being Dörnyei, 1994a, 1994b; Gardner and Tremblay, 1994a, 1994b; and Oxford, 1994). Although Crookes and Schmidt's (1991) paper had been in circulation for almost three years, this debate – and the fact that, upon the invitation of editor Sally Magnam, Robert Gardner joined in the discussion, thereby acknowledging the existence of the 'new wave' – played an important role in establishing the alternative tone in the field of L2 motivation research. Further articulation of this 'new key' was also facilitated by a motivation colloquium at the annual conference of the American Association for Applied Linguistics (AAAL) in 1995, organised by Rebecca Oxford, whose proceedings were published in the following year (Oxford, 1996).

The greatest merit of Oxford and Shearin's study (originally published in 1994 and extended in 1996) was to highlight explicitly the growing gap between L2 motivation theories and the variety of emerging new concepts in mainstream motivational psychology, and to call explicitly for an expansion of the social psychological approach. In a real 'paradigm-seeking' effort, the authors surveyed a wide array of motivation constructs in several branches of psychology (general, industrial, educational, cognitive developmental and sociocultural) in order to draw on them in developing L2 models that would have an increased explanatory power in diverse learning contexts. The new perspective they present is very broad indeed; it covers:

- need theories (personal needs, job satisfaction needs, need for achievement)
- expectancy-value theories (achievement motivation, VIE [valence/instrumentality/expectancy] theory, goal-setting theory)
- equity theories
- reinforcement theories
- social cognition theories
- achievement goal theory
- Piaget's cognitive developmental theory
- Vygotsky's sociocultural theory.

4.2.3 Dörnyei's extended motivational framework

Crookes and Schmidt's (1991) approach of examining motivation at various conceptual levels was taken up by Dörnyei (1994a), who conceptualised L2 motivation within a framework of three relatively distinct levels (see Table 4.1):

- language level
- learner level
- learning situation level.

When drawing up this framework, the intention was to design a comprehensive construct to synthesise various lines of research by offering an extensive list of motivational components categorised into main dimensions/clusters. The tripartite division was based on the empirical results of Clément et al. (1994), which pointed to the existence of three main determinants of the motivation of the L2 learners investigated: *integrativeness*, *linguistic self-confidence* and the *appraisal of the classroom environment* (3.5.3), but in the Dörnyei categorisation the scope of each component was broadened. The resulting three levels coincide with the three basic constituents of the L2 learning process – the target language, the language learner and the language-learning situation – and also reflect three different aspects of language: the social dimension, the personal dimension and the educational subject-matter dimension.

The conceptualisation of the constituent components of the first two levels draws heavily on Gardner and Clément's theories, supplemented with the findings of Dörnyei (1990), whereas the third and most elaborate dimension was largely based on findings reported in the educational psychological literature. More specifically:

- The *language level* encompasses various components related to aspects of the L2, such as the culture and the community, as well as the intellectual and pragmatic values and benefits associated with it.

- The *learner level* involves individual characteristics that the learner brings to the learning process.

- The *learning situation level* is associated with situation-specific motives rooted in various aspects of language learning within a classroom setting:

  Course-specific motivational components are related to the syllabus, the teaching materials, the teaching method and the learning tasks, and can be well described with the framework of four motivational conditions proposed by Keller (1983) and subsequently by Crookes and Schmidt (1991) (interest, relevance, expectancy and outcome; 4.2.2).

  Teacher-specific motivational components concern the motivational impact of the teacher's personality, behaviour and teaching style/practice (cf. 2.2.3 and 3.6.5).

  Group-specific motivational components are related to the group dynamics of the learner group (cf. 2.2.3 and 3.6.5).

The rationale for separating the three motivational levels was that they seem to have a vital effect on the overall motivation independently of each other; that is, by changing the parameters at one level and keeping the other two dimensions constant, the overall motivation might completely change. For example, the same learner in the same learning

Table 4.1   Dörnyei's framework of L2 motivation
(Dörnyei, 1994a: 280)

LANGUAGE LEVEL	Integrative motivational subsystem Instrumental motivational subsystem
LEARNER LEVEL	Need for achievement Self-confidence • Language use anxiety • Perceived L2 competence • Causal attributions • Self-efficacy
LEARNING SITUATION LEVEL *Course-specific motivational* *components*	Interest (in the course) Relevance (of the course to one's needs) Expectancy (of success) Satisfaction (one has in the outcome)
Teacher-specific motivational *components*	Affiliative motive (to please the teacher) Authority type (controlling vs. autonomy- supporting) Direct socialisation of motivation • Modelling • Task Presentation • Feedback
Group-specific motivational *components*	Goal-orientedness Norm and reward system Group cohesiveness Classroom goal structure (cooperative, competitive or individualistic)

situation might show a strikingly different degree of motivation depending on what the target language is. Similarly, when the target language is the same, the same learner's motivation can show vast differences as the function of the learning situation, that is, the appraisal of the language classroom (consider, for example, the effect of a bad or a good teacher). In other words, each of the three levels of motivation exerts its influence independently of the others and has sufficient power to nullify the effects of the motives associated with the other two levels.

4.2.4   Williams and Burden's social constructivist model

Another comprehensive attempt to summarise the motivational components that are relevant to L2 instruction has been made by Marion

Table 4.2   Williams and Burden's framework of L2 motivation (Williams and Burden, 1997)

Internal factors

Intrinsic interest of activity:
- arousal of curiosity
- optimal degree of challenge

Perceived value of activity:
- personal relevance
- anticipated value of outcomes
- intrinsic value attributed to the activity

Sense of agency:
- locus of causality
- locus of control RE process and outcomes
- ability to set appropriate goals

Mastery:
- feelings of competence
- awareness of developing skills and mastery in a chosen area
- self-efficacy

Self-concept:
- realistic awareness of personal strengths and weaknesses in skills required
- personal definitions and judgements of success and failure
- self-worth concern
- learned helplessness

Attitudes:
- to language learning in general
- to the target language
- to the target language community and culture

Other affective states:
- confidence
- anxiety, fear

Developmental age and stage
Gender

External factors

Significant others:
- parents
- teachers
- peers

The nature of interaction with significant others:
- mediated learning experiences
- the nature and amount of feedback
- rewards
- the nature and amount of appropriate praise
- punishments, sanctions

The learning environment:
- comfort
- resources
- time of day, week, year
- size of class and school
- class and school ethos

The broader context:
- wider family networks
- the local education system
- conflicting interests
- cultural norms
- societal expectations and attitudes

most elaborate treatment (at that time) in L2 field of contextual factors

Williams and Bob Burden (1997) as part of a larger overview of psychology for language teachers. In spite of the fact that the coverage of motivation was restricted to only one of the ten chapters in Williams and Burden's book, and therefore could not go into sufficient detail, the construct presented is unique in that it explicitly addresses two of the six fundamental motivational challenges discussed in Chapter 1: those of *context* and *time*. The authors' general approach taken in the whole book is rooted in the social constructivist tradition, and in terms of motivation, their emphasis on contextual influences is very much in accordance with the arguments in 1.5, 2.2 and 3.6. The treatment of the time element by the authors was discussed in 3.8.

> **Quote 4.7** Williams and Burden on the social constructivist conception of motivation
>
> A constructivist view of motivation centres around the premise that each individual is motivated differently.... However, an individual's motivation is also subject to social and contextual influences. These will include the whole culture and context and the social situation, as well as significant other people and the individual's interaction with these people. Thus, the approach we are taking, in keeping with the rest of this book, is social constructivist.
>
> Williams and Burden (1997: 121)

In conclusion to their discussion of L2 motivation, the authors present a detailed framework of motivational factors (Table 4.2). These were all distilled from a review of the mainstream rather than the L2 motivational literature, which places Williams and Burden's work very much in line with the 'paradigm-seeking spirit' of the reform movements in the 1990s. Although the organisation of the listed components does not reflect the authors' temporal considerations (3.8), some aspects of the framework (e.g. external, contextual factors) represent the most elaborate treatment of the particular issue in the L2 literature.

Chapter 5

Motivation and motivating in the foreign language classroom

This chapter will...

- summarise the main motivational areas where the conscious enhancement of student motivation is a realistic option and outline the strategic arsenal available for language teachers;
- present three sets of 'motivational macro-strategies', that is, collections of general guidelines to provide orientation when introducing a motivation-sensitive teaching practice.

With motivation being as important a factor in learning success as argued earlier, teacher skills in *motivating* learners should be seen as central to teaching effectiveness. Evident though this statement may be, the current state of L2 motivation research does not bear witness to it. In Keller's (1983) words, motivation is the 'neglected heart' of our understanding of how to design instruction. Although the education-oriented publications in the 1990s were helpful in that they provided taxonomies of relevant classroom-specific motives, they did not offer a sufficiently serviceable guide to practitioners because the proposed lists of motives themselves were not readily applicable. What teachers usually wish to know is how they can *intervene*, that is, what they can actually *do* to motivate their learners. In other words, for classroom practitioners the real area of interest is not so much the nature of 'motivation' itself as the various techniques or strategies that can be employed to *motivate* students.

The purpose of *motivational strategies* is consciously to generate and enhance student motivation, as well as maintain ongoing motivated behaviour and protect it from distracting and/or competing action tendencies. That is, such strategies are used to increase student involvement and to 'save' the action when ongoing monitoring reveals that progress is slowing, halting, or backsliding. In this chapter I will first discuss the nature and scope of motivational strategies in general, and then present a taxonomy that can serve as an organisational framework for the numerous and diverse strategies in question. The chapter will be concluded by the description of three different sets of motivational *macrostrategies* – that is, collections of general motivational guidelines aimed at raising teacher awareness about how to introduce a more motivation-sensitive teaching approach in one's practice. Although I will include many concrete practical examples throughout the chapter, the intention is not to create a 'recipe book' here but rather to illustrate the wide scope of motivational techniques that teachers can use to enhance their learners' commitment, effort and persistence.

5.1   Motivational techniques, strategies and macrostrategies

In a review of studies examining beginning teachers' perceptions of problems they face, Veenman (1984) has found that teachers ranked problems about *motivating pupils* as the second most serious source of difficulty (the first being maintaining classroom discipline), preceding other obviously important issues such as the effective use of different teaching methods, a knowledge of the subject matter, and the effective use of textbooks and curriculum guides. The question of how student motivation can be increased remains a prevailing issue for seasoned practitioners as well, since student lethargy and non-achievement norms (or 'norms of mediocrity') in the classroom are regularly reported to be basic hindrances to effective teaching (Daniels, 1994). In the light of this, it is hard to believe that until the mid-1990s there had been no serious attempts in the L2 literature to design motivational strategies for classroom application. Since the educational shift in L2 motivation research in the first half of the 1990s, a growing number of publications have described motivational techniques (e.g. Alison, 1993; Brown, 1994; Chambers, 1999; Cranmer, 1996; Dörnyei, 1994a; Dörnyei and Csizér, 1998; Oxford and Shearin, 1994; Williams and Burden, 1997), but the amount of research devoted to the question of motivating learners has still been rather meagre relative to the total amount of research on L2 motivation.

If we look at general motivational psychology, the same tendency can be noted: far more research has been done in the past to identify various motives and validate motivational theories than to develop techniques to increase motivation. There have, however, been some valuable exceptions to this generalisation; examples include Brophy (1987), Burden (1995), Galloway et al. (1998), Good and Brophy (1994), Jones and Jones (1995), McCombs (1994), Raffini (1993, 1996) and Wlodkowski (1986); three particularly noteworthy works in this vein are Brophy's (1998) comprehensive summary of research on motivational strategies, Pintrich and Schunk's (1996) authoritative overview of motivation in education with practical recommendations, and a summary of how to motivate the hard-to-reach students by McCombs and Pope (1994), sponsored by the American Psychological Association.

Quote 5.1 Good and Brophy on motivational strategies in educational psychology

Skill in motivating students to learn is basic to teachers' effectiveness. Like classroom management, however, motivation did not receive such scholarly attention until recently, so that teachers were forced to rely on unsystematic 'bag-of-tricks' approaches or on advice coming from questionable theorising. Much of the latter advice was based on one of two contradictory yet frequently expressed views that are both incorrect (at least in their extreme form). The first view is that learning should be fun and that motivation problems appear because the teacher somehow has converted an inherently enjoyable activity to drudgery. We believe that students should find academic activities meaningful and worthwhile, but not fun in the same sense that recreational games and pastimes are fun. The other extreme view is that school activities are necessarily boring, unrewarding, and even aversive, so that we must rely on extrinsic rewards and punishments in order to force students to engage in these unpleasant tasks.

Good and Brophy (1994: 212)

There is one common feature of all the different motivational approaches both in the L2 field and in educational psychology: they are based on the idealistic belief that 'all students are motivated to learn under the right conditions, and that you can provide these conditions in your classroom' (McCombs and Pope, 1994: vii). This assumption is, at best, arguable and, at worst, naive. Realistically, it is highly unlikely that everybody can be motivated to learn anything. Yet, my belief is that *most* students' motivation can be 'worked on' and increased.

Although rewards and punishments are too often the only tools present in the motivational arsenal of many teachers, the spectrum of other potentially more effective motivational strategies is so broad that it is hard to imagine that none of them would work. The following taxonomy of motivational strategies is intended to demonstrate the variety of different ways by which human achievement behaviour can be promoted, and the subsequent discussion of broader motivational macrostrategies will hopefully help to prioritise within the diversity of specific techniques and procedures.

5.2   A framework for motivational strategies

The central question in designing a practical framework of motivational strategies is to decide how to organise the long list of relevant motivational techniques into separate 'themes'. The following taxonomy is based on the process-oriented model by Dörnyei and Ottó (1998) (3.8). This model offers an important advantage over other potential organising principles, namely *comprehensiveness*. Following through the motivational process from the initial arousal of the motivation to the completion and evaluation of the motivated action seems more reasonable than making somewhat arbitrary decisions about selecting certain central themes and building the material around them. The key units in this process-oriented organisation include:

- *Creating the basic motivational conditions*, which involves setting the scene for the effective use of motivational strategies.
- *Generating student motivation*, corresponding roughly to the preactional phase in our model.
- *Maintaining and protecting motivation*, corresponding to the actional phase.
- *Encouraging positive self-evaluation*, corresponding to the postactional phase.

5.2.1   Creating the basic motivational conditions

Motivational strategies cannot be employed successfully in a 'motivational vacuum' – certain preconditions must be in place before any further attempts to generate motivation can be effective. The most important of these motivational conditions are:

- appropriate teacher behaviours and a good relationship with the students;
- a pleasant and supportive classroom atmosphere;
- a cohesive learner group with appropriate group norms.

Although these three conditions are not independent of each other since they collectively mould the psychological environment in which learning takes place, it is useful to discuss teacher behaviour, classroom climate and learner group separately.

Appropriate teacher behaviours and a good relationship with the students

It was argued in 2.2.3 and 3.6.5 that teachers play a significant role in socialising and shaping the motivation of their students through their

- personal characteristics
- verbal and non-verbal 'immediacy' behaviour
- active motivational socialising behaviour
- classroom management practices.

Indeed, almost everything a teacher does in the classroom has a motivational influence on students, which makes teacher behaviour a powerful 'motivational tool'. This has been confirmed by Dörnyei and Csizér's (1998) study of Hungarian teachers of English, in which the participants rated the teacher's own behaviour as the most important and, at the same time, extremely underutilised, motivational factor in the classroom. Chambers's (1999) study examined a very different population – British secondary school learners of German – and came to the same conclusion: of all the factors that were hypothesised to contribute to the pupils' positive or negative appraisal of L2 learning, the teacher came out on top for all cohorts surveyed.

Motivational teacher influences are manifold, ranging from the rapport with the students to specific teacher behaviours which 'persuade' and/or 'attract' students to engage in on-task behaviours. A key element is to establish relationships of *mutual trust* and respect with the learners (Alison, 1993). This involves finding opportunities to talk with them on a personal level and letting them know that we have thought about them and that their individual effort is recognised. Another factor which many believe to be the most important ingredient of motivationally successful teaching is *enthusiasm* (for more details, see 7.2.2). Students take cues from their teachers about how to respond to school activities. Enthusiastic teachers convey a great sense of commitment to and

---

Example 5.1   Strategy

Model student interest in L2 learning by:

- showing students that you value L2 learning as a meaningful experience that produces satisfaction and enriches your life;
- sharing your own personal interest in L2 and L2 learning with the students;
- taking the students' learning process and achievement very seriously (since showing insufficient commitment yourself is the fastest way to undermine student motivation).

Source: Dörnyei (1994a: 282)

---

excitement about the subject matter content, not only in words but also by body language.

A pleasant and supportive atmosphere in the classroom

This condition requires little justification. Any practising teacher will be aware of the fact that student anxiety created by a tense classroom climate is one of the most potent factors that undermine learning effectiveness and L2 motivation (e.g. MacIntyre, 1999; Young, 1999). Learner involvement will be highest in a psychologically safe classroom climate in which students are encouraged to express their opinions and in which they feel that they are protected from ridicule and embarrassment.

Quote 5.2 Good and Brophy on the classroom environment and the teacher

To be motivated to learn, students need both ample opportunities to learn and steady encouragement and support of their learning efforts. Because such motivation is unlikely to develop in a chaotic classroom, it is important that the teacher organise and manage the classroom as an effective learning environment. Furthermore, because anxious or alienated students are unlikely to develop motivation to learn, it is important that learning occurs within a relaxed and supportive atmosphere. *The teacher should be a patient, encouraging person who supports students' learning efforts.* Students should feel comfortable taking intellectual risks because they know that they will not be embarrassed or criticised if they make a mistake.

Good and Brophy (1994: 215)

Table 5.1 **Factors promoting intermember acceptance and group cohesiveness**

- Time spent together and shared group history
- Learning about each other
- Proximity (physical distance)
- Contact (situations offering spontaneous opportunities to meet)
- Interaction (situations in which people's behaviour influences each other)
- The rewarding nature of group experience
- Cooperation with each other
- Joint hardship experienced together
- Emphasising 'us' and 'them': defining the group against others
- Intergroup competition
- Common threat
- Solidarity against a common enemy
- Developing group legends
- Public commitment to the group
- Personal investment in the group
- Active presence of the leader

Source: Ehrman and Dörnyei (1998: 142)

A cohesive learner group with appropriate group norms

The third basic condition concerns the composition and internal structure of the learner group and the developing norm system that governs group behaviour in general. We have seen in 2.2.3 and 3.6.5 that group characteristics have important motivational bearings, and central to these characteristics is the level of *cohesiveness* among the class members. Indeed, fragmented groups, characterised by uncooperative cliques, can easily become ineffective, thus diminishing the individual member's commitment to learn. There are several factors that promote group cohesiveness (see Table 5.1) and most of these can be consciously 'manipulated' to good effect (see also 5.3, for a set of general group-building guidelines).

Group norms are inherently social products: in an effective group, in order for a norm to be long-lasting and constructive, it should be explicitly discussed and willingly adopted by members. A great deal of research has shown that institutional norms mandated by a teacher are unlikely to become effective group norms unless they are accepted as right or proper by the majority of the class members (Ehrman and Dörnyei, 1998). Consistent with these considerations, Dörnyei and Malderez (1997) argue that it is beneficial to include an explicit norm-building procedure early in the group's life by formulating potential norms, justifying their purpose in order to enlist support for them, having them discussed by the whole group, and finally agreeing on a mutually accepted set of 'class rules', with the consequences for violating them also specified.

5.2.2   Generating initial motivation

In an ideal world, all learners are eager to learn because they are driven by their inborn curiosity to explore the world, and the learning experience therefore is a constant source of intrinsic pleasure for them. Reality, however, rarely lives up to these ideals. The fact is that if students could freely choose what to do, academic learning for many would most likely feature low on their agenda. School attendance is compulsory for students, and the content of the curriculum is almost always selected on the basis of what society – rather than the learners themselves – considers important (Brophy, 1998). It is no wonder, therefore, that Csikszentmihalyi and his colleagues (Schneider et al., 1995; Wong and Csikszentmihalyi, 1991) have found in a large-scale US survey that schoolwork was considered to be the least rewarding activity among adolescents, and the most common adjectives they used to describe their classroom experience were 'boring', 'unenjoyable' and 'constrained'.

> **Quote 5.3** Brophy on the main motivational challenge for teachers
>
> The motivational challenge facing teachers is to find ways to encourage their students to accept the goals of classroom activities and seek to develop the intended knowledge and skills that these activities were designed to develop, regardless of whether or not the students enjoy the activities or would choose to engage in them if other alternatives were available.
>
> Brophy (1998: xviii)

This means that unless teachers are singularly fortunate with the composition of their class group, they need to contribute actively to generating positive student attitudes towards learning the subject matter even if the general motivational conditions described above are in place. I have divided the strategies that can be used to achieve this into four main groups:

- Enhancing the learners' language-related values and attitudes
- Increasing the learners' 'goal-orientedness'
- Making the curriculum relevant for the learners
- Creating realistic learner beliefs.

Enhancing the learners' language-related values and attitudes

The individual's subjective *value system* is a more or less organised collection of internalised perceptions, beliefs and feelings related to one's position in the social world, developed during the past as a reaction to past experiences. These values largely determine the individual's internal preferences and basic approaches to activities, and therefore perhaps the most far-reaching consequences in motivating learners can be achieved by promoting positive *language-related values and attitudes*. Adapting Eccles and Wigfield's (1995) value typology (2.1.1) to the specific domain of L2 learning, we can distinguish between three main value dimensions:

1. The *intrinsic value* of the ongoing process of L2 learning, associated with the interest in and anticipated enjoyment of the language-learning activity. The key issue in generating interest is to 'whet the students' appetite' – that is, to arouse the students' curiosity and attention, and to create an attractive image for the course.

2. *Integrativeness* involves a composite of various L2-related attitudes (social, cultural, ethnolinguistic, etc.), as well as a general interest in 'foreignness' and foreign languages (cf. 3.1.1). The importance of this value dimension suggests that the traditional practice of teaching languages through their cultures and the social reality of their speakers does have some scientific basis and, therefore, there is a need to make the L2 'real' by introducing to learners its cultural background, using authentic materials, and promoting contact with native speakers of the L2.

3. *Instrumentality* refers to the consequences that might arise from the mastery of the L2. Its special importance in many L2 learning contexts lies in the fact that for most students the process of language learning is a means to achieve other goals through the knowledge of the L2 (rather than being an end in its own right). In order to spur students to invest more effort in the task than they might do otherwise, instrumental strategies can

    - make students aware (or remind them) that successful completion of the tasks is instrumental to the accomplishment of their valued goal;

- reiterate the role the L2 plays in the world and its potential usefulness both for themselves and their community;
- establish incentive systems that offer extrinsic rewards for successful task completion (e.g. good grades, prizes, celebration).

Increasing the learners' 'goal-orientedness'

Educational psychological research has found repeatedly that in an ordinary class many, if not most, students do not really understand (or accept) why they are involved in a learning activity: the 'official group goal' (i.e. mastering the course content) set by outsiders (e.g. policy and curriculum makers) may well not be the only group goal and, in extreme cases, may not be a group goal at all. Because of the inherent goal diversity prevalent in any classroom, it would seem beneficial to increase the group's *goal-orientedness*, that is, the extent to which the group is attuned to pursuing its official goal (in our case, L2 learning).

Quote 5.4 Hadfield on increasing the learner group's goal-orientedness

It is fundamental to the successful working of a group to have a sense of direction and a common purpose. Defining and agreeing aims is one of the hardest tasks that the group has to undertake together.

Hadfield (1992: 134)

The most obvious way to achieve this is by initiating a discussion with your students with the objective of outlining 'group goals'. Personalised learning 'itineraries' and 'contracts' have also worked in many classrooms because they allow students to define their own personal criteria for success. Other key issues in goal setting involve the identification of those goal features that increase student performance most; trying to construct activities that can accommodate simultaneous pursuit and attainment of many different kinds of goals; and resolving the common conflict between individual learner goals and institutional constraints. It is important to emphasise that the initial effort to establish a sense of direction and a common purpose for the group needs to be followed up by a recurring review of the original goal(s) in view of the progress made towards them.

Making the curriculum relevant for the learners

The average student in a good school tends to do the work even when a subject does not arouse high intrinsic motivation and even when rewards and punishments are not salient. What, then, is the source of the efforts of such students? One answer to this is that these learners share the belief of the curriculum designers that the programme is desirable and valuable. In order to increase this beneficial effect, much of the motivational advice offered to teachers in the educational literature boils down to the following general principle: *Find out your students' goals and the topics they want to learn, and build these into your curriculum as much as possible.* Students are not motivated to learn unless they regard the material they are taught as worth learning.

Quote 5.5 Chambers on the significance of 'relevance' in L2 teaching

If the teacher is to motivate pupils to learn, then relevance has to be the red thread permeating activities. If pupils fail to see the relationship between the activity and the world in which they live, then the point of the activity is likely to be lost on them. . . . If pupils do not see the relevance of a subject, the teacher has from the outset a major challenge.

Chambers (1999: 37–8)

Creating realistic learner beliefs

Unrealistic *learner beliefs* about how much progress to expect, and how fast, function like 'time bombs' at the beginning of a language course because of the inevitable disappointment that is to follow. It is therefore a key motivational issue to sort out some of the most far-fetched expectations and get rid of the preconceived notions and prejudices that are likely to hinder L2 attainment.

In order to rectify students' erroneous assumptions they

- need to develop an informed understanding of the nature of second language acquisition and reasonable criteria for progress;
- should be made aware of the fact that the mastery of a L2 can be achieved in a number of different ways, using diverse strategies, and therefore a key factor leading to success is for learners to discover for themselves the methods and techniques by which they learn best.

Concept 5.1   **Horwitz's research on learner beliefs**

Horwitz (1988) developed a self-report questionnaire, the Beliefs About Language Learning Inventory (BALLI), consisting of 34 items, to assess student beliefs in five major areas:

- difficulty of language learning
- foreign language aptitude
- the nature of language learning
- learning and communication strategies
- motivation and expectations.

Empirical data obtained from American learners of German, French and Spanish confirmed that certain belief systems are quite common among learners and are consistent across different language groups.

An effective way of initiating discussions towards these goals is to administer the BALLI (see Concept 5.1) to the learners and use the answers as a starting point in analysing the validity of popular beliefs and myths.

5.2.3   Maintaining and protecting motivation

We have seen in earlier sections (2.3, 3.7 and 4.2.4) that unless motivation is actively nurtured and protected during the actional phase of the motivational process – that is, when action has commenced and is well on the way – the natural tendency to lose sight of the goal, to get tired or bored of the activity and to give way to attractive distractions or competing action tendencies will result in the initial motivation gradually petering out. Therefore, an effective motivational repertoire should include motivation maintenance (or 'executive motivational') strategies that can help to prevent this from happening.

Although the spectrum of executive motivational strategies is broad (since ongoing human behaviour can be modified in so many different ways), five areas appear to be particularly relevant for classroom application:

- Setting 'proximal subgoals'
- Improving the quality of the learning experience
- Increasing the learner's self-confidence

- Creating learner autonomy
- Promoting self-motivating learner strategies.

Setting 'proximal subgoals'

> **Quote 5.6** Oxford and Shearin on goal setting in language classrooms
>
> Goal setting can have exceptional importance in stimulating L2 learning motivation, and it is therefore shocking that so little time and energy are spent in the L2 classroom on goal-setting.
>
> Oxford and Shearin (1994: 19)

Individual goal setting is one of the most effective methods to enable students to experience a sense of control over their own learning and perceive themselves as mastering material while incorporating their own interests (Jones and Jones, 1995). It is particularly relevant to language learning because the ultimate purpose of this prolonged process – to communicate with L2 speakers – is several years away and is, in fact, for many learners only moderately realistic (i.e. what if the learner does *not* really want to communicate with L2 speakers?). Therefore, setting *proximal subgoals* has a powerful motivating function by providing advance organisers as well as immediate incentive and feedback.

Locke and Latham's (1990) goal-setting theory has been widely used in many organisational settings to improve employee motivation and performance, and Latham et al. (1997) argue that the theory is just as relevant to educational contexts. In agreement with this claim, Pintrich and Schunk (1996) offer four main principles based on the theory that can be applied in the classroom setting:

1. *Goals should be clear and specific*, referring to concrete outcomes.
2. *Goals should be challenging and difficult, but not outside the range of students' capabilities.*
3. *Both proximal and distal goals should be set.* For example, teachers can design a learning agreement, or a 'contract', with each student that specifies a series of subgoals that lead to larger goals.
4. *Teachers should provide feedback that increases students' self-efficacy for obtaining the goal.* Such feedback can involve informational input or extrinsic rewards that are contingent on actual academic performance.

Improving the quality of the learning experience

Most researchers and practitioners would agree that the higher the quality of the learning experience, the more learner engagement and persistence we can expect. The real question is what we mean by the 'quality of the learning experience'. Drawing on neurobiological research, Schumann (1998) argues that environmental stimuli are appraised along a number of different dimensions (3.4); he distinguishes five major environmental facets: novelty, pleasantness, goal/need significance, coping potential and self and social image. Indeed, learners continuously assess the intrinsic enjoyment they experience and the personal and goal-specific relevance the various tasks offer; they check how well they are doing, how much they are approaching their overall goal, and how their personal and social image is affected by the actions they are expected to take as part of task completion.

Out of the many issues related to the promotion of the quality of the learning experience, let me highlight here two basic issues that must be addressed by any motivationally conscious teaching practice:

1. *Increasing the intrinsic enjoyment of participating in learning tasks.* This is probably the best-known motivational dimension of classroom teaching, and many practitioners would simply equate the adjective 'motivating' with 'interesting'. Accordingly, a great number of recommendations have been made in literature as to how to promote this intrinsic quality dimension, ranging from making the tasks varied and challenging to including novel elements and relating the content of the tasks to the learners' natural interest.

2. *Enhancing the learners' social image.* Maintaining face is a central concern for most school children (2.1.1): for them school is the most important social arena and their peers are their main reference group. Therefore, they will feel ill at ease doing tasks (no matter how conducive those are to learning) that put them in a situation where they are made to look small in front of their contemporaries. Thus, providing opportunities for everybody to play the protagonist's role in one way or another (e.g. by creating situations in which students can demonstrate their particular strength) is an effective method of making the person feel good about the course and the role he or she plays in it. In a similar vein, the learners' social image can be enhanced by avoiding criticisms and corrections that can be considered humiliating, and by 'working on' the group as a whole in order to establish norms of tolerance and acceptance (Example 5.2).

Example 5.2   A set of 'Class Rules' fostering peer acceptance

- Let's try to listen to each other.
- Let's help each other.
- Let's respect each other's ideas and values.
- It's OK to make mistakes: they are learning points.
- Let's not make fun of each other's weaknesses.
- We must avoid hurting each other, verbally or physically.

Source: Ehrman and Dörnyei (1998: 241)

Increasing the learners' self-confidence

Self-efficacy is generally seen as a key factor in determining the amount of effort exerted and the persistence displayed (2.1.1); also, the significance of linguistic self-confidence has long been recognised in the L2 field (3.2.1). The important question, then, is how to maintain and increase the students' self-confidence and self-esteem in a context – the language classroom – which is inherently face-threatening for the learner: they often have to 'babble like a child' in the L2 for a lack of sufficient resources, and further anxiety is usually created by the grading system and the public nature of most teacher–student interaction (Good and Brophy, 1994). In spite of these unfavourable odds, there are several ways of successfully increasing the students' self-confidence, as illustrated by the following five approaches:

1. Teachers can foster the belief in their students that competence is a changeable and controllable aspect of development and they can help to dispel misconceptions and unrealistic fears.
2. Favourable self-conceptions of L2 competence can be promoted by providing regular experiences of success and emphasising what learners can rather than cannot do.
3. Everybody is more interested in proceedings if they feel that they have an important part to play, and therefore even hard-to-reach learners can be motivated by giving them the feeling of making a useful contribution and creating classroom situations where they can demonstrate positive features and come forward to offer help (Alison, 1993).

4. Sometimes a small personal word of encouragement is sufficient.

5. Finally, teachers can reduce classroom anxiety by making the learning context less stressful and by providing learners with strategies to cope with anxiety-provoking situations.

Creating learner autonomy

Contemporary language-teaching methodologies make the assumption (either overtly or covertly) that taking an active, independent attitude to learning – that is, becoming an autonomous learner – is beneficial to learning (cf. Benson, 2000; Little, 1991; Wenden, 1991). This assumption is partly rooted in the principles of humanistic psychology, namely that 'the only kind of learning which significantly affects behaviour is self-discovered, self-appropriated learning' (Rogers, 1961: 276), and partly in educational psychology, which has emphasised the importance of learning strategies and self-regulation (see, for example, a special issue of the journal *Educational Psychologist*, Vol. 30(4), 1995, on self-regulatory learning). How can we foster learner autonomy? Key issues include allowing students real choices, sharing responsibility with the students for organising their learning process and giving them positions of genuine authority, and encouraging student contributions, peer teaching and project work. Benson (2000) distinguishes five different types of practice associated with the development of autonomy:

- *resource-based approaches* (emphasising independent interaction with learning materials);
- *technology-based approaches* (emphasising independent interaction with educational technologies);
- *learner-based approaches* (emphasising the direct production of behavioural and psychological changes in the learner, e.g. strategy training);
- *classroom-based approaches* (emphasising changes in the relationship between learners and teachers in the classroom and learner control over the planning and evaluation of learning);
- *curriculum-based approaches* (extending the idea of control over the planning and evaluation of learning to the curriculum as a whole).

Quote 5.7 Good and Brophy's word of caution about autonomy

For one thing, the simplest way to ensure that people value what they are doing is to maximise their free choice and autonomy – let them decide what to do and when and how to do it. However, schools are not recreational settings designed primarily to provide entertainment; they are educational settings that students are required to come to for instruction in a prescribed curriculum. Some opportunities exist for teachers to take advantage of existing motivation by allowing students to select activities according to their own interests, but most of the time teachers must require students to engage in activities that they would not have selected on their own.

Good and Brophy (1994: 228)

Promoting self-motivating learner strategies

Most of the discussion so far has concentrated on the teacher's responsibility and role in stimulating student motivation. It has been observed, however, that even under adverse conditions and without any teacher assistance, some learners are more successful in keeping up their goal commitment than some others. How do they do it? They *motivate themselves*. Fuelled by this recognition, recent research in educational psychology has turned increasingly to the learners to explore what they can do to 'save' the action when the initial motivation is flagging (Corno, 1993; Snow et al., 1996). An important role of teachers is to raise their students' awareness of relevant strategies and to remind them at appropriate times of the usefulness of these.

Quote 5.8 Ushioda on self-motivation

Self-motivation is a question of thinking effectively and meaningfully about learning experience and learning goals. It is a question of applying positive thought patterns and belief structures so as to optimise and sustain one's involvement in learning. In other words, a capacity for self-motivation may be defined as a capacity for *effective* motivational thinking. . . . this capacity entails taking personal control of the affective conditions and experiences that shape one's subjective involvement in learning. It entails minimising the damage when these experiences are negative, and maximising the subjective rewards when these experiences are positive, and so fostering optimum motivational conditions for continued engagement in language learning.

Ushioda (1997: 41)

Under the label of 'action control strategies', section 2.3 presented a taxonomy of six types of self-motivating strategies developed by Kuhl (1987). Following Kuhl's pioneering research, a considerable array of action maintenance strategies have been documented in the educational psychological literature during the past decade. The most elaborate taxonomy has been developed by Corno and Kanfer (1993). Drawing on Kuhl's (1987) original taxonomy they proposed four large classes of volitional strategies:

1. *Metacognitive control strategies* subsume three strategies suggested by Kuhl (active attentional selectivity, encoding control and parsimony of information processing), involve intentionally ignoring attractive alternatives or irrelevant aspects and adopting a 'let's not ruminate and procrastinate any longer but get down to doing it' attitude (e.g. *think of first steps to take and get started right away*).

2. *Emotion control strategies* involve managing emotional states that might disrupt or inhibit action (e.g. *sing to yourself when you're nervous* or *recall your strengths and your available resources; remember, you've done this kind of thing before*).

3. *Motivation control strategies* involve enhancing the motivational basis of intentions to pursue a goal (e.g. *pat yourself on the back for good work*, or *escalate goals by prioritising and imagining their value*).

4. *Environmental control strategies* involve manipulating aspects of the individual's environment in a way that the resulting socio-environmental pressure or control makes the abandoning of the intention more difficult or by creating safeguards against undesirable environmental temptations (e.g. *move away from noise and distraction*).

5.2.4 Rounding off the learning experience: encouraging positive self-evaluation

A large body of research has shown that the way students feel about their past accomplishments, the amount of satisfaction they experience after successful task completion and the reasons to which they attribute past successes and failures will significantly determine how teachers approach subsequent learning tasks (it is for this reason that the Dörnyei and Ottó model contains a postactional phase; 3.8). By using appropriate strategies, teachers can help learners to evaluate their achievements in a more 'positive light' (i.e. to more appreciate their advances in progress and mastery), and to encourage them to take credit for these accomplishments by attributing them to sufficient ability plus reasonable effort (which, as discussed in 2.1.1, is an important concern in attribution theory). I have selected three areas of postactional strategies whose classroom relevance has received ample confirmation by research findings:

- Promoting attributions to effort rather than to ability
- Providing motivational feedback
- Increasing learner satisfaction and the question of rewards and grades.

Promoting attributions to effort rather than to ability

Past research had identified a certain hierarchy of the types of attributions people make in terms of their motivating nature (2.1.1). It is easy to see, for example, that failure that is ascribed to stable and uncontrollable factors such as low ability hinders future achievement behaviour (*I'm not good enough for this sort of thing . . .*), whereas failure that is attributed to unstable and controllable factors such as effort is generally regarded by learners as less detrimental (*I didn't work hard enough but next time . . .*). In order to promote effort attributions, in failure situations teachers should generally emphasise the low effort exerted as being a strong reason for underachievement because this communicates to students that they can do better in the future. In situations when failure occurs in spite of obvious hard work on the student's part, the best strategy is to point out the skills/knowledge that were missing and communicate to the student that these are unstable and can be mastered. With regard to student success, it should not be attributed entirely to effort (even if the person did work hard) but also to a stable cause such as talent.

Providing motivational feedback

The attributional aspect is only one (although a crucial) element of motivationally effective feedback. There are a number of other important issues to consider in this respect:

- An often mentioned distinction of two types of feedback involves *informational feedback*, which comments on progress and competence, and *controlling feedback*, which judges performance against external standards (Brophy and Good, 1986). It is generally maintained that from a motivational point of view the former should be dominant since it enables students to understand where they are in relation to achieving goals and what they need to do to continue or improve their progress (Jones and Jones, 1995).

- An important source of self-efficacy is *observing models* (2.1.1). Therefore, drawing attention to the fact that others are coping with a certain task and providing relevant positive examples and analogies of accomplishment may be useful in suggesting that task attainment is within the student's means.

- Effective feedback can also contain a *positive persuasive element*, communicating that the teacher believes that the student is capable of reaching certain predetermined goals. Students in general experience high efficacy when told they are capable of attaining success by a trustworthy source such as the teacher (2.1.1).

- A further important component of effective teacher feedback concerns information about how well learners were applying *strategies* and how strategy use is improving their performance. Various learner strategies help students to attend to tasks, focus on important features, structure one's activity, organise material and maintain the productive psychological climate of learning (Pintrich and Schunk, 1996; Zimmerman, 1994). In the L2 field, learner strategies related to the acquisition and production of the target language have been shown to play an important role (e.g. Cohen, 1998; Dörnyei, 1995a; Dörnyei and Scott, 1997; Kasper and Kellerman, 1997; Schmitt, 1997) and one way of ensuring the success of strategy training is by giving regular strategy feedback.

- Finally, certain aspects of teacher feedback can also have negative impact on learner behaviour. Graham (1994) highlights three such instances:
  - communicating pity instead of anger after failure;
  - the offering of praise after success in easy tasks;
  - unsolicited offers of help (particularly 'gratuitous help' such as supplying answers outright).

Increasing learner satisfaction and the question of rewards and grades

There seems to be a general assumption that the feeling of satisfaction is a significant factor in reinforcing achievement behaviour, which makes *satisfaction* a major component of motivation. This has been well reflected in Keller's (1983, 1994) influential model of motivation in instructional

> **Quote 5.9** Keller on satisfaction
>
> The fourth component of the ARCS model – satisfaction – pertains to those things that must be done to reinforce and sustain students' motivation. The use of intrinsically motivating consequences, such as pride of accomplishment and recognition of achievement, and of extrinsically motivating consequences such as grades or special favours, can ensure that the learners have positive feelings about their performance and that they continue to value the given activity.
>
> Keller (1994: 3945)

design (4.2.1), in which one of the four main motivational dimensions is satisfaction (in the latest version of the construct, the ARCS Model, the final letter 'S' stands for 'satisfaction', with the other three letters indicating *attention*, *relevance* and *confidence*).

Motivational strategies aimed at increasing learner satisfaction typically focus on allowing students to create finished products that they can perform or display, encouraging them to be proud of themselves after accomplishing a task, taking stock from time to time of their general progress, celebrating success and using motivationally appropriate rewards. Unfortunately, this latter task is difficult to accomplish because of the overarching importance of grades as the ultimate embodiment of school rewards, providing a single index for judging overall success and failure in school. The problem with grades is that they focus student attention on performance outcomes, such as high test scores, rather than on the process of learning itself. As a result, 'many students are grade driven, not to say, "grade grubbing", and this preoccupation begins surprisingly early in life' (Covington, 1999: 127).

Concept 5.2   The controversy of rewards

Although teachers regularly dispense a variety of rewards to students for good behaviour and academic performance, the effectiveness of rewards has been a controversial issue among educational psychologists. Early research on extrinsic/intrinsic motivation indicated that extrinsic rewards undermined intrinsic interest and therefore were to be avoided. Indeed, we can list many instances in school settings when students lose their natural intrinsic interest in an activity if they have to do it to meet some extrinsic requirement (e.g. even pupils who like reading often dislike compulsory readings). However, the simplistic 'extrinsic = bad and

intrinsic = good' view has been modified (cf. 2.1.3) and sufficiently internalised extrinsic motives are now seen as complementary to intrinsic
interest. This implies that rewards are not necessarily harmful after all
but their effects depend on what the actual rewards are and how they are
presented. Brophy (1998) argues that detrimental effects are most likely
when rewards have the following three characteristics:

- *High salience*, that is, they are very attractive and are presented in a
  highly conspicuous manner.
- *Non-contingency*, that is, the rewards are given for participating in the
  activity rather than being contingent on achieving specific goals (see
  also Raynor's concept of a 'contingent path' in 7.1.3).
- *Unnatural/unusual*, that is, the rewards are not natural outcomes of the
  behaviours but are artificial control devices.

5.3 Motivational macrostrategies

Motivation concerns human behaviour in general, and with human
behaviour being as complex as it is, the number of possible motivational techniques is rather extensive. Human action can be influenced
or modified in so many different ways that even a selection of the most
important strategies will make up a long list if we want to be systematic. While this is understandable, it is at the same time a serious problem from a practical point of view, because if the number of classroom
recommendations is overwhelming in their abundance, this will simply
defeat the purpose of such practical advice. There is very little a teacher
can do with a list of suggestions that takes up many printed pages – all
such a list is likely to achieve is to increase our feeling of inferiority, by
making us realise how many things we do not actually do.

For this reason, in addition to a comprehensive coverage of motivational techniques, we also need a smaller set of 'core' strategies to
which teachers can pay special attention when trying to implement a
motivation-conscious teaching approach. This core set can then be
extended when the techniques have become sufficiently internalised
and automated. This was the rationale for developing the 'Ten commandments for motivating language learners' (Dörnyei and Csizér,
1998), and the positive reception of this list by teachers confirmed to
me that the generation of a distilled set of macrostrategies might
indeed make the concept of motivating learners more teacher-friendly.

In the following I will present three compilation of motivational strategies. First, I will include two sets of macrostrategies that I have developed with colleagues: (1) the 'Ten commandments' mentioned above and (2) a list of recommendations, compiled together with Angi Malderez (Dörnyei and Malderez, 1999), on how to facilitate group development in one's language class. The chapter will be concluded by a list of 12 suggestions drawn up by Marion Williams and Bob Burden (1997) for motivating language learners.

The 'Ten commandments for motivating language learners'

1. Set a personal example with your own behaviour.
2. Create a pleasant, relaxed atmosphere in the classroom.
3. Present the tasks properly.
4. Develop a good relationship with the learners.
5. Increase the learner's linguistic self-confidence.
6. Make the language classes interesting.
7. Promote learner autonomy.
8. Personalise the learning process.
9. Increase the learners' goal-orientedness.
10. Familiarise learners with the target language culture.

(*Source*: Dörnyei and Csizér, 1998: 215)

A set of group-building strategies

1. Spend some time consciously on group processes.
2. Use *ice-breakers* at the beginning of a new course to set members at ease, to get them to memorise each others' names, and to learn about each other; and *warmers* at the beginning of each class to allow members to readjust to the particular group they are now with).
3. Promote peer relations by enhancing classroom interaction (using activities such as pair-work, small group work, role-play, 'mixer' classroom organisation which not only allows, but encourages people to come into contact and interact with one another, as well as helping to prevent the emergence of rigid seating patterns) and by personalising the language tasks (choosing, when possible, activities with a genuine potential for interpersonal awareness-raising to allow members to get to know each other).

4. Promote group cohesiveness by including small-group 'fun' competitions in the classes, by encouraging (and also organising) extra-curricular activities, and by promoting the creation of a group legend (establishing group rituals, bringing up and building on past group events, creating a semi-official group history, encouraging learners to prepare 'group objects' and symbols such as flags, coats of arms, creating appropriate group mottoes/logos, etc.).

5. Formulate group norms explicitly, and have them discussed and accepted by the learners; specify also the violation of any agreed 'rule'.

6. Formulate explicit group goals by having the students negotiate their individual goals, and draw attention from time to time to how particular activities help to attain them.

7. Be prepared for the inevitable conflicts or low points in group life.

8. Take the students' learning very seriously; never forget that the commitment you demonstrate towards the L2 and the group, the interest you show in the students' achievement, and the effort you yourself make will significantly shape the students' attitudes to their group and to L2 learning.

9. Actively encourage student autonomy by handing over as much as you can of the various leadership roles and functions to the group.

10. Prepare group members for the closing of the group by giving members some continuity and helping them to prepare for their new phase of learning after the course.

(*Source*: Dörnyei and Malderez, 1999: 167–8)

A list of suggestions for motivating language learners

1. Recognise the complexity of motivation.
2. Be aware of both initiating and sustaining motivation.
3. Discuss with learners why they are carrying out activities.
4. Involve learners in making decisions related to learning the language.
5. Involve learners in setting language-learning goals.
6. Recognise people as individuals.
7. Build up individuals' beliefs in themselves.
8. Develop internal beliefs.

9. Help to move towards a mastery-oriented style.
10. Enhance intrinsic motivation.
11. Build up a supportive learning environment.
12. Give feedback that is informational.

(*Source*: Williams and Burden, 1997: 141–2)

Chapter 6

Student demotivation

- introduce the notion of 'demotivation';
- summarise the most salient sources of demotivation in L2 studies.

It has been mentioned earlier (e.g. in 1.4 and 3.8.2) that there are both positive and negative forces exerting their influence on ongoing student behaviours. However, if we think about the multitude of motives discussed in that chapter, very few of them concerned the negative forces. This is no accident: past motivation research has typically conceptualised a 'motive' as a kind of 'inducement', that is, as a force whose strength ranges on a continuum from zero to strong, without much being said about 'negative' motives. Is this, however, the complete picture? How can we account for the motivational influences that have a detrimental rather than a positive effect on motivation – that is, instead of energising action, they 'de-energise' it? There is no question that there *are* such negative motives. Classroom practitioners can easily think of a variety of events that can have demotivating effects on the students, for example public humiliation, devastating test results, or conflicts with peers. If we think about it, 'demotivation' is not at all infrequent in language classes and the number of demotivated L2 learners is relatively high.

The importance for teaching of such negative motivational influences warrants a closer look at the 'dark side' of motivation. In this chapter I will first analyse the notion of 'demotivation' and attempt to provide a definition for it. After this, I will review the (little) available research literature outside the L2 field, followed by the description of four investigations that have specifically focused on the analysis of demotivating experiences in L2 learning. These reviews will shed light on several potential motivational pitfalls and danger zones, and therefore it is hoped that this chapter will be useful in a 'that's-how-we-should-*not*-do-it' way.

6.1 'Demotivation' vs 'motivation'

It is relatively easy to reach an initial common-sense understanding of 'demotivation': it concerns various negative influences that cancel out existing motivation. Let us look at some hypothetical examples:

- Jack became demotivated to learn Spanish after his language class was split into two groups, the more and the less able ones, and he found himself among the 'slow' students.
- Jill lost her commitment to French when she did not understand something and the teacher talked to her in a rather brusque and impatient manner.
- For Rupert the final straw was when he suffered an embarrassing experience of having to speak in front of the class.

Thus, a 'demotivated' learner is someone who was once motivated but has lost his or her commitment/interest for some reason. Similarly to 'demotivation', we can also speak of 'demotives', which are the negative counterparts of 'motives': a motive increases an action tendency whereas a demotive decreases it. However, can we label every type of negative influence as a 'demotive'? Not necessarily. To illustrate the problem, here are three negative factors that I would not refer to as demotivation:

1. An attractive alternative action that serves as a powerful distraction (e.g. watching a good film on TV instead of writing one's home work).
2. The gradual loss of interest in a long-lasting, ongoing activity.
3. The sudden realisation that the costs of pursuing a goal are too high (e.g. when someone recognises how demanding it is to attend an evening course while working during the day).

In what way are these negative factors different from the phenomena described above?

1. Powerful distractions are not demotives in the same sense as, say, public humiliation, because they do not carry a negative value: instead of *reducing* the actual motivation towards the original activities, their distracting effect is due to presenting *more attractive* options. In racing terms, this would be the case when a runner is doing very well indeed yet does not win the race because there is someone who is doing even better on that particular day. We can only speak about demotivation proper when something *slows down* the runner.

2. The gradual loss of interest is also different from a proper demotivating event because – again using the racing metaphor – it reflects the runner's losing speed caused by, say, ageing, rather than by a particular incident in a particular race.

3. With regard to the sudden recognition of the costs of an activity, this is the result of an *internal* process of deliberation, without any specific external trigger. If something prompted the termination of action (e.g. the persuasion of an influential friend), that would be a different situation and would be a case of demotivation.

In view of the above considerations, 'demotivation' in the following will concern *specific external forces that reduce or diminish the motivational basis of a behavioural intention or an ongoing action*.

Demotivation does not mean that all the positive influences that originally made up the motivational basis of a behaviour have been annulled; rather, it is only the resultant force that has been dampened by a strong negative component, and some other positive motives may still remain operational. For example, a learner who has lost his or her interest in studying Esperanto because the Esperanto teacher turned out to be a heartless bully may still believe in the important role of Esperanto as a potential lingua franca in the world.

Although the term 'demotivation' is virtually unused in motivational psychology, a related concept, 'amotivation' is a constituent of Deci and Ryan's (1985) self-determination theory (2.1.3) (see Concept 6.1). Are we talking about the same thing? Not quite. 'Amotivation' refers to a *lack* of motivation caused by the realisation that 'there is no point . . .' or 'it's beyond me . . .'. Thus, 'amotivation' is related to general outcome expectations that are unrealistic for some reason, whereas 'demotivation' is related to specific external causes. Some demotives can lead to general amotivation regarding the particular activity (e.g. a series of bad classroom experiences can reduce the learner's self-efficacy) but with some other demotives as soon as the detrimental external influence ceases to exist, other positive, and thus far oppressed, motives may again get the upper hand (e.g. if it turns out that someone who dissuaded the individual from doing something was not telling the truth).

Concept 6.1   **Deci and Ryan's notion of 'amotivation'**

'Amotivation' as defined by Deci and Ryan (1985) refers to the relative absence of motivation that is not caused by a lack of initial interest but rather by the individual's experiencing feelings of incompetence and helplessness when faced with the activity. According to Vallerand's (1997) overview, it can have four sources. People can be amotivated because

- they think they lack the ability to perform the behaviour ('capacity–ability beliefs');
- they do not consider the strategies to be followed effective enough ('strategy beliefs');
- they think the effort required to reach the outcome is far too excessive ('capacity–effort beliefs');
- they have the general perception that their efforts are inconsequential considering the enormity of the task to be accomplished ('helplessness beliefs').

6.2   Research on demotivation in instructional communication studies

Since motivation is a central component in a number of diverse research disciplines which all focus on behavioural issues in one way or another (for an overview, see 11.1), it should not come as a surprise that we find the only systematic line of research on demotivation in a seemingly unrelated discipline, a subfield of (L1) communication studies: *instructional communication research*. This area of investigation is grounded in the assumption that the classroom is a relevant context to study L1 communication (for example, between the teacher and the students) and that the analysis of classroom interaction and instructional outcomes has important theoretical and practical implications (cf. Christophel and Gorham, 1995). In 2.2.3, we already saw how the teachers' use of

immediacy behaviours (i.e. verbal and non-verbal behaviours which
reduce physical and/or psychological distance between teachers and
their students) affects student motivation, and it was a logical extension
of this research paradigm to look at the negative impact of certain
(mainly but not necessarily teacher-related) factors (for reviews, see
Christophel and Gorham, 1995; Gorham and Christophel, 1992).

Two different investigations of demotivation by Christophel and
Gorham (1995; Gorham and Christophel, 1992), using both qualitative
and quantitative techniques, generated consistent results: approximately
two-thirds of the reported sources of demotivation in these studies
were 'teacher-owned', that is, the lack of motivation was attributed to
what the teacher had done or had been responsible for. Gorham and
Christophel (1992) also presented a rank order of the frequency of the
various demotives (conceptualised as broad categories rather than specific
events/behaviours) mentioned by the students. The first five categories
were as follows:

1. Dissatisfaction with grading and assignments.
2. The teacher being boring, bored, unorganised and unprepared.
3. The dislike of the subject area.
4. The inferior organisation of the teaching material.
5. The teacher being unapproachable, self-centred, biased, condescending and insulting.

Although some of the demotivator categories in Gorham and
Christophel's (1992) study would not be considered 'demotives'
according to the definition used in this chapter, the general finding
that negative teacher behaviours were perceived as central to students'
demotivation is fully consistent with the results obtained in the L2
field (see below). The teachers' responsibility in demotivating students
was further confirmed by an additional finding by Christophel and
Gorham (1992), namely that teachers who used appropriate immediacy
behaviours were significantly less frequently mentioned in connection
with demotivation than teachers with non-immediate behaviours.

6.3   Findings in L2 motivation research

Instructional communication researchers have taken an interest in
demotivation because it was found to be a frequent phenomenon

related to the teacher's interaction with the students. The interest in demotivation in L2 studies has been aroused by a different reason. The L2 domain is the area of education that is, I believe, most often characterised by learning failure: nearly everybody has failed in the study of at least one language and it is not uncommon for someone to have failed in two or three languages (personally, my varying successes in English and German have been well counterbalanced by failures in Spanish, Portuguese, Latin and Russian). Thus, language-learning failure is a salient phenomenon and the study of its causes is often directly related to demotivation.

In the following I will present the main findings of four investigations, by Oxford (1998), Chambers (1993), Ushioda (1998) and Dörnyei (1998b). Admittedly, none of them offers a comprehensive inspection of demotivation: two studies (by Oxford and Dörnyei) were conference presentations; one (by Ushioda) provides only very general results as part of a broader discussion on effective motivational thinking; finally, in the only study that was fully devoted to demotivation, Chambers (1993) modestly states that 'there are so many aspects to the problem of motivation that I have not even started to do it justice' (p. 16). However, in spite of their incompleteness, these exploratory works are useful in preparing the ground for future investigations.

6.3.1   Oxford's investigation

Rebecca Oxford (1998) carried out a content analysis of essays written by approximately 250 American students (both in high schools and universities) about their learning experiences over a period of five years. During this time a variety of prompts were used, such as 'Describe a situation in which you experienced conflict with a teacher' and 'Talk about a classroom in which you felt uncomfortable'. In the content analysis of the data, four broad themes emerged:

1. *The teacher's personal relationship with the students*, including a lack of caring, general belligerence, hypercriticism, and patronage/favouritism.

2. *The teacher's attitude towards the course or the material*, including lack of enthusiasm, sloppy management and close-mindedness.

3. *Style conflicts between teachers and students*, including multiple style conflicts, conflicts about the amount of structure or detail and conflicts about the degree of closure or 'seriousness' of the class.

4. *The nature of the classroom activities*, including irrelevance, overload and repetitiveness.

Although some of the prompts used by Oxford specifically referred to the teacher's role in causing demotivation, the general picture emerging from these essays is not unlike the conclusions arrived at in the communication studies presented above.

6.3.2   Chambers's investigation

The basic assumption in Gary Chambers's (1993) study is the general view among language teachers that 'Arguably the biggest problem is posed by those pupils who are quite able but do not want to learn a foreign language and make sure that the teacher knows it!' (p. 13). To find out what goes on inside the heads of pupils who systematically 'dismantled' L2 lessons, Chambers visited four schools in Leeds (UK) and administered a questionnaire to 191 year nine pupils enrolled in eight classes. A questionnaire was also filled in by seven teachers. These teachers had no problem identifying the main characteristics of the demotivated pupil; he or she

- makes no effort to learn, shows no interest, demonstrates poor concentration, produces little or no homework, fails to bring materials to lessons, claims to have lost materials; doesn't respond well to extra help;
- lacks a belief in own capabilities;
- demonstrates lethargy, 'what's the use?' syndrome, and gives negative or nil response to praise;
- is unwilling to cooperate, distracts other pupils, throws things, shouts out.

It is interesting to learn – particularly in view of the earlier evidence pointing to the teachers' responsibility in generating demotivation – that the participating teachers perceived the causes of demotivation as related to a variety of reasons (which, understandably, did not include themselves): psychological, attitudinal, social, historical, geographical. Chambers quotes one teacher stating,

> Some pupils feel forced into choosing a language course. Some cannot cope with the demands of the subject (e.g. the learning which is required). At our school many do not see the relevance of languages to their everyday lives – they are very insular and parochial and languages are not a priority.
>
> (p. 13)

Another teacher draws attention to the social nature of the problem:

> Demotivation is an affliction of our society and must be addressed. Children need to be encouraged more to respond and be praised for their contributions so that they feel their contribution is of value. Often at home they exist and are not spoken to, not stimulated and sit in front of the TV/video. They are brainwashed and become passive.
>
> (p. 14)

As can be imagined, the students' responses were in a different vein. Although only 14% view the modern language component of the curriculum as 'not essential' or a 'waste of time', 50% go on record as not enjoying or loathing language learning. Their reasons are varied. Some blame their teachers for

[margin note: Blame tchrs for:]

- going on and on without realising that they've already lost everybody;
- not giving clear enough instructions;
- using inferior equipment (e.g. for listening tasks);
- not explaining things sufficiently;
- criticising students;
- shouting at them when they don't understand;
- using old-fashioned teaching materials, etc.

Others think the group is too big, the language room is too small and the furniture in it should facilitate different seating arrangements. One pupil would like to have two language teachers. In fact, as Chambers concludes, the data about what students like and dislike most are not conclusive: it seems that what one pupil likes, the next pupil detests.

Based on his data, Chambers could draw only few conclusions about the exact impact of the language-learning experience. It is clear that, in some cases, demotivation originated from home rather than from the classroom ('My brothers told me it would be boring': p. 15) or from the pupils' previous experience in learning languages. Several students simply did not see the point of learning a L2 since their mother tongue was the world language ('Everybody should learn English'; p. 15). In some cases, however, demotivation stemmed from the L2 class and the perception of the teacher. Demotivated learners in the survey appeared to possess very low self-esteem and needed extra attention and praise for what they could do and what they were good at, which they often did not receive ('I am no good so teachers ignore me'; p. 15). As Chambers concludes, 'pupils identified as demotivated do not want to be ignored or given up as a bad job; in spite of their behaviour, they ✓ want to be encouraged' (p. 16). He also reminds us that with some pupils it will appear that nothing works, but the problem in their cases may not necessarily be with learning languages but rather with learning in general, and 'we need to adjust the attitude of parents, friends and society before real success can be achieved' (p. 16).

Quote 6.1 Chambers's conclusion about his study of demotivated pupils

I started off with this little exercise to satisfy my curiosity. Far from being satisfied, I find that I am dealing not with a mole-hill but rather the mountain.... Perhaps this realisation alone will help me come to terms with the inadequacy I and others feel when dealing with demotivated pupils. It is a problem we all have. We cannot solve it alone. Seeking the help of pupils might be a good place to start. They could well be more cooperative than school management!

Chambers (1999: 16)

6.3.3   Ushioda's investigation 1998

As part of a qualitative investigation of effective motivational thinking of 20 Irish learners of French at Trinity College Dublin (cf. also 3.2.2 and 3.7.2), Ema Ushioda asked the participants to identify what they found to be demotivating in their L2-related learning experience. As the author summarises, almost without exception, these demotives related to negative aspects of the institutionalised learning context, such as particular *teaching methods* and *learning tasks*. Ushioda emphasises that the learners in her sample did manage to sustain or revive their positive motivational disposition in the face of the various negative experiences, due to the use of a number of effective self-motivating strategies (5.2.3), such as:

- setting oneself short-term goals,
- positive self-talk,
- indulging in an enjoyable L2 activity that is 'not monitored in any way by the teacher or by essays or exams' (p. 86), such as watching a film or listening to the radio, or even eavesdropping on the conversations of L2-speaking tourists in the shops.

> **Quote 6.2** Ushioda on demotivation and self-motivation
>
> In the follow-up interview, subjects were simply asked to identify what they found to be demotivating in their learning experience. Their responses overwhelmingly targeted negative aspects of the institutionalised learning framework, rather than personal factors such as falling grades or negative self-perceptions of ability. By projecting the responsibility of their loss of motivation onto external causes in this way, learners may be better able to limit the motivational damage and dissociate the negative affect they are currently experiencing from their own enduring motivation for wanting to learn the language. The process of affirming this sense of motivational autonomy becomes the process of self-motivation, or as one subject puts it, the process of *getting your motivation on line again*.
>
> Ushioda (1998: 86)

6.3.4 Dörnyei's investigation 1998

The concluding words of Chambers's (1993) study pointed at the importance of communication and cooperation with the students, and, interestingly, the main lesson Oxford (1998) drew from her investigation was the same: 'We must listen to our students. We must directly address the important teacher- and course-specific aspects mentioned by students if we want students to be motivated to learn.' Therefore, it is perhaps no accident that my own investigation of demotivation grew out of close cooperation with my students. The original idea to focus on demotivated learners came from an MA student, Katalin Kohlmann (1996), during an academic advisory session, and the data for my project were gathered with the assistance of the participants of an MA course on 'Demotivation in Second Language Learning'. In addition, several fruitful discussions with my students, more than a dozen course papers and two additional MA theses by Rudnai (1996) and Halmos (1997) served as further inspiration to my thinking.

The Dörnyei (1998b) study differs from those by Oxford (1998), Chambers (1993) and Ushioda (1998) in that it focused specifically on learners who had been identified as being demotivated, rather than looking at a general cross-section of students and asking them about bad learning experiences. Because the primary objective was to run an exploratory analysis, we followed a qualitative approach by conducting structured long interviews (10–30 minutes) with the participants. For the purpose of these one-to-one interviews we developed a list of core questions that the interviewers were to ask some time during the interviews, but no rigid structure was set and the interviewers were instructed to allow as much free speech on the part of the participants as possible.

Participants were 50 secondary school pupils in various schools in Budapest, studying either English or German as a foreign language, identified by their teachers or peers as being particularly demotivated. The interviews were recorded and the data analysis followed a stepwise theme-based processing procedure. First, all the salient demotivating topics mentioned by the students were marked and common themes were established. We then identified for each student the most important demotivating factors. Finally, these primary demotives were tabulated according to the main categories established earlier. Only the primary demotives were tabulated and not all the negative issues mentioned by the students as I assumed that some of the negative elements were only reflections of already existing demotivation; that is, I speculated that once a student had lost interest in learning the particular L2, everything related to that learning suddenly assumed a slightly negative undertone.

The results of the analysis are presented in Table 6.1, with sample extracts to illustrate the various categories. The table lists all the types of negative influence (nine altogether) which were mentioned by at least two students as the main sources of their demotivation. The nine categories accounted for a total of 75 corresponding occurrences in the transcripts. By far the largest category (with 40% of the total frequency of occurrences) directly concerned the *teacher* (his or her personality, commitment to teaching, attention paid to the students, competence, teaching method, style, rapport with students), which is fully consistent with the results reported by other researchers. A further 15% of the occurrences also concerned the teacher, although indirectly, through the learner's *reduced self-confidence* that was partly due to some classroom event within the teacher's control (e.g. perception of too strict marking). Together these two categories made up for more than half of all the demotivating factors mentioned.

Significant proportions (more than 10%) of the demotives were accounted for by a further two factors:

- *inadequate school facilities* (group is too big or not the right level; frequent change of teachers),
- *negative attitude towards the L2* (i.e. dislike of the way the language sounds and/or operates).

Table 6.1 Main demotivating factors identified by Dörnyei (1998b)

Demotivating factor	N	Examples
1. The teacher (personality, commitment, competence, teaching method)	30	• *The teacher shouted all the time. There wasn't a single class in which he didn't shout at someone.* • *If it is raining or cold or windy, or if the roads are icy, the teacher doesn't come to class.* • *In the very first English class, the teacher said that there was no point in learning English for just two lessons a week and therefore we were not going to try very hard.* • *The teacher always had her favourites, and she always concentrated on them. I was never one of them.*
2. Inadequate school facilities (group is too big or not the right level; frequent change of teachers)	11	• *They said it would be a beginners' group but it wasn't because many classmates already knew some English ... so they had an advantage, and I could never really get into it.* • *It was really offputting that in ten years we had eleven teachers; they kept changing ... everybody tried out a new method ... everybody demanded different things and considered different things important, and I got tired of this after a while. But it wasn't just me, the whole class did. This totally demotivated me.*
3. Reduced self-confidence (experience of failure or lack of success)	11	Interviewer: *How confident are you in learning English?* Student: *Not at all any more.* Interviewer: *And how did that happen? Did you have any confidence when you started ... ?* Student: *Yes, then I still had some. But then I realised that no matter how hard I studied – the teacher was picking on me or something – I would never get anything better than a 'C' or a 'D'. ... I only got about three 'A's during the four years ...*
4. Negative attitude towards the L2	9	*At the beginning I studied quite hard but I realised that I didn't like the whole structure of the German language, the grammar. ... Although I really like the Germans, I simply can't get to grips with the language, because I don't like its sound and its structure. It is sometimes totally incomprehensible to me what's going on and why.*
5. Compulsory nature of L2 study	4	Interviewer: *You said that you had some reservations about German? How did this come about ... ?* Student: *In secondary school we had to choose a foreign language; I didn't really want to choose German, I wanted French. But Mum said that I had*

Demotivating factor	N	Examples
		to choose German because that's the second most useful language.
6. Interference of another foreign language being studied	3	• *It [German] is similar to English in many ways, and this really irritates me because I keep saying German words instead of English....I mix them up and then I get really worried that my English will suffer because of German. English is much more important.* • *English is a more useful language in everyday life than German. And German doesn't sound nice ... It's true that one of my problems with German has been that I started to learn English first and it was easier than German.*
7. Negative attitude towards L2 community	3	*This American culture we get, that is, McDonalds and the American films, is not very attractive to me....I can't say that hardly a day passes that I think 'how nice it would be to go to the US'.*
8. Attitudes of group members	2	*There were quite a few of them [group members] that I didn't like. I always felt embarrassed in the English classes because my English wasn't very good and neither was my pronunciation....I always felt that the others were laughing at me. I didn't like being there in that group. I am much better off in my current group...*
9. Coursebook	2	*We used what I think is the worst coursebook in the world....It was incredibly bad. I have seen several EFL coursebooks and this is one of the worst. Never mind.*

Although the motivational impact of the former is obvious, motivation scholars tend to overlook the fact that objective school conditions can constitute an 'affective filter' that is powerful enough to block even the best intentions on the students' or teachers' part. The second factor, the emerging dislike of the L2, is related to the fact that launching into the study of a L2 is like signing a blank cheque, since learners have only a vague idea at best about what the language will be like. A closer contact with the L2, then, results in strong evaluative feelings (both positive and negative), which in turn affect subsequent commitment to learning the language. The significant variation in student perceptions of different L2s was also confirmed by Ludwig (1983) in a large-scale study of American college students learning French, German and Spanish. In Ludwig's sample, for example, French was typically seen as *attractive* and *romantic*, probably because 'it sounds neat' (p. 225), and the author also reports strong feelings about the grammar of the various L2s under examination.

Other, less frequent but still potent demotivating factors in the investigation included:

- the compulsory nature of L2 studies;
- the interference of another foreign language being studied;
- the negative attitude towards the L2 community;
- the attitudes of other group members;
- the coursebook used in the language class.

In view of past research, it is easy to see how some of these factors decrease motivation. If learners develop *negative attitudes* towards the L2 speakers, this undermines the social dimension of their L2 motivation complex. Although it can be argued that this is not a demotive in the strict sense because the development of negative attitudes is rarely linked to specific events – in this case the unique Hungarian situation seemed to justify the inclusion of this category. After the collapse of communism at the end of the 1980s, there was a very rapid and pervasive spread of western commercialism in the country, which triggered a negative disposition in some learners. The potential damaging effect of *other group members* in creating anxiety and conveying a 'norm of mediocrity' has been discussed with regard to group motivation (2.2.3 and 3.6.5). Due to the amount of time students are to spend working with their *textbooks*, it is also logical that the attitudes towards these have a significant impact on the overall appraisal of the learning process; this was also confirmed by Chambers's (1999) empirical findings, according to which the importance of textbooks is second in importance (after that of the teacher) in determining student attitudes towards the language course.

However, the fact that the *compulsory nature of L2 studies* and the *interference of a L3* qualified as primary demotives came as a surprise, because I am not aware of any mention of their potential motivational impact in the L2 motivation literature. The negative effect of the obligatory character of L2 learning is obviously related to the lack of autonomy and can be seen as the validation of the arguments presented earlier concerning the importance of self-determination (2.1.3 and 5.2.3). With regard to the interference of the L3, our data suggest that in situations where learners are taught two foreign languages at the same time, some students may feel that the successful mastery of their preferred language is threatened by having to study the other language.

6.4 Concluding remarks on demotivation

The main conclusion we can draw from the studies reviewed above is that demotivation is a salient phenomenon in L2 studies and that teachers have a considerable responsibility in this respect. A range of potential demotives is mentioned by the students, but in several cases it is difficult to decide which of these are the real antecedents of the loss of interest and which are simply by-products of disillusion caused by another factor. It is also interesting that in Chambers's (1993) study the participating teachers attributed their students' demotivation to a number of broader, social factors, and in interpreting the student responses we should also bear in mind Chambers's warning that we are living in an age when it is not 'cool' for students to show enthusiasm for anything and 'Boredom is in' (p. 14).

I would like to emphasise that demotivation is a complex issue and the current analysis should be seen as a mere introduction. More research is needed to determine the following:

- How do demotives interplay with more general motivational dispositions and the learners' personality characteristics? Why is it that learners show a considerable variation in the extent of their demotivation under the same adverse conditions?

- Are demotives restricted to the particular situation in which they were generated or are the bad experiences generalised across situations (e.g. will someone resume learning with enthusiasm once the 'loathed' teacher is replaced)? The literature on 'learned helplessness' suggests that one's demolished self-concept is very hard to rebuild, but other types of demotives (such as boring classes) may lend themselves more easily to amendment.

- What consequences does demotivation have on the validity of motivation measurement? Given the significant impact demotivation can have on the learner's overall motivational disposition, we must question the validity of tests that mainly focus on the availability of positive motivational inducements, since it is not obvious that the negative influence of a demotive will be reflected sufficiently in the decrease of the positive scores on the other variables.

Chapter 7

Teacher motivation

This chapter will...

- analyse the unique characteristics of the 'motivation to teach';
- describe what we know about the motivation of language teachers;
- examine how teacher motivation affects the motivation of the students.

The issue of *teacher motivation* has received little attention in educational psychology. There are few publications discussing the nature of the 'motivation to teach' (although some work has been done on related issues such as teachers' job satisfaction, stress and burnout – see Dinham and Scott, 2000; Pennington, 1995), and in a recent article American psychologist Csikszentmihalyi (1997) has stated that he was not aware of a single study relating a teacher's motivation to the effectiveness of his or her teaching and to the motivation of his or her students. This is all the more surprising because, as we have seen earlier (2.2.3, 3.6.5 and 5.2.1), the teacher's level of enthusiasm and commitment is one of the most important factors that affect the learners' motivation to learn. Broadly speaking, if a teacher is motivated to teach, there is a good chance that his or her students will be motivated to learn. Furthermore, I believe that this principle does not only apply to the overall level of motivation but also to more specific aspects of motivation: for example, if a teacher finds a particular academic task meaningful rather than pointless drudgery, this task attitude is likely to be communicated – either directly through deliberate action, or indirectly by means of modelling – to the students, who will in turn adopt a similar position.

This chapter is an attempt to draw together sources from various educational domains to provide an overview of teacher motivation and how it relates to student motivation and learning behaviours. Although teachers show considerable variation across geographical locations, subject matters and the level of education they work at, there appear to be certain commonalties that are sufficiently robust to allow for some generalisations. Yet, we should bear in mind throughout this chapter that far more research is needed to do this important issue justice.

7.1   Conceptualising the 'motivation to teach'

How can we conceptualise the 'motivation to teach'? In what way is it different from the motivation to pursue other activities? In the most general sense, the understanding of teacher motivation requires no special treatment since 'teaching' is just one type of human behaviour and therefore general models of motivation to act should be applicable to describing it. Indeed, scholars have argued that teacher motivation can be best understood in the light of expectancy-value theory (e.g. McKeachie, 1997), expectancy theory (e.g. Mowday and Nam, 1997), self-efficacy theory (e.g. Ashton, 1985), goal-setting theory (e.g. Latham et al., 1997) and self-determination theory (e.g. Csikszentmihalyi, 1997; Deci et al., 1997) – that is, the various approaches closely reflect those in general motivation theories in terms of the underlying principles and their diversity. Researchers have also highlighted the relevance of social contextual factors (cf. the challenge of context in 1.5) (Bess, 1997) and temporal variation (cf. the challenge of time in 1.6) (Blackburn, 1997), which suggests that this subfield of motivational psychology is no less complex than the understanding of motivation in general.

The other side of the coin, however, is that with such a specific professional activity as teaching it might be realistic to expect to find certain unique motivational characteristics – for example, to identify some factors that have a special significance in terms of their impact on the motivation complex underlying teaching. Indeed, a review of the literature suggests that four motivational aspects are particularly featured with respect to teacher motivation:

1. It involves a prominent *intrinsic component* as a main constituent.

2. It is very closely linked with *contextual factors*, associated with the institutional demands and constraints of the workplace, and the salient social profile of the profession.

3. Along with all the other types of career motivation, it concerns an extended, often lifelong, process with a featured *temporal axis* (which is most clearly reflected when talking about career structures and promotion possibilities).

4. It appears to be particularly *fragile*, that is, exposed to several powerful negative influences (some being inherent in the profession).

I will first discuss these four points in more detail, then summarise the research on the motivation of language teachers.

7.1.1   The intrinsic component of teacher motivation

The fact that teaching is more closely associated with *intrinsic motivation* than many other behavioural domains may not come as a surprise to many readers. 'Teaching' as a vocational goal has always been associated with the internal desire to educate people, to impart knowledge and values, and to advance a community or a whole nation. This is very clearly reflected in large-scale survey of over 2,000 teachers in England, Australia and New Zealand by Dinham and Scott (2000), in which the researchers found that the option 'I always wanted to become a teacher' was the most frequently endorsed reason for entering the profession in all three countries (with 45–49% of the teachers agreeing with it). Furthermore, in all three countries the intrinsic rewards of teaching were the most satisfying aspects of the profession. What are these intrinsic rewards? Csikszentmihalyi (1997) separates two sources of such rewards:

• the *educational process itself* (i.e. working with students and experiencing the changes in the students' performance and behaviour attributable to the teacher's action);

• the *subject matter* (i.e. dealing with a valued field and continuously integrating new information in it, thereby increasing one's own level of professional skills and knowledge).

Quote 7.1   Deci, Kasser and Ryan on the intrinsic rewards of teaching

Guiding the intellectual and emotional development of students, whether in nursery school or graduate school, can be profoundly gratifying for teachers, satisfying their psychological needs and contributing to their growth as individuals.

Deci et al. (1997: 57)

In an anticipation of such intrinsic rewards, most people who go into teaching are ready to forgo high salaries and social recognition – a fact that is recognised and abused by many national governments.

Let us stop for a moment to examine the issue of 'psychological needs' mentioned by Deci et al. (1997; see Quote 7.1). As seen in 2.1.3, Deci and Ryan (1985) postulated three basic human needs that are related to intrinsically motivated behaviour:

- *autonomy* (i.e. experiencing oneself as the origin of one's behaviour);
- *relatedness* (i.e. feeling close to and connected to other individuals);
- *competence* (i.e. feeling efficacious and having a sense of accomplishment).

Teaching, ideally, satisfies the first two of these human needs: a teacher is fairly autonomous in dealing with a class, and the school community (both staff and students) provides a rich and intensive human environment. The critical issue, then, is 'competence' or, using a more technical term, the teachers' sense of *efficacy*, which refers to 'their belief in their ability to have a positive effect on student learning' (Ashton, 1985: 142). This, according to Ashton, consists of two hierarchically organised dimensions:

- *teaching efficacy*, referring to the teachers' general beliefs about the possibility of producing student learning in the face of multiple obstacles (e.g. unsupportive home environment);
- *personal efficacy*, referring to the teacher's personal appraisal of his or her own effectiveness as a pedagogue.

Although the intrinsic interest in and enjoyment of teaching is a primary constituent of teacher motivation, Latham et al. (1997) reason that – in line with the main tenets of goal-setting theory (2.1.2) – instructors will be most persistent when they also have clear and feasible *goals* to achieve. This makes sense, since in the case of such a complex process as teaching, one needs explicit guidelines and standards to keep one's behaviour on track. However, Latham and his colleagues also emphasise that wise goal setting alone will not necessarily improve performance or increase the motivation of a teacher, because frequent *performance feedback* is also needed to obtain good results. Combining this with the intrinsic factors discussed above, we have a picture that is in accordance with the dominant view of work motivation in organisational psychology (Hackman, 1991), which maintains that work will be more motivating when

- it is *meaningful* (i.e. it requires a multiplicity of skills, is a whole unit rather than an unintelligible part, and is clearly important to others);
- it allows *autonomy* (i.e. the worker is given control of what, how, and when the work is done);
- it provides *feedback* (i.e. the worker has knowledge of results).

In sum, the intrinsic dimension of teacher motivation is related to the inherent joy of pursuing a meaningful activity related to one's subject area of interest, in an autonomous manner, within a vivacious collegial community, with self-efficacy, instructional goals and performance feedback being critical factors in modifying the level of effort and persistence.

7.1.2   Teacher motivation and social contextual influences

A characteristic feature of most vocation-specific motivation constructs is that they concern a peculiar situation whereby the individual is paid to act according to an externally imposed job description within an organisational framework. And even though young people are often encouraged to select a job that suits their personal interests and intrinsic vocational desires, organisations are 'achievement-laden environments' (Blackburn, 1997: 321), and as organisational workers, teachers make 'commitments to produce that are sustained on the basis of inducements that the organisation offers' (Bess, 1997: 430). Thus, even with the best possible match between a profession and an individual, one's intrinsic motivation will be inevitably 'tainted' by the impact of the external conditions and constraints of the social context of the job. Accordingly, theories of job design in organisational psychology assume that the environment plays a fundamental role in job motivation – that is, it is the work, not the worker, which affects persistence and performance (Walker and Symons, 1997).

Traditionally, extrinsic influences on work motivation have been considered as one broad domain whose salient presence typically caused dissatisfaction but whose absence did not significantly increase job satisfaction. Thus, these contextual influences were seen as the potentially negative counterpart of the positive side of work motivation, the intrinsic domain (Dinham and Scott, 1998). However, in their large-scale international study already mentioned, Dinham and Scott (2000) offer research evidence that contextual influences can be separated into two main categories that affect teacher satisfaction in different ways (see Concept 7.1):

Concept 7.1   **Two levels of contextual influences on teacher motivation: macro and micro**

Similarly to social motivation in general, we can separate *macro-* and *microcontextual influences* on teacher motivation. The former is associated with the general work ethos prevalent at the societal level. This macro-dimension is particularly featured in the case of teaching, because the profession is to accomplish one of the most prominent societal functions: bringing up and educating the next generation of people. For this reason, teaching is exposed to external influences from every layer of society, including politicians, parents and the media.

Microcontextual motives, on the other hand, are more closely related to the organisational climate of the particular institution in which the teacher works and the characteristics of the immediate teaching environment, that is, the classroom and the learner group. Particularly important school effects are exerted by a number of factors such as:

• the school's general climate and the existing school norms;
• the class sizes, the school resources and facilities;
• the standard activity structure within the institution;
• collegial relations;
• the definition of the teacher's role by colleagues and authorities;
• general expectations regarding student potential;
• the school's reward contingencies and feedback system;
• the school's leadership and decision-making structure.

Quote 7.2   **Bess on the sociocultural dimension of teacher motivation**

The motivational states of all workers, including faculty, are importantly affected by unexamined assumptions that are embedded in culturally generated values. Conceptualisations of motivation in different societies are quite different. For example, we have common Eurocentric notions of what work means, what we should 'get out' of it, how 'satisfied' we should be, and whom to blame if we do not derive sufficient rewards from it. We usually compare our own lot with others', and these comparisons very often determine not only the state of our mental well-being but also the effort we are willing to devote to various tasks.

Bess (1997: 426)

- *school-based extrinsic factors* (micro-level) exert a varied impact, ranging between satisfying and dissatisfying, primarily as a function of the school leadership;
- *systemic/societal-level factors* (macro-level) such as the status and image of teachers or the imposed educational changes, over which teachers and school have little control, function as major dissatisfiers.

Among the school factors, overall satisfaction was – not surprisingly – associated most strongly with the amount of workload, which is consistent with results reported by Blackburn (1997), namely that 'perceived expected effort' (that is, the teacher's perception of the institutional demands) is one of the key determinants of teachers' work effort.

Concept 7.2   **Social knowledge**

Blackburn and Lawrence (1995) postulated that *social knowledge* is an important component of teacher motivation, mediating between personal motives (e.g. self-efficacy, interest) and teaching behaviour. Focusing on teachers in higher education, they conceptualised social knowledge variables to include beliefs among teaching staff about their employing institution, such as the adequacy of laboratory and library holdings, grant support, department's commitment to research and teaching, morale, career success, perceived effort the institution expects to be given to a role, the norms of the specific workplace, and the characteristics of the discipline.

7.1.3   The temporal dimension of teacher motivation

Teacher motivation is not just about the motivation to teach but also about the motivation to be a teacher as a lifelong *career*. A career perspective highlights the temporal dimension of motivation in vocational engagements. The interlinked consecutive steps on a career path – defined by Raynor as the 'contingent path structure' (see Concept 7.3) – energise long-term achievement strivings in a very effective manner because they capitalise both on the intrinsic pleasure of being involved in one's profession and on various extrinsic rewards that career advancement brings about. However, if the career path is 'closed', that is, present achievements do not create future career steps, this will have a marked negative impact on the individual's work morale. This issue, as we will see below, is of particular relevance to the teaching profession.

Concept 7.3   Raynor's conception of 'career' as a psychological
construct and the 'contingent path'

Joel Raynor's work on long-term achievement strivings (such as pursuing a career) is very relevant to the understanding of teacher motivation
(Raynor, 1974a, 1974b; Raynor and Entin, 1983). He defines *careers* as
'interrelated sets of skill-demanding activities that are engaged in by individuals over time' (Raynor, 1974b: 371). To understand the motivational
foundation of the pursuit of a career, Raynor introduces the concept of
a *contingent path*, referring to a series of tasks where successful achievement is necessary to be guaranteed the opportunity to perform the next
task, that is, to continue in the path (e.g. one needs to take an exam to be
able to carry on studying towards a further exam and eventually a degree).
This means that in a contingent path 'immediate success is known to
guarantee the opportunity for subsequent career striving, and immediate failure is known to guarantee future career failure through loss of
opportunity to continue that career path' (p. 372).

Raynor emphasises that from a path contingency perspective, external
motives (e.g. money, power, prestige, security, public acclaim, approval
of family and friends) are just as important determinants of career
motivation as intrinsic ones (interest in the profession, acquisition of
special competence, successful task completion). In fact, as he reasons,
it is difficult to imagine any sustained motivational disposition in the
vocational/career context without the mutually supportive existence of
an underlying personal interest and a contingent path structure.

An important element of contingent path theory is the recognition
that many careers are so structured that their hierarchy of advancement has a clearly defined final or upper plateau (i.e. a *closed* contingent
path), while others are seen as essentially *open-ended*. In closed paths,
achievement-related motivation decreases with advancement, whereas
open paths sustain persistence and prolonged effort because additional
possibilities for continued career-related striving become apparent as
the individual moves along the career path.

Blackburn (1997) emphasises that the marked steps in a contingent
path include not only 'rational, long-range, discernible plans in accordance with anticipated career stages' (p. 327) such as advancements in
wealth and rank but also 'personally meaningful, idiosyncratic events'
(p. 327) such as honours/awards, appointments, grant/travel opportunities (e.g. conferences or study trips), memberships in professional
societies, the possibility of preparing teaching materials and professional publications, etc. That is, the availability of seemingly secondary

factors such as an award for 'excellence in teaching', a recognition in a public ceremony or a certificate/plaque is crucial in outlining vocational contingencies.

Pennington (1995: 209–10) presents a 'sample career ladder' to demonstrate that possible advancement contingency paths can be established even in the field of education. Some steps in this structure include

- the increased variety of courses taught;
- contribution to curriculum development;
- monitoring role with new faculty;
- being in charge of developing new courses/programmes;
- making conference presentations and/or preparing professional publications;
- serving as teaching consultant within and/or outside the institution;
- conducting teacher-training workshops (in-service programmes);
- developing materials for use in the home institutions and elsewhere.

If management assigns officially recognised titles and responsibilities to these (and other) developmental steps/stages, the resulting tapestry of 'personally meaningful' advancement opportunities and career subgoals can be sufficiently intricate to serve as a powerful motivation dimension. Some examples of such possible titles include team leader, management team member, curriculum group leader, committee member, director of studies, head of supervision, student liaison officer, public relations secretary, international secretary, staff development officer, timetable organiser, academic coordinator, etc.

7.1.4   Negative influences on teacher motivation

It was argued earlier that teaching can be profoundly gratifying for teachers, satisfying their psychological needs, thereby generating intrinsic pleasure to go with the job. Yet all too often, at each level of education, we find teachers who are frustrated, disaffected, or just plain bored. One hears alarming reports indicating that a great proportion of teachers in many countries are *not* motivated to teach, and that this tendency is actually getting worse. Ashton (1985) presents data from the USA, witnessing that in the 1980s one of every four teachers eventually left teaching, and hardly over 20% of the teachers reported that they would have chosen teaching as a career if they had been able to start again. In the UK, as Pennington (1995) reports (based on a study by Travers and

Cooper), teachers have the lowest job satisfaction of any professional groups studied, are more stressed than other notorious occupational groups (such as doctors, nurses or tax officers), and two-thirds actively consider changing jobs (just as I was writing the manuscript of this chapter, a new teachers' telephone stress hotline was set up in the UK to help to cope with the growing frustration within the profession). Dinham and Scott (2000) found that more than half of the teachers they surveyed in three countries (Australia, England and New Zealand) experienced a decline in satisfaction since beginning teaching. Pennington reviews studies from a number of other countries as well and although there are cross-national differences, by and large these studies also recount a rather gloomy picture.

What's happening? What causes this motivational crisis? Part of the answer, I believe, lies in the fact that – as argued earlier – teaching is a profession whose pursuit is fuelled primarily by intrinsic motives and that there exist a number of detrimental factors that systematically undermine and erode the intrinsic character of teacher motivation. Leaving economic issues (such as low salaries) aside for the moment because they vary from country to country, and without aiming for comprehensiveness, there appear to be five general demotivating factors responsible for the erosion process:

- the particularly *stressful nature* of most teaching jobs;
- the *inhibition of teacher autonomy* by set curricula, standardised tests, imposed teaching methods, government mandated policies and other institutional constraints;
- *insufficient self-efficacy* on most teachers' part due to inappropriate training;
- *content repetitiveness* and *limited potential for intellectual development*;
- *inadequate career structure*.

I am certain that several other jobs also share some of these features, but I cannot think of any other qualified profession where almost every aspect of the motivational power base is being challenged.

Stress

Teaching is one of the most stressful professions. This is due to the combination of various reasons (e.g. bureaucratic pressure, lack of adequate facilities, low salaries) but one crucial contributing factor is that teachers have to spend most of their working hours with groups of children or young adults. Dealing with children is inherently difficult, requiring a constant state of alertness, and mistakes are punished dearly. Furthermore, teachers often deal with learners who are going through the most turbulent phases of their personal lives (e.g. adolescence), which is often reflected in increased rebelliousness and basic behavioural problems. It is difficult enough to control these students and keep them 'happy', but teachers also have to *teach* them subjects that many (or most) students would not have selected for themselves. No wonder that surveys typically reveal chronic stress at every level of education in most countries (for a review, see Pennington, 1995), which in turn results in frequent 'teacher burnout'.

Based on the work of Menzies (1959), Ehrman and Dörnyei (1998) argue that in order to cope with the inherent stress, teaching staffs protect themselves from anxiety by applying a number of defence mechanisms that increase structural rigidity in the social system. Some examples of such mechanisms are

- the splitting up of the teacher–student relationship through specialisation and subdivided tasks, resulting in a situation in which no one is responsible for interacting with students in all dimensions;
- the depersonalisation of the individual student and insistence that no one receives special treatment;
- the development of detachment and cynical attitudes, and denial of feelings (e.g. 'stiff upper lip' norms);
- attempts to reduce the need for decisions by reliance on ritualised task performance (e.g. by following routines and standard operating procedures whether they apply to the situation or not);
- the avoidance of change, inasmuch as the existing system, for all its surface dysfunctions (i.e. rigidity, less-than-effective response to individual student needs, and waste), plays an important role in helping members to cope with anxiety and with each other.

Ehrman and Dörnyei's conclusion is similar to that of Lortie (1975), who holds that stresses stemming from the isolated working conditions, pressures from multiple constituencies, little career development, and minimal support from school authorities result in teacher conservatism, lack of complexity in teacher discourse, a preference for both physical and psychic boundedness, a tendency to orthodoxy, and reduction in a search for better ways to teach.

Although part of the stress is inherent in the teaching process itself, Pennington (1995: 109) argues that on-the-job stresses can be significantly mollified by providing structural support in the way of such resources as:

- an orderly and smoothly functioning environment;
- clean, adequately lit, sufficiently large, and well-equipped work spaces, including offices and classrooms;
- textbooks, teaching equipment and other teaching resources which are plentiful, in good condition, and up-to-date;
- reasonable work responsibilities in terms of workload and nature of teaching assignment;
- moral and work support from administrators.

Restricted autonomy

The experience of frequent stress contributes significantly to the weakening of intrinsic motivation, but – in the light of self-determination theory – a factor that is perhaps even more potent in undermining teacher motivation is the increasing limitation of teacher autonomy. As seen earlier (7.1.2), education is an area that has a high social profile, and governments, educational authorities and various district school boards regularly impose normative constraints on schools in an attempt to bring the behaviour of teachers in line with some *a priori* criteria of effectiveness. This regularisation process can take the form of introducing nationwide standardised tests (the more the merrier!) and national curricula, and the general mistrust towards teachers is also reflected by the increasing administration demands. Leaving aside whether these attempts are justified, it can be concluded from a purely motivational point of view that if the measures that are intended to produce better results introduce growing centralised control, this will impede teacher autonomy (which is one of the cornerstones of teacher motivation) and will therefore lead to the increased demoralisation of teachers. No wonder that Brown (1994: 129) warns L2 teachers: 'Institutional constraints are sometimes the biggest hurdle you have to cross.'

Insufficient self-efficacy

Deci and Ryan (1985) listed *competence* (i.e. feeling efficacious and having a sense of accomplishment) as one of the basic conditions of intrinsic motivation. Do teachers have sufficient competence to go about their jobs with confidence? The answer is usually 'no'. Teacher education has traditionally taken a very one-sided approach by placing most emphasis on subject-matter training, accompanied by some (rather limited) participatory experience in an instructional context that is supposed to provide the practical skills. Teacher-training programmes do not as a rule include any awareness raising about how to manage groups (e.g. they do not cover the main principles of group dynamics and effective leadership strategies, and do not offer any training in interpersonal skills and conflict resolution). As a consequence, most newly qualified teachers are hit hard by the harsh reality of everyday classroom life, often referred to as the 'reality shock' (Veenman, 1984: 143). They are at a loss when something 'goes wrong' in the class, and because they lack any explicit skills in how to handle such inevitable crises, many of them change their original student-centred teaching behaviours into a more authoritarian way (for a review, see Veenman, 1984).

Quote 7.3 Crookes on the insufficient training of language teachers

In many areas of both English as a second language and FL [foreign language] education in the U.S., including my own home state of Hawai'i, educational systems (not to mention private language schools, literacy programs, etc.) refuse to provide even the basic training (and appropriate remuneration) that teachers need to execute their duties effectively.

Crookes (1997: 68)

In sum, I would like to argue that newly qualified teachers are thrown into very deep water, and unless they have a natural 'knack' for dealing with people, they easily misunderstand and mishandle the inevitable fluctuation of both emotions and productivity that social groups regularly experience. As a result of their lop-sided training, many teachers simply lack the skills necessary for doing well in the classroom. For them the task may be overly challenging and thus not intrinsically motivating. This insufficient self-efficacy, of course, also contributes to the stress-generating nature of the profession (discussed above).

Lack of intellectual challenge

In a typical school setting, many teachers teach the same subject matter year after year, without any real opportunity from teaching to discover or acquire new knowledge, skills or abilities. A recurring complaint I have heard from classroom practitioners is that if they simply do their job they get tired of it after a while and 'lose the spark'. Indeed, meeting the prescribed requirements and covering the imposed course content in the same specialised sub-area of the curriculum does not allow many teachers much leeway to include variations and 'intellectual detours', and the classroom procedures can easily get routinised (Pennington, 1995). Naturally, there are exceptions to these generalisations, and successful teachers show a remarkable resourcefulness in making the time spent in the classroom rewarding for the students and for themselves, but for the average instructor teaching can easily become dreary work.

Inadequate career structure

We have seen above that teaching can be – with some exaggeration – a highly stressful and intellectually numbing process in which under-skilled practitioners try to survive against the odds under the suffocating constraints imposed on them. Unfortunately, this is not all; there is another major motivational impediment with regard to most teaching jobs: the lack of an appropriate *career structure* or professional contingent path. For someone who wishes to remain a classroom teacher rather than going into management there are usually very few areas of advancement or further goals to attain. As a result, teachers often feel that they 'got stuck' or 'reached a plateau', and thinking about the time ahead of them before retirement causes absolutely no tingle of excitement. In other words, teaching offers a 'closed contingent path' (see 7.1.3).

While this situation is also characteristic of a great number of other occupations, I believe that teachers – with their high qualifications, ambitions and intrinsic job involvement – find it particularly difficult to live with the notion of 'futurelessness'. On the other hand, I also believe that this 'no-career-ladder' situation could be changed to some extent. Although educational settings will probably never be able to offer such an elaborate advancement path as there are, say, in the military or in certain business areas, we can envisage a sufficiently intricate future-oriented reward system of titles and responsibilities even in educational domains that can potentially fill the motivational hiatus caused by an inadequate career structure (for some examples, see 7.1.3). In a recognition of the importance of this issue, several countries have recently considered introducing titles such as 'super-teachers' or 'master teachers' within the educational hierarchy.

In a review of the psychological literature on work satisfaction, Pennington (1995) makes a further important point concerning the temporal dimension of work motivation. She argues that work dissatisfaction tends to be associated with the concrete, daily characteristics of the employment situation, that is, the 'here and now' aspect; in contrast, work satisfaction is generally focused more broadly on the larger outlook of a whole career, such as future plans and goals. This implies that the inadequate career path contingency for most teachers increases their dissatisfaction with the generally less-than-perfect work condition by turning their attention away from the larger, more idealistic and intrinsically coloured outlook of their profession.

Quote 7.4 Pennington on the role of future career perspectives in compensating for concerns with actual work conditions

Where an employee's future-oriented, long-term outlook is positive, there is less attention to the more immediate, quotidian framework. However, where the broad outlook is unsatisfactory and there seems little chance of career aspirations being met in a given work context, the employee's attention shifts to the immediate frame of reference, which assumes comparatively great importance.

Pennington (1995: 19–20)

7.1.5   The motivation of L2 teachers

The literature on the motivation of language teachers is even more scarce than on teacher motivation in general. One important exception is a series of studies conducted by Martha Pennington and her colleagues on teachers of English and a monograph she has written to summarise the findings and place them within a broader theoretical framework (*Work satisfaction, motivation, and commitment in teaching English as a second language*; Pennington, 1995). In the following, I will first describe Pennington's findings, then I will summarise a research project on factors affecting teacher motivation by Terry Doyle and Young Mi Kim (Doyle and Kim, 1999; Kim and Doyle, 1998), to whom I also owe special thanks for directing me to a number of related sources.

Pennington's analysis of the motivation of ESL teachers

Being fully aware of the paucity of relevant theoretical and field-specific information, Martha Pennington (1995) has set out to provide 'a first approximation, or initial model, of the ESL work environment that will be elaborated and refined by others in the future' (p. 7). Her specific focus is the work satisfaction and motivation of teachers of English as a Second Language, but she also provides a more general review of research on work and teacher satisfaction/motivation.

Pennington (1995) gives a detailed summary of the empirical work she has conducted with various colleagues on the topic in different parts of the world. In 1991, Pennington and Riley sent a standardised work satisfaction questionnaire (the Minnesota Satisfaction Questionnaire) to 100 randomly selected members of the US-based organisation 'Teachers of English to Speakers of Other Languages' (TESOL), which is the world's largest international association of L2 teachers. The questionnaire measured satisfaction with 20 different work facets (5 items each) and the ESL practitioners' responses showed considerable interscale variation. The two highest rated facets were *Moral Values* and *Social Services*, which is in accordance with the theoretical arguments about the intrinsic, ideologically loaded character of teacher motivation. These two facets were followed by *Creativity*, *Achievement* and *Ability Utilisation*, which are also related to intrinsic job satisfaction. The two lowest rated facets were *Advancement* and *Compensation*, which is again consistent with earlier arguments, followed by two *Supervision* scales and one of *Company Policies and Procedures*, indicating that the respondents did not find their institutions generally supportive.

In 1991, Pennington and Riley also conducted a second, similar study but this time sending out another well-known work satisfaction questionnaire, the Job Descriptive Index, which focuses on five job facets (pay, promotion, co-workers, supervision and the nature of the work) and contains an additional general job satisfaction scale. Although the division of the work facets examined was different in the two instruments, the results of this second study were consistent with those of the first: the highest ratings occurred in the categories of *Co-workers* and *Work*, with the lowest in *Promotion* and *Pay*. Pennington also conducted research among Chinese bilingual high school English teachers in Hong Kong, and the findings again confirmed the general trends outlined earlier. As she concluded, these teachers had reduced commitment due, among other things, to high stress, low autonomy, poor resources and minimal work incentives such as promotions.

> **Quote 7.5**   Pennington on the work satisfaction of ESL teachers
>
> ESL practitioners are motivated in a positive direction in their jobs and careers by intrinsic work process and human relations factors. These positive motivators guarantee that the level of overall satisfaction will be sufficiently high within ESL so as to sustain a core of experienced educators in teaching and related practices and to continue to attract a steady stream of enthusiastic newcomers to fill the increasing need for ESL practitioners around the globe.... At the same time, the global picture is one of considerable dissatisfaction with long-term career opportunities within the field, with the compensation and recognition received for the work performed, and with administrative and supervisory policies and practices that limit professional responsibility and growth.
>
> Pennington (1995: 139–40)

Doyle and Kim's investigation

The work of Terry Doyle and Young Mi Kim differs from the line of research reported by Pennington (1995) in that it takes a less positivist approach. Although the authors also use questionnaire data, they complement these with extensive qualitative interviews with teachers, and also draw heavily on critical language pedagogy as a basic theoretical orientation (e.g. Crookes, 1997; Pennycook, 1989). By doing so, their objective is to attempt to achieve a critical analysis of the 'social, cultural and political reasons which diminish teacher motivation and cause dissatisfaction and low morale' (Kim and Doyle, 1998) by means of analysing data from Korean (9 interviews, 99 questionnaires) and American teachers of English (5 interviews, 100 questionnaires).

Doyle and Kim (1999) discuss their results by focusing on three main themes:

1. *Intrinsic motivation.* The authors report a general consensus among the participating teachers that the main motivating factor for them is the intrinsic interest in teaching and helping students; as one American teacher explicitly stated, if 'it's not fun for you, you really should get out of it because it's not financially rewarding'. Another teacher emphasised the importance of being in charge of one's own class: 'What increases my motivation, and what is certainly one of your questions, is the fact that, a one thousand percent plus of the job is that it's your class. It really is your class, right? I feel like this is my class.'

2. *Factors leading to dissatisfaction.* The high intrinsic commitment of language teachers is (as one teacher explicitly stated) known and taken advantage of by school administrators. Similarly to English teachers in many other contexts (cf. Crookes, 1997; Johnston, 1997), Doyle and Kim's data reveal that the adverse external factors associated with the job have an eroding effect on some of the teachers; for example, 43% of the American sample agreed that their salary affects their motivation in the classroom and 34% stated the same thing about their advancement opportunities. Further dissatisfaction is caused by the lack of respect from the school administration and even department heads; the unfavourable employment conditions; the lack of advancement opportunities; and the perceived gradual devaluation of the teacher's role.

3. *Mandated curricula and tests.* Kim and Doyle (1998) report three sources of curriculum-related pressures observed in their study, all impeding teachers' autonomy. The first is the obligation to teach a *set curriculum* ('I teach students, not a curriculum'), a point which is often mentioned with regard to other subject areas as well in the educational psychological literature. In Korea, this pressure was also augmented by the limited choice of textbooks prescribed by the national textbook committee and by the fact that the prescribed methodology was imposed by western experts abroad. The second type of pressure is to use *standardised tests*, which – apart from the fact that they are restricting – were also regarded by some teachers as 'condescending' (e.g. in the sense that they highlighted low-level service jobs, a criticism that was also mentioned about the curriculum in general) and sometimes 'culturally insensitive'. The third source of pressure is the interference from *government-mandated directives*; for example, mandatory attendance at 'politically correct workshops' was seen to lead to dissatisfaction.

It is noteworthy that although Doyle and Kim's (1999) sample consisted of two sets of teachers of very different types – western instructors in a second language acquisition context and oriental instructors in a foreign language learning context – the results showed more commonalties than differences.

7.1.6   Summary of the 'teacher motivation' construct

Although the amount of past research on teacher motivation (let alone L2 teacher motivation) is far too little relative to its importance, the relevant bits and pieces that we can find in various educational domains suggest a consistent picture, with teachers working in diverse geographical and subject-matter areas sharing certain powerful motivational themes that add up to a general 'teacher motivation' construct. Accordingly, we can describe the teaching profession as a body of highly qualified professionals with an intrinsically motivated and ideologically coloured commitment to pursue what they see as a by and large fulfilling job. The profession, however, is struggling with serious difficulties that overshadow the satisfaction with the inherent qualities of the job, such as

- the exceptionally high stress level;
- the increasing restrictions of teaching autonomy (by externally imposed curricula, tests, methods and other directives);
- the fragile self-efficacy of practitioners, most of whom are undertrained in areas concerning group leadership and classroom management;
- the difficulty of maintaining an intellectual challenge in the face of repetitive content and routinised classroom practices;
- an inadequate career structure to generate effective motivational contingent paths;

Example 7.1   A set of self-motivating strategies for teachers

- Reflect immediately after a lesson on how it went and make mental notes on what to do differently next time.
- Imagine being named teacher of the year and how satisfied that would make you.
- Observe other teachers as a learning tool.
- Marshal inner resources and remember you've been through more than this and made it.
- Analyse why you feel so anxious about aspects of your work and think through ways to overcome these feelings.
- Embellish your teaching – keep changing what you do – so it's more interesting for you to teach it again.
- Rearrange the classroom layout for maximal attention from students.
- Call teacher study groups to resolve problems cooperatively.

Based on Corno and Kanfer (1993: 312–13)

- the economic conditions that are usually worse than those of other service professions with comparable qualifications (e.g. lawyers and doctors).

Thus, the unique benefits of doing an inherently fulfilling job that can satisfy one's higher-order psychological needs have increasingly been challenged by adverse conditions (both internal and external) that prevent teachers from fully experiencing the intrinsic rewards of their chosen occupation (Pennington, 1995).

7.2 The relationship between teacher motivation and student motivation

Although the analysis of 'motivation to teach' is an intriguing and largely uncharted domain, it is only relevant to this book inasmuch as teacher motivation affects the motivational disposition of the learners. As was mentioned in the introduction of this chapter, hardly any research has been conducted to examine this relationship specifically; nevertheless, there is some indirect evidence and a certain amount of theorising available to confirm that teacher motivation has a direct impact on student motivation and achievement. I will first describe the indirect empirical support, which concerns the impact of teacher expectations on student achievement, and then present the relevant theoretical arguments related to the link between teacher enthusiasm to teach and learner enthusiasm to learn.

7.2.1 Teacher expectations and student achievement: the 'Pygmalion effect'

One component of the 'motivation to teach' complex involves the teacher's expectation about the students' learning potential, a factor that can be considered closely related to the more general 'expectancy of (teaching) success' component discussed earlier (2.1.1). This teacher expectation factor has been shown to affect the students' rate of progress, functioning to some extent as a *self-fulfilling prophecy* (also referred to as the 'Pygmalion effect' after Bernard Shaw's play), with students living up or 'down' to their teachers' expectations.

There have been several models postulated in educational psychology to explain the self-fulfilling process (for a review, see Brophy, 1985;

Concept 7.4   Rosenthal and Jacobson's experiment to document the 'Pygmalion effect'

In a famous experiment, Rosenthal and Jacobson (1968; summarised by Pintrich and Schunk, 1996) administered an intelligence test to primary school children at the start of the academic year. Teachers were told that the purpose of this test was to predict which students would 'bloom' intellectually during the academic year. The researchers, however, deceived the teachers because instead of providing them with the true test scores, they identified 20% of the sample as potential 'intellectual bloomers' randomly, that is, regardless of their actual intellectual potential. The results of the experiment were quite remarkable: by the end of the year there were significant differences between the 'bloomers' and the control students whereas at the beginning of the year they were similar in every respect except in the way they were labelled by the researchers. Rosenthal and Jacobson explained the emerging difference by arguing that the (false) information about the students created differential teacher expectations concerning them and these expectations acted as self-fulfilling prophecies in that students lived up to them.

Good, 1994). There is a consensus in that initial teacher expectations trigger off various events and teacher behaviours which, in turn, influence student performance in a corresponding fashion: These mediating influences can be

- *direct* (e.g. extra learning opportunities or increased challenges), or
- *indirect* (e.g. improved rapport and more detailed performance feedback which, in turn, change student attitudes and motivation).

If they are consistent over time, these influences are likely to affect the student's self-concept, level of aspiration, achievement strivings, classroom conduct and interaction with the teacher. The cumulative effect of these changes will, then, be a change in the student's achievement.

Although Rosenthal and Jacobson's original study (see Concept 7.4) only looked into positive expectations, the Pygmalion effect can also involve negative expectations (i.e. teachers expect less than what the student is capable of) and in these cases the false evaluation of/beliefs about the students can become harmful. Brophy (1985: 180) lists eight concrete ways by which negative expectancy-driven teacher behaviour can reduce student motivation:

1. Giving up easily on low-expectation students (e.g. not waiting long enough for their answers).

2. Criticising them more often for failure.

3. Praising them less often following success.

4. Praising inappropriately (e.g. after routine responses).

5. Neglecting to give them any feedback following their responses.

6. Seating them in the back of the room.

7. Generally paying less attention to them or interacting with them less frequently.

8. Expressing less warmth towards them or less interest in them as individuals.

In the light of the Pygmalion effect, teachers need to be very careful about the psychological acceptance and evaluation of their students: non-subject-matter-related biases and stereotypes can easily be transformed into disadvantageous learning conditions along the above lines, even without teachers being conscious of the fact that they are transmitting expectation-mediated discrimination.

The self-fulfilling prophecy phenomenon exists not only at the individual level but also at the group level. Pintrich and Schunk (1996) reported on an experiment by Schrank (1968), in which teachers were told (again without any basis of truth) that their classes were made up of students of particularly high or low learning potential. Similarly, as in the Rosenthal and Jacobson study, students in the high-potential condition were found to learn more than their peers in the low-potential group. This link between teacher beliefs and student behaviour is particularly noteworthy in view of the fact that ability grouping has become a standard practice in contemporary education. Schrank's results indicate that students assigned to low-ability groups are at a multiple disadvantage, as their and their peers' (allegedly) limited capabilities are accompanied by the teacher's reduced commitment to their learning. This may send the children on an ever downward spiral of low achievement and low expectations. In fact, as Chambers (1999) summarises, recent national examination results in the UK pointed to a growing gap between 'the more and less able', which was widely attributed by the media to the schools neglecting those pupils who were not likely to feature in the national league tables for A–C passes.

7.2.2   Teacher enthusiasm – learner enthusiasm

In a thought-provoking article, Csikszentmihalyi (1997) points out that the most influential teachers – those who are remembered and who make a real difference in their students' development – are not the ones who have most status and power, and they may not even be the most intelligent or knowledgeable instructors a student has. Instead, they are usually the ones who love what they are doing, who show by their dedication and their passion that there is nothing else on earth they would rather be doing. They are the 'nutcases' whose involvement in the subject matter is so excessive that it is bordering on being crazy. 'Yet', the author goes on, 'it is such fools who keep the fabric of knowledge from unravelling between one generation to the next. If it weren't for them, who would believe that knowledge really mattered?' (p. 78).

Quote 7.6 Csikszentmihalyi on the effects of teacher motivation

Young people are more intelligent than adults generally give them credit for. They can usually discern, for instance, whether an adult they know likes or dislikes what he or she is doing. If a teacher does not believe in his job, does not enjoy the learning he is trying to transmit, the student will sense this and derive the entirely rational conclusion that the particular subject matter is not worth mastering for its own sake. If all the teachers they are exposed to are extrinsically motivated, students might well conclude that learning in general is worthless in and of itself.

Such a reaction on the part of young people is eminently adaptive. Why should they want to spend their lives being bored? Why should they emulate a model who is already alienated from his or her life activity? The young are in general less resigned than adults to the prospect of a meaningless life. They look around them for adults who seem to enjoy their jobs, who believe in what they are doing, and take them as models.

Csikszentmihalyi (1997: 77)

The point Csikszentmihalyi (1997) makes touches upon the core of the teacher–student relationship. Effective teachers are not necessarily the ones who are successful in the business of transferring cognitive information. Instead, the positive impact of good teachers is due to the strength of their commitment towards the subject matter which becomes 'infectious', that is, instils in students a similar willingness to pursue knowledge. As Csikszentmihalyi summarises: 'The best way to get students to believe that it makes sense to pursue knowledge is to believe in it oneself' (p. 72).

Quote 7.7 Good and Brophy on teacher enthusiasm

In suggesting that teachers project enthusiasm we do not mean pep talks or unnecessary theatrics. Instead, we mean that *teachers identify their own reasons for being interested in the topic or for finding it meaningful or important and project these reasons to the students* when teaching about the topic. Teachers can use dramatics or forceful salesmanship if they are comfortable with these techniques, but if not, low-key but sincere statements of the value that they place on a topic or activity will be just as effective.

Good and Brophy (1994: 240)

Deci et al. (1997: 68) report on an experiment by Wild et al. (1992) which provides some empirical confirmation to Csikszentmihalyi's argument. In this study, some participating students were led to believe that the teacher conducting a special lesson had been paid to do so (and thus was extrinsically motivated), whereas others were led to believe that the same teacher had volunteered to be of service (and thus was intrinsically motivated). Although all the students participated in exactly the same lesson, the perceptions of the class and the teacher were markedly different in the two groups. Those who thought that the teacher was intrinsically motivated reported enjoying the lesson more, said they would like to learn more and explore their new skills more than the ones who thought that the teacher was 'merely' a paid worker. Furthermore, not only was the first group more influenced by the 'intrinsically motivated' teacher, they also thought that this teacher demonstrated greater enthusiasm and motivation. That is, their perception about the teacher's commitment not only shaped their emotional response to the received teaching but also coloured their actual observation of the teacher, presenting him in a better light. Deci et al.'s final conclusion is very similar to that of Csikszentmihalyi (1997), namely that effective instructors should act as an inspiration and resource, encouraging and supporting students' intrinsic motivation to create, explore, learn and experiment. In order to achieve so, they need to be 'enthused and involved in the teaching process and in the material they are teaching' (p. 69).

> **Quote 7.8** Deci, Kasser and Ryan on the interactive relationship between the motivation of students and teacher
>
> The relationship between students and faculty is an interactive one that can be either positively or negatively synergistic. Students affect the faculty's motivation and behaviour just as faculty affect the students'. But it is important to keep in mind that part of the task of teaching is to engender in students the enthusiasm that facilitates a positive rather than a negative cycle. For teachers to recognise that students' lack of enthusiasm affects them negatively can be important and useful information for their own self-regulation, but it does not absolve them of responsibility for not devoting themselves to teaching.
>
> Deci et al. (1997: 68)

In conclusion, although we do not as yet have a precise understanding of the exact mediating factors and processes between teacher motivation and student achievement, the available research evidence and theorising suggest that teachers' values, beliefs, attitudes and behaviour, as well as the general level of their commitment towards the students, their learning and the subject matter, constitute some of the most prevailing influences on student motivation. Of course, as Deci et al. (1997) emphasise, the relationship between teacher and student motivation is an interactive one that can be either positively or negatively synergistic. Yet, the fact is that teachers *are* the designated leaders of the class groups and therefore they have a special responsibility for maintaining their own commitment to the teaching process. If they abandon this responsibility, this will result in their 'psychological absence' from the teaching process, which is the fastest way to undermine the motivational base of the learners.

III Researching motivation

Chapter 8

Making motivation a researchable concept

This chapter will...

- describe the main features of motivation research and summarise the difficulties inherent in it;
- discuss the main decisions one has to take before launching into a research project.

Having looked into the nature of L2 motivation in the previous chapters and having analysed its educational relevance, in Section 3 we will turn our attention to a third aspect of the issue of motivation, its *researchability*. L2 motivation research is aimed at understanding the operation of motivational factors/processes in the learning of second languages as well as exploring ways to optimise student motivation. These objectives are clearly relevant to many professionals working in the L2 field and, hopefully, the following discussion on conducting inquiries into motivational matters will not be restricted to established researchers but will also be useful for language teachers and graduate students who are planning to conduct their own investigations.

Research is nothing but trying to *find answers* to questions – an activity everybody does regularly, both in their personal and professional life. What distinguishes scientific research from the everyday activity of exploring the world around us is that in scientific research we place a special emphasis on being *systematic* and reducing the effects of personal subjectivity and other influencing factors to a minimum. That is, 'research' in the scientific sense is *finding systematic answers to questions*;

or, in other words, research is *disciplined inquiry*. In the most general sense, there are two ways of finding answers to research questions:

1. By looking at what other people have said about the particular issue. This is usually called *secondary* or *conceptual research* and is an essential form of inquiry because it would be a complete waste of time and energy to 'reinvent the wheel' again and again.

2. By conducting one's own investigation, which involves collecting some sort of information (or 'data') and drawing some conclusions. This is called *primary research* and is important for two main reasons:

   • No two learning situations are exactly the same and therefore the guidelines offered by external sources rarely provide the exact answers to one's specific questions.

   • It is an exciting and illuminating process to find one's own answers, and being engaged in this process can be one of the most effective forms of professional development. In addition, other people may also benefit from one's research endeavours.

Quote 8.1 Wallace on professional development and action research

It is assumed that most language teachers wish to develop themselves professionally on a continuous basis. They have access to a wide variety of methods of doing this. One method is by reflecting on interesting and/or problematic areas in a structured way ... through the systematic collection and analysis of data. This is what I have called 'action research'.

Wallace (1998: 18)

The three chapters in this section will focus on the second type of investigation only, that is, on primary, data-based research. My overarching goal is twofold:

• to turn the abstract notion of motivation into a tangible and researchable topic;

• to turn motivation research into a practical activity.

First, I will outline the main difficulties inherent in motivation research, then look at the most important initial decisions that must be made by anyone wishing to pursue such research. Subsequent chapters will discuss specific research methodological questions pertaining to research design and questionnaire development, and describe the main lines of investigation that L2 motivation researchers have adopted in the past. As an illustration of the various research traditions, I will include some selected sample studies from the field, describing their aims, their methodology and the main results. In order to inspire more thinking and empirical work on L2 motivation, I will also offer suggestions about further researchable topics and relevant research questions. It is important to point out that, due to space limitations, the material in this section is necessarily sketchy and reflects my personal research history and experience. My background – following the dominant tradition set by Robert Gardner, Richard Clément and their associates – is in quantitative research methodology, which, despite my best efforts, inevitably creates an imbalance in the treatment of quantitative versus qualitative issues.

Further reading

Research methodology

I have found the texts by Brown (1988), Hatch and Lazaraton (1991), Johnson (1992), Oppenheim (1992), Pedhazur and Schmelkin (1991) and Seliger and Shohamy (1989) very useful. I would also recommend the qualitative and quantitative research methods series of Sage Publications Ltd, which has separate, high-quality books and booklets addressing virtually every major facet of research methodology; one booklet that has helped me a lot when dealing with qualitative data was McCracken (1988). I have also frequently turned to the statistics guide of the SPSS (Statistical Package for the Social Sciences) Manual.

8.1   Inherent problems in motivation research

Doing motivation research can be a most rewarding but at the same time formidable task. There are three features of 'motivation' in particular that pose a challenge to the researcher:

1. *Motivation is abstract and not directly observable*. 'Motivation' is an abstract term that refers to various mental (i.e. internal) processes and states. It is therefore *not* subject to direct observation but must be inferred from some indirect indicator, such as the individual's *self-report accounts*, *overt behaviours* or *physiological responses* (e.g. change of blood pressure). This means that there are *no* objective measures of

motivation; all the motivation indices used in research studies are inherently subjective, and one of the most difficult tasks of the motivation researcher is to keep this level of subjectivity to a minimum.

2. *Motivation is a multidimensional construct.* Motivation is a multi-faceted concept that cannot be represented by means of simple measures (e.g. the results of a few questionnaire items). Researchers need to bear this in mind when conceptualising and assessing motivation variables, and should also be aware of the fact that the specific motivation measure or concept they are focusing on is likely to represent only a segment of a more intricate psychological construct.

3. *Motivation is inconstant.* Motivation is not stable but changes dynamically over time. It is therefore questionable how accurately a one-off examination (e.g. the administration of a questionnaire at a single point of time) can represent the motivational basis of a prolonged behavioural sequence such as L2 learning.

Although the unobservable, multifaceted and dynamically changing nature of motivation makes its study admittedly complicated, there is a variety of research methodological tools at our disposal to help us with our enquiries and to avoid the pitfalls. I firmly believe that if we make informed decisions about which aspect of motivation to focus on and which methods to use when collecting and analysing our data, motivation research can produce meaningful and valid results even for the novice researcher.

Quote 8.2 Williams on motivation research

✓   There is no room for simplistic approaches to such complex issues as motivation.

Williams (1994: 84)

8.2   Initial decisions to make

Graduate students often come to academic advisory sessions with only very broad research intentions in mind, such as 'to study the motivational basis of L2 learning'. In order to proceed further, such broad intentions need to be narrowed down. There are three initial decisions to be made at this point:

- Which aspects of motivation will the study focus on?
- What kind of research method will be employed?
- What kind of research instruments/tools will be used?

8.2.1   Deciding on the particular aspect of motivation to focus on

Because of the broad spectrum of the various components of motivation, the starting point in any research in this area is the clarification of how 'L2 motivation' will be conceptualised in the particular study, that is, which aspects of L2 motivation will be specifically targeted. Although this may sound obvious, the failure to consider this issue explicitly has resulted in a great deal of disappointing results and frustration in past research. For example, L2 motivation studies have traditionally targeted the more general and stable aspects of motivation, such as language attitudes, beliefs and values. These aspects, according to Dörnyei and Ottó's (1998) process-oriented conceptualisation (3.8), are primarily associated with the *preactional stage* of the motivated behavioural process and are, therefore, particularly useful in predicting issues such as *language choice* or the initial intention to *enrol in a language course*. They are less adequate for predicting actual L2 learning behaviours demonstrated in the classroom (e.g. rate of attendance, level of attention paid, degree of task engagement) because learner behaviours during the *actional stage* tend to be energised by a second set of motivational influences: *executive motives*. These are largely rooted in the situation-specific characteristics of the learning context and, following Heckhausen (1991; cf. 2.3), I believe that they show few overlaps with motives fuelling the preactional stage (for empirical results supporting this claim, see Dörnyei, 1996; Dörnyei and Kormos, 2000). Thus, studies that attempt to relate language attitudes and other general motivational aspects to classroom-specific criterion measures, such as student performance, are likely to produce depressed results.

The above example illustrates the importance of selecting the appropriate aspect of motivation to target and it also highlights the key issue in trying to achieve this: the need to define the *behavioural domain* that one is interested in. Motivation – by definition – is related to action and therefore motivational relevance can only be specified in the light of the target behavioural domain.

Concept 8.1   **Steps in choosing the relevant motivational aspects to target**

1. *Define the target behavioural domain* (i.e. the actual aspect of L2 learning in which you are interested) as narrowly as possible. Broad domains such as 'L2 learning' involve so many diverse behaviours (e.g. participating actively in the language class, paying attention to lectures/explanations, writing up home assignments or memorising new vocabulary) that their usefulness for research purposes is very limited (cf. also the discussion on how to select the criterion variable in 9.1.4).

2. *List the various motivational influences* that are likely to affect the behaviours in question. The taxonomies in Figures 3.6–3.10 and Tables 4.1 and 4.2 can serve as checklists for selecting the potential motives.

3. *Set up priorities among the relevant motivational influences*; because it is unlikely that any single project can cover all the relevant factors, narrowing down the motivational focus is justifiable as long as the process is explicitly described and explained (rather than merely stating in the report that 'motivation was measured by means of . . .').

8.2.2   Selecting the method of inquiry

There is no 'best' method for researching motivation; each type of research has advantages and disadvantages. In 9.1, I will provide an overview of some basic methodological considerations regarding research design and Chapter 10 will describe the main types of L2 motivation research. Let me summarise here some general guidelines for the methodological selection.

As stated earlier, the main purpose of primary research is to collect original information about a topic and to draw inferences from the obtained material. The original information obtained is usually referred to as 'data'. The main difference between distinct types of research methods/approaches lies in the different types of data gathered and the different procedures and instruments employed for data collection and analysis. Section 9.1 presents two basic issues to be addressed at this stage:

1. Do we want to collect *quantitative data* (e.g. by using tests and questionnaires) or *qualitative data* (e.g. drawing on interviews and learning journals)? This is not merely a technical question and neither

does it depend entirely on the research topic because most topics can be examined meaningfully following both approaches; important factors to consider are the researcher's general orientation (e.g. world view) and inclination (e.g. aptitude for dealing with numbers or people), as well as the kind of support that is available (e.g. from supervisors and advisers). It is also worth considering a combination of the two approaches (cf. 10.7).

2. Do we want to spend an extended period following the participants' development, thereby collecting *longitudinal data* (e.g. a case study over a term) or do we want/need to restrict data collection to examining a *cross-section* of the participants' thoughts and emotional stances at a particular point in time (e.g. a survey study)? Making a decision regarding this issue involves practical considerations (e.g. resources and time available) in addition to those that are content-based.

Once these initial decisions have been made, the concrete research method to be used can be selected. Chapter 10 summarises the most common methods used in L2 motivation research in the past. However, because I believe that motivation research has reached a stage when it would benefit from complementing the traditional research techniques with novel methodologies, it may not be the best strategy to stick to the traditions in a servile manner. For this reason, I have also included in Chapter 10 certain potentially fruitful research paradigms that have been underutilised in past L2 motivation research.

8.2.3   Obtaining the necessary measuring tools

Motivational data can be gathered in a number of ways (focusing on, as we have seen, the learners' various forms of self-report accounts, overt behaviours or physiological responses), but by far the most common data collection method has been the use of attitude/motivation questionnaires with primarily closed items (9.2.1). Thus, the obvious first problem for many novice researchers is 'how to get hold of an objective motivation test'.

Unfortunately, there are no universally applicable, standardised L2 motivation tests. Gardner's AMTB (3.1.3) comes closest to this criterion, but due to the prominent social dependability of L2 motivation (2.2 and 3.6), even this standardised battery cannot be used mechanically (i.e. without making considerable adjustments) in contexts other than where it was developed. In this respect, motivation questionnaires differ significantly from tests of language aptitude or proficiency.

> **Quote 8.3** Gardner and Tremblay on the Attitude/Motivation Test Battery (AMTB)
>
> The fact is that the AMTB refers to a collection of variables, and often the items are developed to be appropriate to the context in which the study is being conducted. Whenever individuals write requesting copies of the AMTB, this point is made as clear as possible. People are encouraged not to simply take a set of items and administer them unthinkingly in any context.
>
> Gardner and Tremblay (1994b: 525)

Thus, every questionnaire-based research project requires the development of its own assessment tool that is appropriate for the particular environment and sample. Of course, this does not exclude drawing on item pools developed by other researchers in the past, but we must bear in mind that the items in our study may not have the same psychometric properties as in the population for which they were originally devised (particularly if they need to be translated to the learners' L1). This implies that researchers need to submit 'borrowed' items to the same item analysis procedures as the newly written ones. We will come back to the issue of preparing and administering self-report questionnaires (including 'on-line' questionnaires to study motivational dynamics) in 9.2 in detail, and Section IV (12.3) will contain sample items and scales from questionnaires I have used in the past.

Chapter 9

Methodological issues and considerations

This chapter will . . .

- discuss some key issues concerning the research design of motivation studies;
- describe how to devise, administer and analyse motivation questionnaires.

This chapter addresses a number of research methodological questions that I have found particularly important with regard to L2 motivation research. I have grouped the various points under two subheadings:

- 'research design'
- 'self-report motivation tests/questionnaires'.

The first part will cover issues pertaining to the method of data collection and the type of data collected, while the second part will focus on one particular type of data collection instrument which has a special significance in L2 motivation research. Other types of data-gathering methods and procedures will be discussed in Chapter 10.

9.1 Research design

The *research design* of a study is a detailed plan that includes guidelines for all the research-related activities of the researcher. It specifies what needs to be done, with whom, when and where, and of course why.

Because primary research is all about data, a central aspect of any research design is to provide the specifications of the data to be gathered and to describe how the data will be processed and analysed. In the following I will focus on three basic design issues:

- qualitative vs quantitative research;
- longitudinal vs cross-sectional research;
- selecting the dependent/criterion variable.

9.1.1 Qualitative vs quantitative research

One of the most general and well-known distinctions in research methodology is that between *qualitative* and *quantitative* research. As Davies (1995) emphasises, it signifies more than merely using 'figures' versus non-quantitative data (such as open-ended interviews or natural data); the dichotomy refers to two very different philosophical approaches to the exploration of the world and to the construction of meaning. This means that the terms 'qualitative' and 'quantitative research' denote, at the same time, the manner of theory construction, the method of data collection and analysis, and the general ideological orientation underlying the study. Because of this very broad interpretation, some researchers (e.g. Grotjahn, 1987) prefer to avoid these terms altogether. For example, in one of the most well-known summaries of qualitative research methods, Erickson (1986) immediately sets out by explaining why he will use the term *interpretive* instead of 'qualitative' – one obvious reason being that quantification of particular sorts can often be employed in so-called 'qualitative' studies.

The essential characteristic of *quantitative research* is that it employs categories, viewpoints and models as precisely defined by the researcher in advance as possible, and numerical or directly quantifiable data are collected to determine the relationship between these categories, to test the research hypotheses and to enhance the aggregation of knowledge. L2 motivation research has traditionally followed the research principles of quantitative social psychology, relying heavily on survey methods (10.1): most of the motivational data in the L2 field in the past have been gathered by means of questionnaires typically employing quantifiable rating scales without any open-ended items, and the responses have usually been processed by means of various descriptive and inferential statistical procedures. This positivist approach has some. major advantages:

- it is precise;
- it produces reliable and replicable data;
- statistically significant results are readily generalisable, thus revealing broader tendencies. *well ... depending on context of generalising population*

On the other hand, the downside of quantitative methods is that they average out responses across the whole sample or subsample, and by working with concepts of averages it is impossible to do justice to the subjective variety of an individual life. Similar scores can result from quite different underlying motivational processes, and quantitative methods are generally less sensitive to uncovering the motivational dynamics involved than qualitative techniques. There is no question that a deep interview with a language learner can provide far richer data than even the most detailed questionnaire.

In contrast to quantitative studies, *qualitative research* focuses on the participants' rather than the researcher's interpretations and priorities, without setting out to test preconceived hypotheses; this means that analytic categories tend to be defined only *during*, rather than prior to, the process of the research (McCracken, 1988). Different types of qualitative studies (for a review, see Lazaraton, 1995) share the common objective to make sense of a set of (cultural) meanings by trying to identify *systematic patterns* in the observed phenomena and by grounding any interpretation in a rich and sensitive description of events and participant perspectives. The exploratory nature of this type of research largely excludes the collection of numerical data, since figures presuppose the existence of well-defined advance categories (within which the numbers become interpretable). Instead, qualitative studies in the L2 domain rely on field data such as

- *observations* recorded in field notes, journal and diary entries;
- *interviews* recorded on audio or video cassette;
- *authentic documents of communicative behaviour* (e.g. recorded speech samples, written texts).

Although these data are not gathered with the purpose of being directly counted or measured in an objective way, subsequent processing and analysis can define categories through which certain aspects of qualitative data can be quantified.

Qualitative/interpretive research appears to be particularly useful when researchers are interested in the structure of events rather than their overall distributions, and when the goal is to explore new linkages

> **Quote 9.1** McCracken on the contrast between qualitative and quantitative research
>
> Qualitative research normally looks for patterns of interrelationship between many categories rather than the sharply delineated relationship between a limited set of them. This difference can be characterised as the trade-off between the precision of quantitative methods and the complexity-capturing ability of qualitative ones. The quantitative researcher uses a lens that brings a narrow strip of the field of vision into very precise focus. The qualitative researcher uses a lens that permits a much less precise vision of a much broader strip.
>
> McCracken (1988: 16)

and causal relationships, external and internal influences, and internal priorities inherent in a particular social context. Studies conducted in this vein typically yield rich sources of data conducive to raising 'new questions and new slants on old questions that often are missed by traditional methods' (Pintrich and Schunk, 1996: 12). Although qualitative techniques are not without disadvantages (e.g. in terms of their reliability, representativeness and generalisability), education research has moved increasingly towards adopting such approaches in recent years. It may also be time for L2 motivation researchers to start considering the potentials of qualitative methods – personally, I would be pleased to see more interview and case studies. In addition, as will be argued in 10.7, the combination of qualitative and quantitative methods might be a particularly fruitful direction for future motivation research.

9.1.2   Longitudinal vs cross-sectional research

Longitudinal studies observe the participants for an extended period in order to detect changes and patterns of development over time that are due to (Keeves, 1994):

- biological influences (e.g. age)
- environmental influences
- planned learning experiences.

In contrast, *cross-sectional studies* typically sample the participants' thoughts, behaviours or emotional stances at one particular point in time.

Longitudinal research describes a family of methods (Menard, 1991) whose common features are as follows:

- Data are collected for each variable at least twice without any manipulation (i.e. without offering any treatment in between).
- The cases (participants) analysed are the same or are comparable (i.e. drawn from the same population) from one period to the next.
- The analysis involves some comparison of data between periods.

Thus, besides the 'classic' longitudinal design of *panel studies* in which the same participants are investigated on two or more occasions, longitudinal research is often meant to include *repeated cross-sectional designs* (or 'trend studies') of the same population. In addition, some researchers (cf. Keeves, 1994) also include simultaneous cross-sectional studies of different age groups and experimental studies which have pre- and post-tests. In the L2 field, perhaps the best-known longitudinal project has been a ten-year investigation of the study of French in the UK led by Clare Burstall (e.g. Burstall et al., 1974), which also included a featured focus on language attitudes.

Which type of analysis should we prefer: longitudinal or cross-sectional? Economic reasons suggest cross-sectional designs: longitudinal studies require a major initial investment of time and energy (i.e. the collection of the field data over a significant period) before any meaningful results can be obtained, and it is also rather costly to maintain contact with a significant number of sample members over an extended period of time (in case of a panel study). Regrettable, as the relative absence of longitudinal studies in L2 motivation research indicates, few researchers have the necessary resources or chose to accept the long waiting period associated with longitudinal designs. On the other hand, most scholars would agree that longitudinal studies can offer far more meaningful insights into motivational matters than cross-sectional ones, particularly in view of the temporal challenge to motivation research described in 8.1 – only by collecting longitudinal data can we fully explore the dynamic nature of the mental processes underlying motivation.

Quote 9.2 Menard on longitudinal studies

Unless there is good reason to believe otherwise ... it should be assumed that longitudinal data are necessary to estimate the parameters, efficiently and without bias, of any dynamic process in the social sciences.

Menard (1991: 68)

Research 9.1   Topics researchable via longitudinal research design

- *The dynamic interplay between motivational factors and the day-by-day events in a language course* (comparison of the level of observed motivation at the beginning of, during and at the end of the course, as well as before and after certain featured events such as foreign trips, major tests/exams and project work).
- *The effects of teacher behaviours on student motivation* (establishing relations among motivational socialisation experiences provided by teachers and students' adoption and internalisation of the teacher-mandated values, goals and norms).
- *The change of motivation during chronological development* (e.g. age changes in the structure and impact of motivational components during critical periods of the learners' lives such as puberty or adolescence).
- *The change of motivation as a function of the development of L2 proficiency.*
- *The dynamics of motivation during an extended stay in the host environment* (e.g. during study trips, exchange programmes).
- *The analysis of the motivational basis of 'persistence' in the face of difficulties over an extended period.*
- *The micro-analysis of motivational development during the process of task-completion* (from pre-task activities through task performance to post-task activities; cf. 'on-line' questionnaires in 9.2).

(handwritten margin note: Like you'd know in advance of extended difficulties?)

Study 9.1

Marianne Nikolov (1999) 'Why do you learn English?' 'Because the teacher is short.' A study of Hungarian children's foreign language learning motivation. *Language Teaching Research* 3: 33–56

Purpose
To look at the attitudinal/motivational changes of young Hungarian learners of English between the ages of 6 and 14.

Participants
A total of 84 children in three cohorts, 45 of them included for the full length of eight years.

Instrument

Short questionnaire consisting of six open-ended questions, asking about the reason for learning English and the children's likes and dislikes concerning the learning situation.

Procedures

The questionnaire was administered to the children once every year during an English class, after which there was a follow-up session in which the teacher (who was also the researcher) discussed the responses with the children, and took notes of the main issues raised.

Data analysis

Answers to the questions were analysed according to the main themes they contained, and the frequency of similar themes was tabulated. Following this, the results obtained from the three age groups (ages 6–8, 9–11 and 12–14) were compared.

Results

The most important motivating factors for all the age groups were situation-specific (i.e. attitudes towards the learning context, the teacher, the tasks and the materials), and these had a stronger motivational impact than integrative or instrumental motives. Knowledge as an aim gradually over-took the role of extrinsic factors like rewards and approval. Instrumental (utilitarian) motives emerged around the age of 11–12 but remained vague and general.

9.1.3   Selecting the criterion/dependent variable

A large proportion of L2 motivational studies have looked at the relationship between motivation and learning achievement, using some measure of performance/accomplishment (e.g. grades or test scores) as the *criterion* or *dependent variable*. The interest in this connection is justifiable, since – following the spirit of the saying, 'The proof of the pudding is in the eating' – the ultimate goal of a great deal of research in applied linguistics is to explain the observed variation in L2 learning success. However, motivation-achievement relationships should be treated with caution because we cannot assume a direct cause–effect link there (see Concept 9.1) and the absence of some expected results can simply be due to the wrong criterion measure selected for the study. If we want to draw more meaningful inferences about the impact of various motives, it is more appropriate to use some sort of behavioural measure as the criterion/dependent variable (cf. e.g. the sample study in 10.3.3). Examples of potential criterion variables of this sort include:

- language choice
- course attendance
- enrolment in the next course
- volunteering answers
- extent of task engagement
- direct measures of motivated L2 behaviour (such as the number of words used in a task, or the quality and quantity of home assignments)
- extracurricular language use.

That, is, there is a great range of manifestations of motivation that can be used as criterion variables in a motivation study instead of the global and less direct measures of course achievement or language proficiency.

Concept 9.1 On the relationship between motivation and achievement

From a theoretical point of view, the relationship between motivation and achievement is not straightforward. Motivation – per definition – is the antecedent of *action* rather than achievement. It is true that motivated learners will demonstrate more effort and persistence in their task behaviour, which in turn can lead to increased achievement, but this relationship is *indirect*, because achievement is also influenced by a host of other factors, most notably by

- the learners' ability;
- learning opportunities;
- the instructional quality of the learning tasks.

As an extreme, for example, we can imagine a situation when learners spend all their time performing a 'learning' task with great vigour, yet they will show no resulting development because the task in question was not adequate for the purpose of learning. In this case, to interpret the insignificant correlation between motivation and achievement as the indication of a lack of motivational impact would be incorrect.

9.2 'Self-report' motivation tests/questionnaires

As mentioned earlier (8.1), any attempt to measure motivation – an unobservable construct – requires the making of inferences from some observable indicator. Although these indicators can, in theory, include the individual's overt behaviours or physiological responses, almost all motivation assessment uses some sort of 'self-report' measure, that is, elicits the respondent's own accounts from which to make inferences. The popularity of such measuring tools warrants a more detailed discussion of how to devise, administer and process them.

Concept 9.2   **Designing 'on-line' motivation questionnaires**

Because motivation is not stable but changes dynamically over time, it is questionable how accurately a cross-sectional survey (e.g. the administration of a questionnaire at a single point of time) can represent the motivational basis of a behavioural sequence such as L2 learning. One way of tapping into the dynamic nature of motivation is to administer *on-line questionnaires* at various phases of completing a learning task, for example:

- before the task;
- after receiving the instructions but before actually starting working on the task;
- during the process of task completion;
- after completing the task.

In order not to interrupt the process too much, these questionnaires need to be short; based on Boekaerts's (1988) pioneering on-line motivation questionnaire, Julkunen (1989) developed and successfully applied a questionnaire for the context of L2 studies that consisted of 12 Likert scale items. The focus of such short instruments should vary according to the research topic, but the list of motives associated with the different phases of the process model described in 3.8 (cf. Figures 3.6–3.10) can be used as content guidelines.

9.2.1   Techniques of attitude measurement

During the past 70 years, social psychology has developed several methods to make self-report measures of *attitudes* reliable and valid, and these techniques can also be adapted to assessing more general beliefs and values. These measures (referred to as *scaling techniques*) contain closed items (i.e. in which respondents have to mark a choice rather than write answers to open-ended questions) that are based on the individuals' responses to a series of sentences or adjectives. Because of the strong social psychological influence on L2 motivation research (cf. 3.1), the use of scaling techniques is now an established practice in the L2 field; two scaling techniques have become particularly popular:

- *Likert scales* (and their adaptations)
- *semantic differential scales*.

Likert scales

Likert scales (named after their inventor) consist of a series of statements, all of which are related to a particular target (e.g. the L2 community), and respondents are asked to indicate the extent to which they agree or disagree with these items by marking one of the responses ranging from 'strongly agree' to 'strongly disagree'. For example:

Motivation research offers numerous sources of physical and intellectual enjoyment.

| Strongly agree | Agree | Neither agree nor disagree | Disagree | Strongly disagree |

After the scale has been administered, each response option is assigned a number for scoring purposes (e.g. 'strongly agree' = 5, 'strongly disagree' = 1); with negatively worded items the scores are usually reversed before analysis.

The statements on Likert scales should be 'characteristic', that is, expressing either a positive/favourable or a negative/unfavourable attitude towards the object of interest. Although the Likert scale was originally developed to measure attitudes, we can extend its scope by writing statements that refer to interests (i.e. preferences for particular activities; e.g. *I love reading plumbing manuals*) and values (i.e. preferences for 'life goals' and 'ways of life'; e.g. *We should help the poor*). Furthermore, by replacing the standard set of response options representing the degree of agreement, Likert scales can be turned into general *rating scales*, which use flexible descriptive terms pertaining to the factor in question (e.g. frequency categories, as in Oxford's [1990] 'Strategy Inventory in Language Learning': 'never or almost never true of me' → 'always or almost always true of me'). Some rating scales use only numbers (e.g. 1–10), with one end of the continuum indicating the good/positive pole and the other the bad/negative pole.

Semantic differential scales

Instead of Likert scales we can also use *semantic differential scales* for certain measurement purposes. These are very useful in that by using them we can avoid writing statements (which is not always easy); instead, respondents are asked to indicate their answers by marking a continuum between two bipolar adjectives on the extremes. For example:

> *Sheep are:*
> **intelligent** ___:___:___:___:___:___:___ **stupid**

These scales are based on the recognition that most adjectives have logical opposites and where an opposing adjective is not obviously available, one can easily be generated with 'in-' or 'un-' or by simply writing 'not . . .'. The scope of the items is more limited than that of Likert scales but they are very easy to construct and bipolar adjectives appear less offensive than complete evaluative statements when talking about sensitive issues. For example, the AMTB (3.1.3) included semantic differential scales to evaluate the language teacher and the language course because, as Gardner and Smythe (1981) stated, representatives of educational institutions found this approach less objectionable. Nunnally (1978) describes several factor-analytic studies investigating the content structure of semantic differential scales, and concludes that there are three major factors of meaning involved in them:

really?

- *evaluation* (e.g. good–bad, wise–foolish)
- *potency* (e.g. strong–weak, hard–soft, thick–thin, large–small)
- *activity* (active–passive, tense–relaxed, quick–slow).

Scales are normally constructed to contain items focusing on each of the three dimensions; however, scales measuring the three evaluative aspects tend to correlate with each other.

9.2.2   Constructing motivation scales

Having seen some useful techniques to measure attitudes/beliefs/values, it may seem fairly easy to construct a L2 motivation scale: why not simply ask learners to respond to the following trigger sentence '*I am motivated to learn English*' by marking an agree/disagree response option? Although one can intuitively feel that there is something wrong with such a simplistic method, there are actually examples in the literature when such a single-item approach was used (e.g. in the Pimsleur Language Aptitude Battery; Pimsleur, 1966). The main theoretical problem with simply asking learners how motivated they are is that this question will be interpreted by different learners in very different ways and many learners' interpretations will not coincide with the researcher's originally intended meaning. Because in self-report scales everything depends on how the trigger sentence is interpreted (since the scores will be based on the evaluative responses to these trigger statements), motivation test constructors need to do at least four things to ensure the reliability and validity of their items:

1. Following the argument in 8.2.1 concerning the need to decide which aspects of motivation to target, researchers need to break up the umbrella term 'motivation' into a number of *subcomponents* and address each component as a separate item.

2. Instead of using single items to focus on a specific motivation aspect, researchers need to construct *summative scales*, that is, sets of several differently worded items focusing on the same target (e.g. five items on instrumental orientation, five items on sociocultural orientation, etc.) so that any idiosyncratic interpretation of an item will be averaged out during the summation of the item scores (i.e. when obtaining a total scale score by adding scores on individual items).

3. Researchers need to *pilot* the items before launching into the 'real' study. This involves administering the items to a trial group of respondents similar to the participants with which the final instrument will be used, and discussing with them the wording and the perceived meaning of each item.

4. Finally, *post hoc item analysis* needs to be conducted in order to screen out items that have not worked properly.

In the following, we are going to look into two of these issues, *writing multiple items* focusing on a target and *item analysis*, in more detail.

Writing items

Before we can get down to writing motivation questionnaire items, we need to have established clearly which aspect of motivation we wish to focus on, and identified the main constituent elements of the particular domain (by drawing up a concrete list of various sub-areas). Because of the fallibility of single items, we then need to prepare more than one item to address each identified sub-area, all aimed at the same target but drawing upon slightly different aspects of it (the AMTB [3.1.3], for example, contains 4–10 items for each scale). It is dangerous to

> **Quote 9.3** Oppenheim on writing rating scale items
>
> The writing of successful attitude statements demands careful pilot work, experience, intuition and a certain amount of flair.
>
> Oppenheim (1992: 180)

go below 3–4 items per sub-area because if the *post hoc* analysis (see below) reveals that certain items did not work in the particular sample, their exclusion will result in scales that are too short (or single-item).

If we want to write Likert-type items, we need to produce *characteristic statements* that people can easily understand and relate to (either positively or negatively). Oppenheim (1992) argues that the most important rule in writing attitude statements is to make them 'meaningful' and 'interesting' to the respondents. As he points out, 'There are many attitude scales which falter because the items have been composed in the office according to some theoretical plan and fail to arouse much interest in the respondents' (p. 179). The best items are those that seem to have been taken from actual interviews, and Oppenheim encourages item writers not to refrain from using contentiously worded statements that include phrases relating to 'feelings and emotions, hopes and wishes, fears and happiness' (p. 180). Neutral items do not work well on a Likert scale because they do not evoke salient evaluative reactions; on the other hand, extreme items are also to be avoided. Past research has generated some further item-wording principles to be observed (see Concept 9.3).

Concept 9.3   **Item-wording guidelines for writing attitude scales**

- Devise 'characteristic' statements; avoid neutral or extreme formulations.
- Avoid statements that may be interpreted in more than one way.
- Avoid statements that are likely to be endorsed by almost everyone or almost no one.
- Select items that are believed to cover the entire range of the affective scale of interest in a balanced manner.
- Include both positively and negatively worded items.
- Keep the language of the items simple, clear and direct; items should be short, rarely exceeding 20 words; they should preferably be in the form of simple rather than compound/complex sentences and should contain only one complete thought each.

- Use simple words; avoid acronyms, abbreviations, colloquialisms, proverbs, jargon and technical terms; beware of loaded words (e.g. 'democratic', 'modern', 'natural', 'free', etc.).
- Items containing universals such as 'all', 'always', 'none' and 'never' often introduce ambiguity and should be avoided; similarly, words such as 'only', 'just', 'merely' should be used with care and moderation.
- Avoid the use of double negatives because the 'disagree' response to these is likely to create difficulties.

Based on Anderson (1985) and Oppenheim (1992)

Item analysis

The rationale behind devising multi-item scales to address each motivational sub-area is that by doing so, in Skehan's (1989) words, 'no individual item carries an excessive load, and an inconsistent response to one item would cause limited damage' (p. 11). However, multi-item scales are only effective if the items work together in a homogeneous manner, that is, if they measure the same target area. In psychometric terms this means that each item on a scale should correlate with the other items and with the total scale score, which has been referred to as Likert's criterion of 'Internal Consistency' (Anderson, 1985). The objective of item analysis is to ensure that this criterion is fully met.

Internal consistency is expressed by means of the *Cronbach alpha reliability coefficient*, which is dependent on two scale characteristics:

- the average correlation among items,
- the number of items.

Cronbach alpha ranges between 0 and +1, and if it proves to be very low, either the particular scale is too short or the items have very little in common. Internal consistency estimates for well-developed attitude scales containing as few as ten items ought to approach 0.80. L2 motivation researchers typically want to measure many different motivational areas in one questionnaire, and for that reason they cannot use very long scales (or the completion of the questionnaire would take several hours), which necessarily depresses the alpha coefficient. However, even with short scales of three or four items we should aim at reliability coefficients in excess of 0.70, and if the Cronbach alpha of a scale does not reach 0.60, this should sound warning bells.

Modern statistical computer programs make it relatively easy to conduct item analysis. The 'Reliability' procedure of SPSS (Statistical Packages for the Social Sciences), for example, not only provides the

Cronbach alpha for any given scale but also computes what the alpha coefficient would be if a particular item was deleted from the scale. By looking at the list of these 'would-be' alphas for each item, we can immediately see which item reduces the internal consistency of the scale and should therefore be considered to be left out. For an alternative method, using factor analysis to help to eliminate items, see Noels et al. (2000).

9.2.3   Issues concerning the format of rating scales

Nunnally (1978) states that one of the *least* important considerations regarding rating scales is their physical appearance. Whether we use boxes to be ticked or options to be encircled appears to make little difference in the important psychometric properties of ratings as long as the layout of a questionnaire is clear and orderly and there are sufficient instructions and examples to orientate the respondents. However, one aspect of the layout that I personally consider essential is *space-economy*, which is based on my experience that respondents are much more willing to fill in a two-page rather than a four-page questionnaire even if these have exactly the same number of items. Two formats – a rating scale and a Likert scale – that I have successfully used in the past are presented as an illustration in Examples 9.1 and 9.2.

Example 9.1   Rating Scale Format

We would like to ask you to help us by answering the following questions concerning foreign language learning. This is not a test so there are no 'right' or 'wrong' answers and you don't even have to write your name on it. We are interested in your personal opinion. Please give your answers sincerely as only this will guarantee the success of the investigation. Thank you very much for your help.

In the following section we would like you to answer some questions by simply giving marks from 1 to 5.

5 = very much   4 = quite a lot   3 = so-so   2 = not really   1 = not at all

For example, if you like 'hamburgers' very much, 'bean soup' not very much, and 'spinach' not at all, write this:

	Hamburgers	Bean soup	Spinach
How much do you like these foods?	5	2	1

Please put one (and only one) whole number in each box and don't leave out any of them. Thanks.

5 = very much   4 = quite a lot   3 = so-so   2 = not really   1 = not at all

	German	French	Russian	English	Italian
1. How much do you like these languages?					
2. etc.					

Source: Dörnyei et al. (1996)

Example 9.2   Likert Scale Format

Following are a number of statements with which some people agree and others disagree. We would like you to indicate your opinion after each statement by putting an 'X' in the box that best describes the extent to which you agree or disagree with the statement. Thank you very much for your help.

For example:

Pickled cucumbers are unhealthy.

☐	☐	☐	☐	☐	☐
– – –	– –	–	+	+ +	+ + +
Strongly disagree	Disagree	Slightly disagree	Partly agree	Agree	Strongly agree

If you think, for example, that there is something to this statement but it is somewhat exaggerated, you could put an 'X' in the fourth box.

– – –	– –	–	+	+ +	+ + +

1. Sometimes I feel that language learning is a burden.   ☐ ☐ ☐ ☐ ☐ ☐

2. etc.   ☐ ☐ ☐ ☐ ☐ ☐

Source: Dörnyei and Kormos (2000)

An important technical issue concerns the *number of steps* on rating scales. Original Likert scales contained five response options, ranging from 'strongly agree' to 'strongly disagree'. Some researchers, however, prefer to use an even number of response options (e.g. in Example 9.2) because of the concern that some respondents might use the middle category ('so-so' in Example 9.1) to avoid making a real choice, that is, to take the easy way out. This, again, appears to be a relatively unimportant question that is not expected to modify the results significantly (Nunnally, 1978).

9.2.4   Potential problems with self-report instruments

Although appropriate item analysis and a clear and effective presentation layout can make self-report questionnaires fairly reliable, the validity of such instruments has been questioned by many. Without going into details – Brown (1988: ch. 4) provides an excellent summary of the various threats to validity – it is obvious that people do not always provide true answers about themselves. Motivation items are usually rather 'transparent', that is, respondents can have a fairly good guess about what the desirable/acceptable/expected answer is, and some of them will provide this response even if it is not true (Skehan, 1989). In addition, some people may be reluctant to say anything less than positive about a person or topic that they like in general, or they may wish to present themselves in an unrealistically good light, and we can list a number of further sources which can induce participants to respond 'unnaturally' (e.g. instructions to the participants, prior information about the research, and even very subtle aspects of the interaction between the participants and the questionnaire administrator). (For the most well-known attack on self-report measures in L2 motivation research, see Oller and Perkins, 1978a, 1978b.)

While no one would deny that self-report instruments are vulnerable to extraneous influences, we must also face the fact that there is no better way of measuring the unobservable constructs of attitudes and motivation. As stated earlier, we could also make inferences from the individuals' *overt behaviours*, but that would mix the antecedent (motivation) and the consequence (behaviour) in a theoretically confusing way. With regard to the third option, drawing inferences from *physiological responses*, the only motivation construct accommodating such reactions that I am aware of has been offered by Cattell (cf. Cattell and Kline, 1977) but at the moment neither the technology nor the sound theoretical basis for this type of inquiry is available. Thus, we

How so?

have to live with self-report questionnaires and do our best to control the extraneous influences on them.

9.2.5 Administering motivation questionnaires

One area where a motivation survey can go very wrong, and which has been rarely discussed in the L2 literature, concerns the *administration of the questionnaires*. This is often considered to be a mere technical issue relegated to the discretion of the research assistants. In contrast, the psychological literature is quite explicit about the significant role questionnaire/test administration procedures play in the quality of the elicited responses. Four issues that are particularly relevant to L2 motivation research are:

- the question of the *self-selection of the participants* due to some administration procedure;
- the issue of *instructions*;
- the *generation of positive attitudes towards the questionnaire*;
- the issue of *confidentiality*.

Self-selection of the participants

Self-selection of the participants can have many forms. For example,

- researchers invite *volunteers* to take part in a study (occasionally even offering money to compensate for the time spent);
- the design allows for a high degree of *dropout* (or 'mortality'), in which case participants self-select themselves *out* of the sample;
- participants are free to choose whether they fill in the questionnaire or not (e.g. in *postal surveys*).

yes - or absentee Ss!

The main problem shared by all the different types of self-selection is that there is a good chance that the resulting sample will not be similar to the population (Brown, 1988). Volunteers may be different from non-volunteers in their aptitude for the task, their motivation (which is a particularly acute problem for motivation research) or some other characteristic, and the dropouts may also share some common features that will be underrepresented in the sample with their departure. Consequently, the sample may lose its representative character, which is a prerequisite to any generalisability.

Instructions

The nature of the *pre-task instructions* may have a considerable impact on the participants' performance in at least two ways:

1. It is a general experience that pupils do not tend to read the written directions, and unless the administrator reads them aloud (while the respondents read the text silently), some important information is likely to get lost.
2. The manner in which the questionnaire/test is presented also matters. Clemans (1971), for example, reports on a study in which the same test was introduced to three different groups as an 'intelligence test', an 'achievement test' and as a 'routine test', respectively, and because of the obvious connotations and inherent motivating characteristics of these three sets of instructions, there was a significant difference between the test results (with the 'intelligence test' group doing best, followed by the 'achievement test' group and finally the 'routine test' group).

Generating positive participant attitudes

The different impact of the three introductions described above already touches upon the motivational level induced by them, but the question of participant attitudes towards the questionnaire/survey is more far-reaching. If the respondents are reluctant to put in effort or do not take the survey seriously, they are likely to give insincere or careless answers, which can seriously damage the validity of the results and can even wreck the entire research project. This issue is particularly relevant in motivation studies, since in most cases there is absolutely no reason for respondents to be keen on the survey: they do not benefit from the task in a direct and obvious manner, some of the items may look face-threatening and the administration of the questionnaire may be seen as an intrusion, both literally and metaphorically. For this reason the arousal of suitable motivation for students to participate should be a key concern for the researcher. To achieve this is no easy task, but if we pay conscious attention to the issue, it is possible to secure the cooperation of most respondents (Clemans, 1971).

Concept 9.4 Important factors in generating positive participant attitudes towards the questionnaire

1. *Attitudes conveyed by teachers, parents and other authority figures.* Data gathering is almost always done in somebody's 'home grounds'. Participants are quick to pick up their superiors' (form masters', teachers') attitude towards the survey and only acquiesce if the message they receive is positive. Similarly, parental dispositions can also have a major impact. It is therefore an imperative to win the support of all these authority figures.

2. *Providing advance information.* One way of enlisting participant co-operation is by 'selling' the purpose of the survey to them. An effective method to accomplish this is to announce the tests a few days in advance and to give each participant a printed leaflet that explains the purpose and nature of the questionnaire and contains a few sample items. This also raises the 'professional' feel of the survey, which in turn promotes positive participant attitudes.

3. *The behaviour of the questionnaire/test administrator.* The administrators of the questionnaire are, in many ways, identified with the whole survey. Their behaviour and projected attitudes play an important role in 'pulling along' the respondents. They should exhibit keen involvement in the project and show an obvious interest in the outcome. They should establish rapport and give encouragement. Because administrators also represent the professional and serious character of the survey, they are most effective if they conduct themselves in a business-like manner, while remaining natural and approachable.

4. *The style and layout of the questionnaire.* Respondents are normally willing to spend time and effort on an activity if they believe that the issue is important. One factor that plays an important role in convincing them about this is the professional quality of the questionnaire. The tone and content of the printed instructions, the layout and the typesetting of the items, and small things such as thanking the participants for their cooperation can all contribute to the formation of a general good impression about the survey, which in turn affects the quality of the responses. Furthermore, as mentioned earlier, lengthy questionnaires can have a demoralising/disheartening effect on some students.

Confidentiality

L2 motivation questionnaires often contain sensitive items such as the evaluation of the language teacher or course. Students cannot be expected to provide honest information about such issues (and perhaps make critical statements) unless we manage to convince them about the confidentiality of the investigation. Simply saying that the data will be treated confidentially or making the questionnaires anonymous may not be enough for some respondents. In a study that focused on situation-specific motives (Clément et al., 1994), we made a big 'fuss' about handing out envelopes to the participants and asking them to put the completed forms in these and seal them; the administrator (who was external to the school) then stamped every single envelope in front of the students with a university stamp.

9.2.6   Processing questionnaire data

Without trying to give a comprehensive account of various data-processing techniques (some more information will be provided below when discussing particular research techniques), I would like to address three general issues about how to go about processing the completed motivation questionnaires:

- the question of standardising the scores;
- the reduction of the number of variables;
- the labelling of the variables.

Standardising the data

not adequately explained!

If we intend to submit the data to correlation-based analyses such as correlation analysis, factor analysis, discriminant analysis and structural equation modelling (LISREL), we may consider using standardised rather than raw data. This is permissible because when computing correlations we can carry out certain mechanical conversions of the raw scores without these affecting the resulting coefficients. The advantage of using standard scores is that it helps to avoid incorrect results that are due to the heterogeneous nature of the subgroups examined. It is noteworthy that Gardner (who is a professor of psychometrics) has performed this standardisation in *all* of the studies with which he has been concerned (for more information, see Gardner, 1985: 78–80).

Concept 9.5   **Standardised scores**

The standardisation of raw scores involves the conversion of the distribution within a sample in a way that the mean will be 0 and the standard deviation 1. Thus, standard scores express how much each raw value is different from the subgroup mean, and by having equalised the means, scores obtained from different subsamples (e.g. different classes in the school) are readily comparable. Gardner (1985) presents a detailed argument that when we have heterogeneous sources of data (e.g. responses from different schools, proficiency levels, classes, etc.), the use of raw scores for correlation may depress the coefficients. He illustrates this with a hypothetical example in which a motivation measure correlates with achievement in two classes when computed separately, but becomes non-significant when the data are pooled.

Reducing the number of variables

I have argued earlier that a good questionnaire intentionally contains many more items than the number of actual motivational variables it focuses on. Furthermore, even if we did not consciously include parallel items, the number of the real motivation factors underlying the responses will probably be far fewer than the number of items included. For this reason (and also for practical reasons, since it is confusing to work with too many variables in subsequent analyses) the first step in processing a questionnaire is usually to reduce the number of variables by computing *multi-item scales*. The procedure to compute a multi-item scale is simple – all it takes is to calculate the mean of the constituting items; the difficult part is to decide *which* items to merge. One effective method for making such a decision is to use a stepwise procedure (for an example, see Dörnyei and Csizér, 1998, included as a sample study in 10.1.2):

1. First we form a hypothesis about which items belong together (based on theoretical considerations or on an initial factor analysis – cf. 10.2).
2. Then we apply item analysis (9.2.2), during which we exclude all the items from the hypothesised scales which actually reduce the internal consistency of the particular scale.

Variable labels

A serious difficulty in obtaining an integrated overview of the field of motivational psychology is caused by the fact that various authors introduce their own labels for certain constructs even though similar constructs have already been recognised under different labels (cf. the partly overlapping notions of self-confidence, self-efficacy, self-competence, task-specific self-concept, self-worth, academic self-esteem). Alternatively, it is just as confusing when one term is used by different authors in different senses (e.g. 'goal' is a notoriously ill-defined construct). Thus, imprecise terminology, that is, using different terms to denote the same concept and one term to denote different concepts, is one of the most serious hindrances to advancement in the social sciences.

Quote 9.4 Gardner and Tremblay on the problem of different terminologies

There seems to be a general agreement among the authors of the three reviews discussed here [Crookes and Schmidt, 1991; Dörnyei, 1994a; Oxford and Shearin, 1994], as well as ourselves, that motivation plays a major role in second language learning. Disagreement arises, however, when we try to capture the essence of the motivation construct. One of the problems is that researchers often differ in the language they use to explain the same phenomenon. When working with latent constructs such as motivation, substantial effort needs to be directed toward construct validation. This step cannot be bypassed if we want to explain the big picture rather than remote and often redundant segments of motivation.

(Gardner and Tremblay, 1994a: 366)

The issue of using the appropriate terminology occurs at two concrete levels in L2 motivation research:

- when importing concepts from related disciplines;
- when labelling composite multi-item scales.

An example of the first case is when authors (inspired by self-determination theory) talk about *intrinsic* and *extrinsic* motivation to learn a L2 without specifying how these relate to *integrative* and *instrumental* motives. With regard to the second case, in order to illustrate how difficult it can be to decide on the proper label, let me refer to a study with which I have been involved: Clément et al. (1994) found a factor that was determined by indices of social attitudes, motivational intensity, need for achievement and social identification indices. This was identified as an 'Integrative Motive', even though one of the major ingredients of the 'integrative motive' as defined by Gardner (1985)

– 'attitudes toward the learning situation' – was absent from it because it emerged as a separate factor. Thus, when we concluded that 'integrative motivation' and the 'appraisal of the classroom environment' were two separate constituents of L2 motivation, this was not in accordance with Gardner's established terminology (where the second is subsumed by the first). Because many of the motivation models in the L2 fields are empirically grounded (3.5), the emergence of composite variables that are similar but not exactly the same as variables in other researchers' paradigms is not uncommon. The labelling of these variables requires special care.

And ___? Do you feel your term should change?

Chapter 10

Main types of L2 motivation research

This chapter will . . .

- describe the main research traditions in the investigation of L2 motivation;
- present sample research studies from the field as illustrations;
- list a number of researchable issues and topics in the field following each tradition.

In this, the third and final chapter to focus on research methodology, I will summarise the main research traditions followed by L2 researchers in the past. I have set up four main categories to describe existing research:

- survey studies
- factor analytical studies
- correlational studies
- studies using structural equation modelling.

To these four categories I have added a further two which describe research directions that have not been pursued much in the past but which I think have vast potentials:

- experimental studies
- qualitative studies.

Finally, I will conclude this section with a call for research that combines the virtues of quantitative and qualitative studies in an additive manner.

It is important to point out that the purpose of this chapter is not to provide a comprehensive review of past research. The focus will be on the research methods rather than on the actual studies, and after introducing each method/approach I will

- summarise its role in past L2 motivation research;
- discuss some key methodological/technical (e.g. statistical) issues, including possible limitations and pitfalls;
- describe the kind of questions it is best suited to answer and list a number of researchable topics;
- present a sample study for illustration.

10.1   Survey studies

Survey studies aim at describing the characteristics/attitudes/opinions of a *population* by examining a subset of that group, the *sample*, at a single point of time. The main data collection method is the use of questionnaires (8.2.3 and 9.2) but conducting structured interviews (such as the ones used in opinion polls) is also a practical option. The results are typically processed by means of descriptive statistical analyses to provide frequencies, means, percentages, ranges, etc. The data, then, can be further analysed by inferential statistical procedures (e.g. correlation analysis; 10.3) to explore relationships between the variables, but for a real survey study the descriptive findings are sufficiently interesting themselves without further processing. One logical extension of a survey design is to analyse several subpopulations and then compare their results (e.g. motivation patterns in different types of language teaching institutions) by means of *t*-tests or analyses of variance. The main methodological issues concerning surveys are the *representativeness of the sample* and *questionnaire design*. The latter was covered in Chapter 9 (9.2) and will not be repeated here, while the discussion of the former goes beyond the scope of this book.

10.1.1   Role in L2 motivation research

Survey studies have regularly been used in L2 motivation research to assess the attitudinal/motivational disposition of L2 learners in various geographical, sociocultural and institutional contexts, and to compare the results of various subpopulations of learners. Readers are referred to Dörnyei (1998a), Fotos (1994) and Gardner (1985) for reviews of descriptive studies.

10.1.2 Relevant research questions and topics

Survey studies are used when the descriptive results concerning an issue obtained from a population are interesting themselves. Such topics may include

- the language preferences in a community;
- the proportion of affective/integrative/intrinsic versus instrumental/ utilitarian/extrinsic motives;
- the main reasons (orientations) for studying a language.

On the other hand, the sheer description of the actual strength of motivational variables (e.g. the mean of the scores for instrumental motivation as measured on a five-point scale) is less meaningful since it is hard to interpret the practical significance of such raw scores. For this reason, such scores are normally provided in comparison with

- similar scores obtained from another sample (e.g. comparing learners from different nationalities or different types of learning environment);
- similar scores obtained for another target language.

In such cases the significance of the differences is also calculated.

Study 10.1

Zoltán Dörnyei and Kata Csizér (1998) Ten commandments for motivating language learners: Results of an empirical study. *Language Teaching Research* 2: 203–29

Purpose
To examine language teachers' appraisal of the importance of a selection of motivational strategies and to assess how often each strategy was used in the participating teachers' own practice.

Participants
200 teachers of English in Hungary (which is about 2% of the estimated English teacher population), working in various locations within the country in a range of different teaching contexts, having a varied amount of teaching experience. Apart from ensuring a large enough sample size and as much

diversity as possible within the sample, the selection of the participants was done by 'opportunity/convenience sampling'.

Instrument

Two questionnaires, each containing the same 51 motivational strategies that were taken from Dörnyei (1994a). In the first questionnaire respondents were asked to rate the importance of each strategy on a seven-point semantic differential scale with 'not important' and 'very important' being the two poles. The second questionnaire used the same format but the two poles were 'hardly ever' and 'very often'. In order to avoid interference, each respondent was given only one of the questionnaires. The questionnaire was piloted with 20 respondents and, consequently, the wording was revised in several places: some strategies were omitted from the list and some new ones that the respondents considered important were added.

Procedures

In order to ensure their cooperation, all the participants were approached and given a copy of the questionnaire by someone they knew. Respondents filled in the questionnaires on their own and returned them to the contact person.

Data analysis

By applying a stepwise process of item analysis, ten multi-item scales were formed and eight strategies remained individual item variables. The scales were not 'summative scales' in the strict sense (because the constituent items targeted related but not exactly the same issues) and therefore the *importance index* of a scale was taken to be the highest coefficient of all the individual items constituting it (rather than the scale mean). All the variables were rank ordered according to their importance indices and the first ten variables formed the basis of the 'Ten commandments for motivating language learners'.

With respect to the frequency items, we were interested in the variables' *relative frequency*, which provides an index of the frequency of the use of a strategy in the light of its importance. This was achieved by *standardising* the importance and frequency scores for each strategy and computing their difference. The final measure thus indicated how the importance of a strategy related to its frequency, thereby determining underuse or overuse.

Results

The 'Ten commandments' are presented in 5.3. The frequency analysis revealed that the most underused strategies were: promoting the learners' *goal-orientedness*, modelling motivation through the *teacher's own behaviour*, providing the students with feeling of *challenge* and *success*, and giving clear *instructions*.

10.2 Factor analytical studies

Factor analysis is rather complex mathematically but fairly straightforward conceptually. In order to uncover the latent structure that underlies large data sets, it reduces the number of variables submitted to the analysis to a few values that will still contain most of the information found in the original variables (Hatch and Lazaraton, 1991). The outcome of the procedure is a small set of underlying dimensions, referred to as *factors* or *components*, and the computer produces a table – the 'factor matrix' – which contains the correlations between these factors and the original variables from which the factors have been extracted. These correlations are the *factor loadings* and they show the extent to which each of the original variables has contributed to the resultant factors. Factor analytical studies exploit the 'pattern-finding' capacity of the procedure by sampling a wide range of items and then examining their interrelationships and the common underlying themes. Because factor analysis is useful in making large data sets more manageable, the procedure is also used as a preparatory phase in data processing to some further analyses.

10.2.1 Role in L2 motivation research

Factor analysis was the key technique used at the genesis of L2 motivation research. The pioneering article in the field, 'Motivational variables in second-language acquisition' by Gardner and Lambert (1959) was entirely based on this procedure, and the famous notion of 'integrative orientation' was introduced because one factor denoted a 'willingness to be like valued members of the language community' (p. 271). Factor analysis was also used in *all* the investigations described in Gardner and Lambert's (1972) seminal book and, in his 1985 volume, Gardner still regards the use of factor analysis as one of the primary research strategies in studying the interrelationship of attitudinal, motivational and achievement measures in a L2. During the last decade structural equation modelling (10.4) has increasingly replaced factor analysis, but some important studies in the 1990s (e.g. the studies in 3.5, and also Coleman, 1996; Gardner et al., 1997; Laine, 1995) still utilised the procedure.

10.2.2 Statistical issues

Although factor analysis is conceptually straightforward, there are certain pitfalls we must be aware of concerning its application. Furthermore, because factor analysis is mathematically complex, the statistical computer programs offer several options to the researchers, and without any background information there is a danger of making the wrong choice. Let us have a look at the most 'notorious' issues.

Items submitted to the analysis

It is easy to believe that if we submit a wide enough range of items related to a broad target domain to factor analysis, the final factor structure will provide a fair representation of the main dimensions underlying the domain. This is incorrect. The final factor structure will describe only the *items submitted to the analysis*. If we originally did not include in our questionnaire items concerning a key feature of the domain, that particular domain component has no chance to emerge as a statistical factor. That is, our selection of items fundamentally determines the final factor structure. Therefore

- we need to sample items as widely as possible for the particular domain (and, naturally, the narrower and more specified the target domain is, the more comprehensive we can be);
- we need to be careful not to make unfounded generalisations to the domain dimensions when reporting the results.

Selecting the type of factor analysis (extraction and rotation)

Factor analysis employs a stepwise procedure. The first step involves *factor extraction*, that is, condensing the variables into a relatively small number of factors. The second step is *factor rotation*, that is, making the factors more easy to interpret by employing mathematical techniques. There are several alternative methods for both procedures and therefore we must make a decision as to which method to employ. In practice the necessary decisions can be restricted to choosing between

- two extraction methods – 'principal component analysis' and 'maximum likelihood analysis';
- two rotation methods – 'orthogonal (varimax)' or 'oblique (oblimin) rotation'.

Space limitations do not allow an explanation of these procedures, particularly because there is still a great deal of controversy concerning which of the four possible combinations is preferable. In the educational psychological and L2 motivational literature we can find examples of all the four combinations; my personal slant is towards a maximum-likelihood analysis with oblique rotation. Nunnally (1978) argues that if there is a strong multidimensional structure underlying the data, any method will detect it and there will be only minor variation in the individual loadings. This means that if the various methods produce essentially the same results, we can be assured that the factor structure is valid. However, if the data are such that different approaches lead to very different solutions, this should be the source of concern.

Determining the number of factors to be extracted

The most difficult issue in factor analysis is to decide on the number of factors to be extracted. The computer program will provide a ready-made answer; however, it is not an objective solution but just a 'default' that has been artificially set. The typical default principle is that the extraction process should stop at factors which would explain less vari-ance than each individual item submitted to the analysis (i.e. its eigen-value is smaller than 1) because then, in effect, the factor is not better than a single item. This, however, is not necessarily the best solution: sometimes fewer, sometimes more factors may lead to a better result. There is no perfect way of setting the optimal factor number, but there are several useful indicators for the researchers to take into account:

1. Cattell's (1966) *scree test*. By plotting the variance associated with each factor (which the computer can do for us), we obtain a visual representation of the steep decrease – the 'slope' – and the gradual trailing off – the 'scree' – of the factors. According to the scree test, only the factors on the 'slope' should be considered.

2. Aiming for a *simple structure*: that is, choosing a factor solution in which each variable has salient loadings (i.e. loadings above 0.3) only on one factor (i.e. there are no cross-loadings).

3. Aiming for a solution where each factor receives salient loadings from at least *two variables* (which is usually desirable to have well-defined factors).

4. With maximum-likelihood analysis the computer also produces a *goodness of fit* measure to help to appraise the adequacy of the factor structure.

Identifying and naming factors

In 9.2.6, I emphasised the difficulty of labelling composite multi-item scales. Researchers face the same problem when identifying and naming the factors that emerge in the final factor solution. Because each factor is determined by the variables that have the highest loadings on it, the task in interpreting a factor is to identify the common features among these variables, that is, to understand the theme that brought the cluster of variables together. The name of the factor, then, should reflect this common theme as closely as possible. In some cases labelling a factor is fairly straightforward but in cases where the factor receives salient loadings from seemingly different variables, the final factor label can reflect the researcher's subjectivity and, thus, can be highly contestable. Independent labelling and subsequent discussion by more than one person is an obvious way to reduce the personal biases.

10.2.3   Relevant research questions and topics

Factor analysis is an indispensable tool to study any complex psychological construct – intelligence research, for example, has relied heavily on it in the past to identify the major constituents of this multifaceted latent concept (cf. Carroll, 1993). With motivation being similar to intelligence in its abstract and multidimensional character, L2 researchers have also used factor analysis widely to explore the internal architecture of L2 motivation. Because factor analysis can identify only broad clusters of the submitted variables, and because structural equation modelling (10.4) is more suited to investigate causal and hierarchical relationships, my feeling is that factor analysis is gradually losing its importance in analysing the whole of the L2 motivation complex, and the main use of the procedure in contemporary research lies more in the detection of underlying dimensions of narrower subdomains, such as:

- the various language learning goals (or orientations) of the learners;
- the appraisal of the L2 teacher;
- influences stemming from the social milieu (e.g. the effects of friends, parents or various reference groups);
- language contact effects, either indirect (e.g. the influence of L2 films, books or music) or direct (e.g. meeting L2 speakers in various capacities);
- attitudes to various formal properties of the L2 (e.g. complexity of grammar, flexibility of use, perceived ease of learning, aural character).

The identified dimensions, then, can be used for the purpose of clustering variables into multi-item scales, which can, in turn, be further analysed by means of other techniques.

Study 10.2

Richard Schmidt, Deena Boraie and Omneya Kassabgy (1996)
Foreign language motivation: Internal structure and external
conditions. In Rebecca Oxford (ed.) *Language learning motivation:
Pathways to the new century.* University of Hawai'i Press, Honolulu,
HI, pp. 9–70

Purpose
To identify the components of L2 motivation for a population of adult
EFL learners in Egypt, and to identify relationships between the components of motivation and preferred classroom learning activities and learning
strategies.

Participants
1,464 adult learners of English at the American University in Cairo, Egypt
(ages 15–70, but over 80% under 35). They were evenly distributed
across six proficiency levels from basic to advanced.

Instrument
A 100-item self-report questionnaire consisting of six-point Likert scales.
50 items concerned motivation, the rest focused on preferences for classroom activities and learning strategies. The content of the motivation section
reflected the researchers' explicit goal to sample a wide variety of concepts,
and it also included, besides the traditional categories of L2 motivation
questionnaires, items representing the major mainstream psychological
models of motivation.

Procedures
Students completed the questionnaire in a single class period during the
first week of term.

Data analysis (of the motivational items)
Principal component analysis with varimax rotation was used, with the
following factor extraction criteria: (a) minimum eigenvalue of 1, (b) each
factor to account for at least 3% of total variance, (c) each factor to
contain individual items with a minimum loading of 0.45.

Results
The results of the analysis of the motivation section of the questionnaire
are included in 3.5.1. Correlations between the motivational factors and
factors derived from other parts of the questionnaire turned up numerous
significant relationships which, for space limitations, cannot be detailed
here.

10.3 Correlational studies

Correlational studies examine the relations between existing variables observed in the sample, without any attempt to alter them (which is a main difference between correlational and experimental studies [10.5], with the latter also manipulating some of the variables). *Correlation coefficients* are computed between two variables at a time, and can range between +1 and −1. A high coefficient means a strong relationship (i.e. if an individual scores high on one variable, he or she is also likely to score high on the other); a coefficient of 0 suggests no relationship between the two variables; and negative coefficients suggest inverse relationships. In L2 motivation studies the usual strength of the meaningful relationships detected is between 0.30 and 0.50. *& above –*

& on a starting point

10.3.1 Role in L2 motivation research

Because correlation analysis can be performed with questionnaire data (the most common type of data in motivation studies) to clarify the relationship between certain variables and to alert us to important associations, it has been very frequently employed in L2 motivation studies by virtually every quantitative researcher, either as the main technique of data analysis or as an accompanying procedure. Furthermore, factor analysis and structural equation modelling are also correlation-based techniques, in which the 'correlation matrix' (i.e. all the possible pairs of interrelation) of all the variables entered in the analysis is further examined to detect higher-order patterns.

10.3.2 Statistical issues

Computing correlation coefficients is relatively straightforward (particularly because the computer program takes care of the mathematical issues), but there are some questions that are worth addressing briefly.

Types of correlation

Five common types of correlation are used in educational research:

1. Correlation can be computed between 'continuous' variables (with 'interval data') and in such cases the most common type is the *Pearson product-moment correlation*. Usually when we talk about 'correlation' in general, this is what we mean.

2. Correlation coefficients can also be calculated when one or both variables are dichotomous (i.e. have only two values, e.g. 'gender') – there is no need to worry about this because computer programs usually automatically adjust the calculation accordingly and compute *point-biserial* correlations or *phi coefficients*.

3. Correlation can also be computed when we have 'ordinal' data (i.e. a rank order of the values without being certain that the distance between the consecutive values is always the same; e.g. a scale of 'never', 'sometimes', 'often' and 'very often'). We must specifically indicate this when setting up the program parameters for the particular calculation so that the computer computes *Spearman rank-order correlations*.

4. A very useful techniques is *partial correlation*, which examines the relationship between two variables after removing the correlation which is due to their mutual association with a third variable (e.g. a background variable such as the learners' intelligence/aptitude, which can easily modify the scores when computing correlations between motivation and, say, achievement).

5. Finally, statistical techniques are also available to compute *multiple correlations*, that is, the correlation between one variable and a group of variables. This type of correlation can be used, for example, when we want to see the composite effects of all our motivational variables on the criterion measure.

The issue of cause–effect relations

A major disadvantage of correlational research is that it *cannot identify cause and effect*. When two variables show significant positive inter-relation, we cannot claim that this is because one causes or influences the other. All we can say is that they are *interrelated*, since the higher one variable gets, the higher the other is likely to be. It can, for example, be the case that an observed positive association between two variables is only caused by their relationship with a third variable (e.g. football skills are negatively correlated with child-bearing ability only because the former is more common among males and the latter is restricted to females). We must therefore exercise caution when reporting correlational results; on the other hand, because there *may* be (and often *is*) a causal relationship between the two variables, correlation analysis can suggest directions for subsequent experimental research.

The amount of variance explained

To make the actual strength of a correlation more tangible, it is common to *square* the value of the correlation coefficient, because the result thus obtained represents the proportion of the variation in the scores on one variable which is accounted for by the other. For example, a correlation of 0.60 means that 36% of the variance in the scores is explained by the relationship between the two variables rather than by chance or by some other cause(s).

10.3.3   Relevant research questions and topics

Correlation analysis is a versatile technique that can be used to examine a wide range of relationships. Correlation coefficients can be computed, for example, between motivational measures and various *criterion variables,* such as:

- effort (assessed either by means of a self-report measure or some behavioural reflection, e.g. amount of volunteering, quantity of home assignments, level of attention or attendance);
- persistence (e.g. enrolment in the next course, length of time of doing a task, or studying the L2 in general, without giving up in spite of opportunities to do so);
- some aspect of performance (e.g. use of learner strategies or the amount of L2 used in small group tasks);
- language learning achievement.

Correlation is also appropriate to investigate the relationship between motivation and different *background characteristics,* such as:

- the learners' language aptitude or level of L2 proficiency;
- other participant characteristics, such as personality traits (e.g. extroversion), learning styles and self-esteem;
- situational characteristics, such as the amount of L2 contact available for the learners.

Finally, we can also investigate the *interrelationships* of various motives/motivational components, for example:

- parental influence and learner commitment;
- attitudes towards the task and the teacher;
- self-confidence and task attitudes.

Study 10.3

Zoltán Dörnyei and Judit Kormos (2000) The role of individual and social variables in oral task performance. *Language Teaching Research* 4

Purpose
To explore the effects of a number of motivational and social variables on L2 learners' engagement in oral argumentative tasks.

Participants
46 Hungarian students (aged 16−17) studying English at an intermediate level in five classes in two Budapest secondary schools.

Instrument
Two self-report questionnaires. The first addressed attitudinal/motivational issues, consisting of 32 Likert-type items, based on Clément et al.'s (1994) instrument specifically developed for Hungarian learners (cf. 12.3.3). The second questionnaire contained a scale assessing the level of group cohesiveness in the students' learner groups; three standard sociometric questions examining the interrelationships among the learners; and a scale assessing the participants' 'willingness to communicate' (WTC) in the L1 (cf. 11.2).

Procedures
The questionnaires were administered to the students by their English teachers during an English class. The communicative tasks (from which the criterion measures were derived) were conducted in dyads and were recorded by small portable dictaphones.

Data analysis
The recordings were transcribed and task engagement was taken to be reflected by the number of words and turns produced by the learners. All the data from the questionnaires were computer coded, and the number of variables to be analysed was reduced to 11 multi-item scales by summing the thematically corresponding items (while checking their internal consistency; cf. 9.2.2). Because there was considerable between-group variation in the learners' language output, the raw scores were standardised within each class (cf. 9.2.6).

Results (concerning the motivational variables)
Motivational variables (particularly the situation-specific motives) were found to make a significant impact on the learners' task performance, with several of the correlation coefficients approaching 0.50. Correlations were considerably higher in the high task-attitude half of the sample than among students who did not consider the particular task interesting and useful.

10.4   Studies using structural equation modelling (LISREL)

Structural equation modelling (SEM), also referred to as 'causal modelling' or 'LISREL' (after the most well-known computer program for conducting SEM), is a relatively recent procedure which allows researchers to test cause–effect relationships based on correlational data. Thus, it is a very powerful analytical tool as it attempts to combine the versatility of correlation analysis and the causal validity of experimental research (10.5). Because SEM is concerned with the adequacy of hypothesised theoretical constructs (i.e. abstract or latent variables), it is particularly suitable for studying motivational issues.

> **Quote 10.1**   Gardner on structural equation modelling
>
> In addition to forcing researchers to be more explicit about hypothesised measurement errors, assumed causal pathways and the like, this procedure [structural equation modelling] offers a way previously not available to assess different models directly. Causal modelling procedures, therefore, is a strong analytic ally for researchers in this area, and it is recommended that future investigations capitalise on the power of this technique.
>
> Gardner (1985: 174)

To start applying SEM to the data, researchers need an explicitly stated theoretical model in which the main variables are quantified and their directional relationship is clearly stated. Thus, the procedure is not an exploratory but a confirmatory technique, although it is capable of suggesting certain adjustments to the model tested by providing 'modification indices' and tests of significance of estimated parameters. When setting up the model, researchers need to do two things:

1. Describe the *relationship* between the *measured* variables and the hypothesised *latent* variables (e.g. specify that the theoretical construct of 'self-confidence' is measured by, say, three variables: L2 use anxiety, perceived self-competence and a self-report confidence scale), which results in a 'measurement model'.

2. Posit the *casual links* between the latent (theoretical) variables, which results in a 'structural model'.

SEM then tests the adequacy of both models, provides goodness-of-fit measures for the full (i.e. combined) model, and produces modification indices for the purpose of improvement.

Quote 10.2 Pedhazur and Schmelkin on the formulation of a causal model

In sum, the formulation of a causal model is an arduous and long process entailing a great deal of critical thinking, creativity, insight and erudition.

Pedhazur and Schmelkin (1991: 699)

10.4.1 Role in L2 motivation research

LISREL models have been used in L2 motivation research since the early 1980s (e.g. Colletta et al., 1983; Gardner, 1985; Kruidenier and Clément, 1986). However, the early versions of the LISREL program were rather 'user-unfriendly', which limited the popularity of SEM in the L2 field. With the various SEM programs becoming easier to handle and more readily available (e.g. as part of SPSS), we can expect a rapid increase in the utilisation of the procedure. Recent studies employing SEM techniques include Gardner et al. (1997; included as a sample study in 10.4.3), Laine (1995) and Tremblay and Gardner (1995).

10.4.2 Statistical issues

Structural equation modelling is a powerful technique, ideally suited to the study of L2 motivation. However, it has certain limitations; particularly two issues need to be borne in mind:

1. *Goodness of fit and possible alternative models.* SEM provides several indices to show how satisfactory the fit of the final model is and these can be used to compare alternative models and to reject ill-fitting models. However, even a solution with an adequate fit is only one of many that might fit the data equally well. Thus, SEM is not the 'be-all and end-all to research endeavours concerned with inferring causation from correlational data' (Gardner, 1985: 155). It does *not* identify causation but only informs the researcher whether a hypothesised cause–effect relationship is conceivable based on the total amount of data.

2. *Oversimplification of causal relationships.* Causal models with unidirectional relationships can oversimplify the complex relationships of certain psychological variables which operate in an interactive mode in a continuous, cyclical fashion. Such interactive relationships are very common in the motivational domain, because motivation at any time both causes behaviour and is affected by it (Winne and Marx, 1989). One example of this is the synergistic relationship between teacher and student motivation (7.2.2) and another is the recurring issue as to success causes motivation or the other way round (cf. Burstall et al., 1974; Gardner and MacIntyre, 1993a).

10.4.3   Relevant research questions and topics

Structural equation modelling is used to interpret the relationship among several variables within a single framework. It is appropriate to test 'grand' theories, that is, comprehensive models made up of a number of complex, interrelated variables. The main restriction to the use of SEM is that it presupposes a well-developed theoretical model in which the relationship between the different variables is explicitly marked (including the direction of the relationships). It is not easy to produce such a well-defined model, and we should note that almost all the models that satisfy these criteria have been proposed by researchers associated with Gardner and Clément's research laboratories at the University of Western Ontario and the University of Ottawa (a notable exception being Laine, 1995). It is hoped that SEM will also be employed in other contexts in the future. Some concrete areas where conducting SEM would be feasible are:

- the motivational basis of task performance in instructional settings;
- the motivational antecedents of language choice;
- motivational factors underlying learner strategy use;
- motivational determinants of 'continuing motivation', that is, 'the tendency to return to and continue working on tasks away from the instructional context in which they were initially confronted' (Maehr, 1976: 443).

Study 10.4

Robert C. Gardner, Paul F. Tremblay and Anne-Marie Masgoret (1997) Towards a full model of second language learning: An empirical investigation. *Modern Language Journal* 81: 344–62

Purpose
To investigate the interrelationship of a large number of learner character-istics (including various attitudinal measures and language achievement) in a unified framework.

Participants
102 Canadian university students enrolled in introductory French (although 86% or them had at least nine years of prior French training).

Instrument
Three self-report questionnaires focusing on a total of 34 variables within the domains of attitudes, motivation, achievement, perceived French competence, anxiety, learning strategies, aptitude, field dependence/independence and language history.

Procedures
Participants were offered $15 for volunteering to take part in two data collec-tion sessions (90 minutes each), and their French grades were also obtained.

Data analysis
Both factor analysis and structural equation modelling were conducted (the former will not be reported here), the latter by means of the Amos 3.51 program. The modification indices of the Amos program suggested one added link to the initially proposed model, and having taken this into account, a causal model with reasonable goodness of fit indices was obtained.

Results
- 'Language Attitudes' were seen to cause 'Motivation' (the latter referring to a combination of 'attitudes towards learning French', 'motivational intensity' and 'desire to learn French'; cf. 3.1);
- 'Motivation' caused both 'Self-confidence' and 'Language Learning Strategies';
- 'Motivation', 'Language Aptitude' and 'Language Learning Strategies' caused 'Language Achievement';
- 'Field Independence' correlated significantly with 'Language Aptitude';
- 'Language Achievement' caused 'Self-confidence';
- An unexpected result was the negative path between 'Language Learning Strategies' and 'Language Achievement', suggesting that strategy use, as measured by the 'SILL' (Oxford, 1990) is associated with low levels of achievement.

10.5　Experimental studies

Most research studies in applied linguistics are intended to uncover *causal links* by answering questions of the 'Why . . . ?', 'What's going on . . . ?', 'What's the reason for . . . ?', 'What happens if/when . . . ?' and 'How can we make it happen . . . ?' type. The main difficulty in establishing cause–effect relationships is that every cognitive, affective or behavioural outcome is the function of the interplay of several factors and it is hard to isolate the individual contribution of these. However, research methodology has succeeded in developing a way of getting around this problem by means of the *experimental design*. The idea is ingenious in its simplicity:

1. Take a group of people, administer some intervention (or 'treatment') to them and check the outcome; naturally, as stated above, even if there are some significant results, there is no way to tell the extent to which the treatment was responsible for generating them.

2. Compare the results with those obtained from a group that is similar in every respect to the treatment/experimental group *except for the fact that it did not receive the treatment* (this group is usually called the 'control group'). If there are any differences between the results of the two groups, these can now be unambiguously attributed to the only difference between them, the intervention/treatment variable.

Although experimental research has variations, a typical experimental design would be an 'intervention study', in which some sort of instructional treatment (e.g. special communicative L2 training) is administered

---

Quote 10.3　Pedhazur and Schmelkin on the notion of 'causation'

The notion of causation is so ingrained in our thoughts and conceptions that attempts to understand myriad phenomena or to communicate about them without resorting to it are practically inconceivable. Envision, if you can, attempts to understand change or to communicate about it without explicit or implicit reference to causation, or consider attempts to understand or communicate about, say, . . . personality and human behaviour . . . without the implication of causation. . . . In sum, regardless of his/her philosophical stance about causation, the scientist *qua* scientist seems to find a causal framework indispensable when attempting to explain phenomena.

Pedhazur and Schmelkin (1991: 696–7)

to a group of learners and the observed effects of the training are compared to the rate of development in a control group that has not received the treatment. If there is significantly more development in the experimental group than in the control group (which can be determined by using 'analysis of covariance' with the pre-test results being the covariates; or computing 'analysis of variance' of the 'gain scores', i.e. the difference between the post-test and pre-test scores), we can conclude that the intervention was successful and that the treatment variable has caused the outcome. It must be emphasised that experimentation is a natural human way of inquiry: this is the basis of 'trying out something to see what happens', that is, putting ideas to the test (e.g. changing the daily routines of a child if he or she has problems, say, going to sleep at night).

Thus, in an experimental study, the researcher does not only look at the relations between existing variables, but actually *alters* one (or more) variable and determines the effects of this change on other variables. The main role of the control group, then, is to eliminate other variables as potential causes of the outcome. Because of the unequivocal character of the conclusions offered, for many years the true experiment was considered the ideal model for rigorous research (Johnson, 1992). Indeed, many types of quantitative study can be seen merely as reduced or simplified versions of the full experimental designs (e.g. by lacking control groups, pre-tests or specifically manipulated treatment).

Of course, there are many serious methodological challenges behind the 'simplicity' of the experimental design, most notably the issue of how to make the control group similar to the treatment group. As Cook and Campbell (1979) summarise, one of the great breakthroughs in experimental design was the realisation that – if there is a sufficient number of participants – the *random assignment* of participants to experimental and control groups can provide a way of making the average participant in one group comparable to the average participant in the other group before the treatment is applied.

10.5.1   Role in L2 motivation research

Experiments are not as common in L2 studies as in other scientific disciplines because of at least two reasons:

1. Many of the topics L2 researchers are interested in have nothing to do with 'treatment' or 'intervention', that is, do not easily lend themselves to manipulation (e.g. gender differences, personality traits, ethnolinguistic variation).

2. Experimental research is rather narrow in scope as only one or a few variables are altered at a time. On the other hand, language classrooms are complex environments where many factors operate simultaneously, and significant changes can often only be achieved if several variables work *in concert* or *in special combinations* (e.g. Dörnyei and Kormos, 2000, found that 'need for achievement' was a significant motivating influence but only for those students whose task-attitude was high, that is, who were keen to participate in the task). An experimental design, however, is inadequate to address such multivariate patterns.

While these limitations are valid, we must also stress that in many situations experimental studies would be feasible and undoubtedly superior to the less labour-intensive correlational or survey studies that are usually conducted.

In L2 motivation research there have been a number of experimental studies investigating the motivational effects of bicultural excursion programmes, methodological interventions, intensive language programmes and study trips abroad (for reviews, see Gardner, 1985: ch. 5; MacFarlane and Wesche, 1995; Morgan, 1993). These studies vary in their degree of the 'conscious manipulation' of the treatment variable by the researcher (and therefore some are more like longitudinal studies than experiments) and some do not include control groups.

10.5.2   Technical and methodological issues

As any research method, the experimental design is also associated with a host of problem issues (for a very through methodological overview of intervention studies in educational research, see Pressley and Harris, 1994a, 1994b). Let me highlight what I consider the two most basic ones:

- the lack of random assignment of participants, resulting in *quasi-experimental designs*;
- situations in which the outcome of an otherwise solid experiment is not caused by the treatment variable but by the fact that a treatment has been applied, regardless of its nature (i.e. the *Hawthorne effect*).

Quasi-experimental design

In most educational settings, random assignment of students by the researcher is rarely possible and therefore researchers often have to resort to a *quasi-experimental design*. Quasi-experiments are similar to true experiments in every way except that they do not use random assignment to create the comparisons from which treatment-caused change is inferred (Cook and Campbell, 1979). Because of the practical constraints, working with 'non-equivalent groups' has become an accepted research methodology in any field studies where randomisation is impossible or impractical. However, in such cases we cannot rely on the neat and automatic way the true experiment deals with various threats to validity but have to deal with these threats ourselves. In practical terms, in order to be able to make causal claims based on a quasi-experimental study, the effects of the initial group-differences need to be taken into account. This requires that we measure the main sources of difference between the treatment and control groups, such as aptitude, L2 proficiency, initial motivation or past task experience. Once we have these measures, various computer procedures allow us to make statistical adjustments accordingly, that is, to screen the unwanted effects out of the outcome measure (e.g. by means of analysis of covariance).

The Hawthorne effect

The *Hawthorne effect* is named after the research site (in Chicago) where it was first documented: investigating an electric company, the researchers found that work production increased when they were present, regardless of the conditions to which the workers were subjected. The reason for this effect is that sometimes the excitement and the increased attention caused by the fact that there is a research project going on may affect the participants' output beneficially (e.g. if we compare a run-of-the-mill language course to another in which the researchers enthusiastically employ what they believe is a 'revolutionary' method, the chances are that the experimental group will have better proficiency gains even if the method is not particularly 'revolutionary'). In order to counterbalance the Hawthorne effect, researchers often administer some sort of 'placebo treatment' (which is unrelated to the original treatment variable) to the control group with a convincing level of conviction and enthusiasm.

10.5.3   Relevant research questions and topics

Because of the dynamic nature of motivation, several of the longitudinal research topics mentioned in 9.1.2 can be studied using an experimental design if we manipulate and control some of the change conditions (instead of merely observing the developments/changes). More specifically, experimental studies can focus on:

- the effects of certain instructional procedures on student motivation (e.g. comparing the motivation of learners who participate in different instructional activities);
- motivational change as a function of induced L2 contact (e.g. a trip to the L2 environment);
- the analysis of motivational change in various task conditions (e.g. the role of different types of pre- and post-task activities, task instructions/introductions and other task organisational factors such as methods of grouping).

An area that has received a great deal of attention in educational psychology is:

- the effects of different forms of feedback on the students' motivational disposition (cf. 5.2.4).

One recent motivational domain where experimental studies are indispensable is:

- the testing of the effectiveness of *motivational strategies* (i.e. testing whether the application of certain motivational strategies does indeed result in a higher level of student motivation); however, at the moment I am aware of only one unpublished study of this type by Reilly (1994).

Study 10.5

Ofra Inbar, Elana Shohamy and Smadar Donitsa-Schmidt (1999) The effect of teaching spoken Arabic on students' attitudes, motivation and achievements. Paper presented at the AAAL '99 Convention, Stamford, March

Purpose
To examine the effect of an experimental programme of teaching spoken Arabic (Palestinian dialect) on Israeli learners' attitudes, motivation and achievement, and to investigate parental attitudes towards the project.

Participants
Experimental group: 539 students in grades 4–6 (ages 9–11) in 9 schools and 218 parents; control group: 153 students in 5 schools and 144

parents. The schools (all in Tel-Aviv) were selected by using stratified random sampling, with the strata being socio-economic status and religious vs secular. Within these schools all the pupils participated whose parents filled in and returned the consent forms (return rate: 35%).

Instruments (motivation-related)

- The *student questionnaire* (17 four-point rating scales; 2 open-ended questions; 3 selection and rank-ordering items) focused on the exposure to Arabic, family background in Arabic, attitudes towards the Arabic language and its culture, appraisal of the importance of Arabic in Israel, satisfaction of the students with Arabic classes, and motivation to continue studying Arabic in junior high school.
- The *parent questionnaire* (11 five-point rating scales; 2 multiple choice items; 2 language background items) focused on the knowledge of Arabic, exposure to the Arabic language and its culture, appraisal of the importance of studying Arabic, and the preferred starting age for studying literary and spoken Arabic.

Procedures
Students filled in the questionnaires in class. Parents filled in the questionnaires together with the consent form.

Data analysis
Analysis of variance of the post-test results in the two experimental conditions; chi-square analysis of the responses in the experimental and control groups that were summarised in percentages; regression analysis of the variables predicting motivation to continue studying Arabic.

Results (selected)
The significant outcome differences between the experimental and treatment group have indicated that the teaching of spoken Arabic:

- positively affects the attitudes towards the language and its culture, and increases the motivation to study the language;
- improves the motivation to study the language for peace and pragmatic (utilitarian) reasons, rather than because of the surrounding countries and in order to deal with Israel's enemies (areas where the control group's scores were significantly higher).

The best predictors of the intention to continue studying Arabic were:

- the quality of the teaching programme;
- student attitudes towards Arabic and its culture;
- students' perception of parental support.

10.6 Qualitative studies

Although there is a range of qualitative/interpretive research techniques, two methods occupy a central position in qualitative research methodology:

- interview studies
- case studies.

Earlier I have described the characteristic features of qualitative research (9.1.1); the following discussion is to complement that discussion by focusing specifically on interview and case studies.

Interviews can be divided into four broad categories, the first three involving a one-to-one format, the fourth a group format:

1. In a *structured interview* the researcher closely follows a preprepared interview schedule/guide, which contains a list of questions to be covered closely with every interviewee, and the elicited information shares many of the advantages (e.g. comparability across participants) and disadvantages (e.g. limited richness) of questionnaire data.

2. The other extreme, the *unstructured interview*, allows maximum flexibility to 'follow' the interviewee into unpredictable directions, with only minimal interference from the research agenda. The intention is to create a relaxed atmosphere in which the respondent may reveal more than he or she would in more formal contexts.

3. *Semistructured interviews* offer a compromise between the two extremes: although there is a set of preprepared guiding questions and prompts, the format is open-ended and the interviewee is encouraged to elaborate on the issues raised in an exploratory manner.

4. *Focus group interviews* involve groups of (usually 6–12) people discussing some shared concern, with the interviewer (labelled as the 'moderator') taking on the group leader's role. This format is based on the collective experience of group brainstorming, that is, participants thinking together, inspiring and challenging each other, and reacting to the emerging issues and points.

The key notion with regard to *case studies* is flexibility and, in fact, a considerable proportion of the obtained data is often impressionistic in the sense that it does not get recorded (Stake, 1995). Because a case study involves an extended period spent with the participant, such investigations are often longitudinal. In order not to become overwhelmed with the huge amounts of detail, it may be useful to have a *data-gathering*

Concept 10.1   A framework for processing interview data

Following the recommendations of Rubin and Rubin (1995) and McCracken (1988), the analysis of the recorded and transcribed interview data is a stepwise process, involving the following broad phases:

1. The initial *coding* of the transcripts, often utterance by utterance, based on discrete observations.
2. The formation of *broader categories* – based on core ideas, assumptions and concepts emerging from the texts – that allow the researcher to compare what different people have said.
3. Identifying *patterns* in the responses and reassembling the information into overarching and hierarchical *themes* and *arguments*.
4. By selecting from the main themes, determining the *interview theses*, that is, the theoretical and practical implications of the insights gained.

---

plan, which defines the case, the research questions, the data sources and the allocation of time. Some of the data are usually interview-based and some observation-based, but the data sources in a case study may also include various documents and elicited discourse samples produced by the participants. As Johnson (1992) summarises, one strength of the case study approach is the variety of the combination of elicitation techniques and contexts available. The main purpose of the analysis is similar to that of interview data – that is, to discover meaningful themes and patterns – but due to the greater variety of the data sources, no simple and uniform framework for data processing can be provided.

10.6.1   Role in L2 motivation research

Because of the strong initial influences of quantitative social psychology on L2 motivation research, qualitative studies have traditionally not been part of the research repertoire in the field. Ushioda (1994, 1996b) has been one of the few to advocate qualitative approaches to the study of L2 motivation, arguing that the quantitative framework is necessarily limiting with regard to this dynamic construct. In the present state of L2 motivation research, which is characterised by searches for a new understanding of the intricate and multilevel construct of motivation, the adoption of qualitative research methods would seem to be very timely. The richness of qualitative data may provide 'new slants on old questions' (Pintrich and Schunk, 1996), in a similar vein to the studies on L2 demotivation (reported in 6.3).

Quote 10.4 Ushioda on the need for qualitative approaches to the study of L2 motivation

The generally positive impact of high levels of motivation on levels of L2 achievement has been extensively documented in the existing quantitative research tradition. A more introspective approach to the perceived dynamic interplay between learning experience and individual motivational thought processes may offer a better understanding of how these high levels of motivation might be effectively promoted and sustained.

There is clearly much potential in the theoretical development of a dynamic concept of L2 motivation. The concept of motivational change after all brings with it the notion of motivational control, or self-motivation. In this respect, a qualitative approach may be the most fruitful means of exploring the role of motivation thought processes over the language learning time span.

Ushioda (1994: 83; and 1996b: 245)

10.6.2   Relevant research questions and topics

The most stimulating aspect of qualitative research for me is its open-ended and exploratory character. Describing a small-scale interview study, Ushioda (1994) has emphasised the wide range of motivational perspectives that emerged in spite of the small size of the subject sample and the unity of the learning context and language of study. My experience is similar: the amount of new insights gained from a recent interview study with 50 learners (6.3.3) was most convincing with regard to the potential value of qualitative research in L2 motivation research. In contrast to the quantitative tradition, whose strength lies in detecting general trends across learners, this line of investigation is more appropriate to uncover the complex interaction of social, cultural and psychological factors within the individual learner. Past L2 motivation research has distilled a set of valuable concepts and principles that have stood the test of time; qualitative studies, in turn, can reveal

- how these general principles are reflected in actual people's lives;
- what patterns emerge as a result of the dynamic interplay of (a) motivational forces, (b) time, and (c) personal priorities;
- what other, thus far undetected or underrated, confounding factors shape student motivation (e.g. demotives; Chapter 6).

Study 10.6

Marion Williams and Robert Burden (1999) Students' developing conceptions of themselves as language learners. *Modern Language Journal* 83: 193–201

Purpose
To investigate the development of learners' attributions for their perceived successes and failures in L2 learning.

Participants
36 learners of French in three English schools. An equal number of boys and girls were selected randomly from four age groups (12 pupils from year 6 (ages 10–11); 12 from year 7 (ages 11–12); 6 from year 9 (ages 13–14); and 6 from years 10–12 (ages 14–17), stratified by three ability bands (low, moderate and high)).

Instrument
Short interview guide consisting of four questions.

Procedures
Semistructured one-to-one interviews of about 20–25 minutes with each participant in a quiet area in his or her school.

Data analysis
The tape-recorded and transcribed data were content analysed in a grounded manner; that is, no predetermined categories were imposed on the data. The students' responses were listed in specific descriptive phrases, after which the two researchers independently searched for natural groupings and overreaching constructs. These were then compared and discussed until a consensus on the groupings was reached.

Results
The results of the analysis are included in 3.5.1.

no 3.7.1

10.7 Towards a combined use of quantitative and qualitative studies

Research studies usually apply either a qualitative or a quantitative paradigm, without combining the two. This is understandable since the two approaches are associated with different personal beliefs about scientific truth and objectivity, and also require different expertise and orientation on the researchers' part. To put it broadly, quantitative and qualitative researchers often find that they do not speak the 'same language'. However, during the past decade there has been a growing recognition at conferences and other professional meetings of the fact that a combination of qualitative and quantitative designs might bring out the best of both approaches while neutralising the shortcomings and biases inherent in each paradigm. Given that collaborative research is very widespread in the L2 field, such a combination is not at all inconceivable within research teams that contain both quantitative and qualitative experts. Because I believe that combined method studies have a lot of potential in L2 motivation research, I will conclude the section on research methodology by examining some ways in which such quantitative–qualitative combinations can be implemented.

Based on a review of the literature, Creswell (1994) offers three models that advance useful prototypes for combining designs:

1. *Two-phase designs* have separate qualitative and quantitative phases. For example, the main theses of a qualitative project can be tested in a survey study to determine the distribution and frequency of the phenomena that have been uncovered.

Quote 10.5 McCracken on the cooperative use of qualitative and quantitative methods

The first principle [in qualitative research] is that 'less is more'. It is more important to work longer, and with greater care, with a few people than more superficially with many of them. For many research projects, eight respondents will be perfectly sufficient. The quantitatively trained social scientist reels at the thought of so small a 'sample', but it is important to remember that this group is not chosen to represent some part of the larger world. It offers, instead, an opportunity to glimpse the complicated character, organisation, and logic of culture. How widely what is discovered exists in the rest of the world cannot be decided by qualitative methods, but only quantitative ones. It is, precisely, this 'division of labour' that makes the cooperative use of qualitative and quantitative methods so important to the qualitative investigator. It is only after the qualitative investigator has taken advantage of quantitative research that he or she is prepared to determine the distribution and frequency of the cultural phenomenon that has come to light.

McCracken (1988: 17)

2. *Dominant-less dominant designs* draw on a single paradigm with one
   small component of the overall study drawn from the alternative
   paradigm. For example, the material gathered in a relatively small-
   scale exploratory interview study can be used to design a quantitative
   motivation questionnaire to be used in a large-scale survey.

3. *Mixed-methodology designs* attempt to achieve a real mixture of the
   two paradigms at all, or many, methodological steps in the designs.
   An example would be the case study of the motivational foundation
   of a language-teaching programme in a particular school in which
   an equal weight would be assigned to gathering and analysing quantitative questionnaire data, quantifiable observational data, elicited
   speech samples and interviews with learners and teachers. Such a
   research design is in line with the general concept of 'triangulation'.

10.7.1   Two examples of a multimethod design for studying L2 motivation

As argued in 8.2.3, the most common data collection method in the
study of L2 motivation has been the use of questionnaires with closed
items. Thus, for most fellow researchers 'motivation research' in effect
equals designing, administering and processing questionnaires. How
could this approach be combined with a qualitative analysis? In the
following I will outline two design ideas that offer such a combination:

1. *Systematic sampling of interviewees.* My main concern about qualitative interview studies is the somewhat ad hoc nature of selecting the
   interviewees. Although it was stated above that sample representativeness is not a compelling issue in qualitative studies, I cannot help
   wondering about just how idiosyncratic the experiences and insights
   of individual informants are in an area which is characterised by
   considerable micro- and macrocontextual variation. However, this
   concern could be eliminated by applying a *two-phase design*:

   - In *Phase 1*, a short questionnaire is administered to a substantial
     sample, and on the basis of the responses the researchers identify
     certain individuals who represent either typical or extreme cases
     from certain key aspects of the study.

   - In *Phase 2*, these learners are invited to participate in a qualitative
     interview, thereby making the selection of the sample systematic.
     (We should note that this design does not work if the ques-
     tionnaires are anonymous, which may be a problem in certain
     contexts.)

2. *Questionnaire study with retrospection*. A very versatile technique to study the respondents' thought processes, feelings and experiences is *retrospection,* which is a type of 'verbal reports' (cf. Færch and Kasper, 1987; Kasper, 1998; Kormos, 1998). A typical use of this procedure in L2 studies involves the participants first completing a communicative task (which is recorded) and then listening to the recording of their own speech while making running commentary (which is again recorded). Grotjahn (1987) demonstrated that retrospection can also be used for the purpose of validating language tests, and in a similar vein we can conceive of a study in which respondents first complete a standard motivation questionnaire and then are asked to go through the responses with an interviewer and provide retrospective comments on the reason for their particular response in each item. Thus, in this design the participant's own item responses serve as prompts for further open-ended reflection and, at the same time, the coverage of all the items ensures systematicity and comprehensiveness.

IV Resources and further information

Chapter 11

The locus of motivation research: Linkages to other topics and disciplines

This chapter will . . .

- summarise the disciplines that are related to L2 motivation research in the social sciences and provide some key references to them;
- discuss the place of L2 motivation research within applied linguistics.

The study of L2 motivation is an interdisciplinary field as it requires some degree of expertise in three scholarly domains:

- language education
- (applied) linguistics
- psychology.

Because of this interdisciplinary nature of the domain, L2 motivation researchers can find materials relevant to their subject in a number of related disciplines within the social sciences where the understanding of human behaviour is a focal issue. Some of these areas, like motivational psychology, are obvious 'feeder disciplines'; however, there are also some other fields that contain useful information that one would normally not turn to. In order to help to locate these fields, in the following I will map the terrain of the social sciences with respect to the thematic linkages to L2 motivation research. First I will look outside the L2 field, then I will discuss the place of motivation research within L2 studies.

11.1   Language-learning motivation and related disciplines in the social sciences

The study of L2 motivation has always had strong ties to disciplines outside the boundaries of L2 studies. The 'pioneers' of the field in Canada – Robert Gardner, Richard Clément and Wallace Lambert – have all approached the issue from a psychological perspective, looking at the study of L2 motivation as a sub-area within social psychology. These scholars have been first and foremost social psychologists who had an interest in the affective basis of second language acquisition and interethnic communication. Although the next generation of L2 motivation researchers have identified themselves more closely with applied linguistics and L2 studies, L2 motivation research has maintained its permeable boundaries: Even the 'great paradigm shift' in the 1990s (4.1) was characterised by an outward-looking orientation as researchers surveyed a wide array of motivation constructs in several branches of psychology in order to draw on them in developing new L2 models.

Because of the inherently interdisciplinary nature of the subject, anyone wishing to do research on L2 motivation needs to look both inside and outside the field of L2 studies for the relevant literature. The question, then, is: 'Where shall we look?' In my past research I have found valuable material in the eight domains detailed below.

Motivational psychology

This obvious link to L2 motivation research has been a thriving specialisation area within general psychology during the past century. Chapters 1 and 2 review many key publications in the field, and Eccles, Wigfield and Schiefele (1998) and Weiner (1992) offer comprehensive and highly informative overviews of the main trends and theories.

Educational psychology

Although 'motivation' refers to human behaviour in general, particularly two behavioural domains have been subject to extensive research: the motivation to *achieve* in general and the motivation to achieve in educational environments, that is, the motivation to *learn*. The findings in these two areas show many similarities and have often been transferred to the other. Yet, there are also some important differences between motivation in educational and other (e.g. work) contexts, and consequently the study of student motivation has been a prominent subject in educational psychology. Authoritative summaries can be found in Brophy (1998), Pintrich and Schunk (1996), Stipek (1996) and Wigfield et al. (1998).

In addition to the research focusing explicitly on motivation within educational psychology, there is a second area that has a considerable relevance to the understanding of the motivational basis of instructed learning: the study of the *psychological environment* of the classroom. Fraser and Walberg (1991) provide a detailed account of the various research directions, instruments and findings, and Burden and Williams (1998) discuss their connection with the L2 field.

Educational studies

Although educational psychology and educational studies show a considerable overlap, there are three traditional educational areas that are relevant to motivation research:

- *classroom management* (e.g. Burden, 1995; Jones and Jones, 1995);
- *instructional design* (for a review of the motivational aspects, see Keller, 1994);
- *research on teachers* (for the 'classic' summary, see Wittrock, 1986; for a more recent discussion, see McCormick, 1994).

Social psychology: attitude research

Social psychologists have been interested in human action because of the recognition that various aspects of the individual's sociocultural context have a considerable impact on the person's cognitions, emotions, behaviours and achievement. The most explicit treatment of this effect has been within an 'attitude-causes-action' framework, in accordance with a key tenet in social psychology that someone's attitude towards a target influences the overall pattern of the person's responses to the target. Three texts that offer insightful discussions of various related issues are Ajzen (1988), Eagly and Chaiken (1993) and Geen (1995).

Social psychology: theories of social identity and social cognition

There are two further areas within social psychology that concern the sociocultural influences on human behaviour and thus, indirectly, social motivation:

1. *Social identity theory*, focusing on the effects of various social group memberships (e.g. ethnic, ethnolinguistic, professional) on the individual's self-image and aspirations.
2. *Social cognition theory*, focusing on how individuals process and store information about other people and how these mental processes affect their interaction with them.

For a recent review of the interrelationship of the two perspectives, see Abrams and Hogg (1999); for an explicit treatment of motivational issues within a social identity perspective, see Hogg and Abrams (1993).

Group dynamics

Membership in various small groups such as learner groups, project teams, work parties, etc., has a powerful impact on the group members' motivation and behaviour, for example through

- the socionormative influences of peer pressure;
- the directive influence of group goals;
- the general effects of group cohesiveness on group performance.

Such issues have been the subject of a great deal of research in an interdisciplinary field within the social sciences, *group dynamics*. For a comprehensive account of the field, see Forsyth (1998); for a summary of group dynamics in education, see Schmuck and Schmuck (1997); for an overview of the L2 educational implications of group dynamics, see Ehrman and Dörnyei (1998).

Organisational psychology: work motivation

Employee motivation is understandably a key issue within work settings and therefore a great deal of research within organisational and industrial psychology has been directed at understanding

- which aspects of work design motivate employees;
- how this motivation can be enhanced;
- how worker dissatisfaction can be reduced.

The following three volumes offer comprehensive overviews: Hersey et al. (1996), Pinder (1997) and Steers and Porter (1991).

Communication studies

'Communication studies' is a thriving discipline within the social sciences, covering a variety of topics related to L1 language use, ranging from media studies to intercultural communication. The field in general has relevance to L2 studies that has not been sufficiently exploited by L2 researchers, and one particular subfield, *instructional communication studies*, specifically targets classroom motivation as a function of 'teacher immediacy' (i.e. verbal and non-verbal behaviours which reduce the physical and/or psychological distance between teachers and their students). An extension of this research direction within instructional communication studies has been the analysis of student motivation and 'demotivation', particularly in the light of the teacher's role in demotivating learners. For reviews, see Christophel (1990), Christophel and Gorham (1995) and Rubin and Rubin (1992).

11.2   The place of motivation research in applied linguistics

Motivation research (and individual difference research in general) has a somewhat ambiguous position within the field of applied linguistics. Although most summaries of the area acknowledge its importance, L2 motivation research is rarely given more than a marginal treatment in general overviews. For example, in the most comprehensive survey of the field of second language acquisition (SLA) to date, Ellis (1994) devotes only 13 out of a total of 700 pages to the discussion of motivational issues, even though he begins the section on motivation as follows: 'Language teachers readily acknowledge the importance of learners' *motivation* . . . SLA research also views motivation as a key factor in L2 learning' (p. 508).

The ambiguous treatment of motivation in L2 studies is due to at least two main reasons:

1. Even though the understanding of the complex mental processes involved in L2 learning is just as much a psychological as a linguistic issue, most researchers in the field have a background in

linguistics, and postgraduate courses focusing on second language acquisition are also usually dominated by a linguistic approach. This predisposes L2 researchers towards concentrating on the linguistic aspects of the topic.

2. There have been few theories proposed in the L2 field that could accommodate both linguistic and psychological constructs in a unified framework. Thus, the study of language processing did not organically orientate researchers towards using combined psycholinguistic paradigms in an integrated manner.

Recently, however, there have been some important changes in the L2 field in these respects. Certain cognitive-psychological and psycholinguistic research directions have reached a 'mainstream' status in the study of L2 acquisition (e.g. Schmidt's (1995) 'noticing hypothesis' and Skehan's (1998a) psycholinguistic/cognitive account of L2 processing), and psychological theories have increasingly been drawn on when studying a number of important topics in applied linguistics, such as

- *fluency* (e.g. Schmidt, 1992);
- *communication strategies* (e.g. Kasper and Kellerman, 1997; Dörnyei and Kormos, 1998);
- *repair* (e.g. Kormos, 1999);
- *formulaic speech* (e.g. Ellis, 1996);
- *learning strategies* (e.g. MacIntyre and Noels, 1996; O'Malley and Chamot, 1990);
- *learning styles* (e.g. Ehrman, 1996; Reid, 1997);
- the relationship between *language aptitude*, *L1 skills* and *L2 learning* (e.g. Sparks and Ganshow, 1999; Sparks et al., 1995).

Thus, the imbalance between linguistic and psychological approaches has been gradually decreasing, thereby creating a more fertile research environment for the study of L2 motivation.

In addition, there have been some important recent attempts at setting up *integrated frameworks* for investigating various L2-related phenomena; two examples of this research effort are:

- *task-based research*
- *L2 performance modelling.*

The theoretical significance of *task-based approaches* (for reviews, see Crookes and Gass, 1993a, 1993b; Skehan, 1998b) lies in the fact that focusing on tasks as basic conceptual units allows researchers to break down the complex L2 learning process into discrete segments with well-defined boundaries, thereby creating meaningful 'anchor points' in discussing the various dimensions of L2 processing. Skehan and Foster (1997, 1999) – see also Skehan (1998a) – have successfully used a task-based framework for studying the cognitive aspects of L2 processing; Bygate (1999, 2000) has provided a psycholinguistic analysis of L2 task performance drawing on Levelt's (1989) model of speech production; and Dörnyei and Kormos (2000; cf. 10.3.3) applied a task-based approach to examine the sociodynamic and motivational foundation of L2 learners' task engagement. In view of the significant amount of accumulated linguistic knowledge on interaction in communicative tasks (e.g. Gass and Selinker, 1994; Gass and Varonis, 1994; Pica, 1994), the extension of the task-based paradigm to include a psychological dimension offers a potentially fruitful, comprehensive framework to the study of L2 learning and use.

Attempts at conceptualising *L2 performance* have been, in McNamara's (1996: 85) words, 'loosely psychological in orientation', focusing on various knowledge dimensions. The main challenge has involved adding a dynamic character to the static, competence-based models of communicative competence so that the resulting constructs can be used for the purpose of assessing situated L2 speech. For example, Bachman (1990) and Bachman and Palmer (1996) have proposed a model in which a complex construct of 'language knowledge' is mapped onto performance through the operation of *strategic competence*, which is made up of metacognitive strategies, to explain the capacity of L2 speakers to create and interpret discourse. McNamara (1996) and Skehan (1998c) have drawn up an elaborate model of oral test performance in which the *interactive* nature of performance is emphasised.

Finally, based on the recognition that performance is also a function of the participants' *willingness* to engage in the act of communication, MacIntyre et al. (1998) have made an attempt to conceptualise *willingness to communicate (WTC) in the L2*. Inspired by research on L1 WTC in communication studies (e.g. McCroskey and Richmond, 1991), we have extended the trait-like conceptualisation of L1 WTC to cover situated L2 speech events as well, thereby explaining the individual's 'readiness to enter into discourse at a particular time with a specific person or persons, using a L2' (p. 547). The L2 WTC construct, conceived as having several layers, is made up of a hierarchical complex of both linguistic and psychological variables that include:

- self-confidence (both state and trait);
- desire to affiliate with a person or persons;
- interpersonal motivation;
- intergroup attitudes, motivation and climate;
- parameters of the social situation;
- communicative competence and experience;
- personality traits.

Thus, the model attempts to draw together a host of learner variables that have been well established as influences on second language acquisition and communication in varied sub-areas, resulting in a construct of WTC in which psychological and linguistic factors are integrated in a hitherto unprecedented degree in applied linguistics.

Chapter 12

Sources and resources

This chapter will...

- summarise the various information sources and databases relevant to the study of L2 motivation;
- offer a collection of motivation questionnaire items that have been used successfully in the past.

12.1   Relevant journals and magazines

There is no particular L2 journal or magazine that specialises in motivational issues; rather, most of the main L2 periodicals publish relevant articles from time to time. Having said that, there are certain differences in priorities among the various research organs. During the past two decades, the *Modern Language Journal* has been the most supportive forum for articles (both data-based and conceptual) that addressed the affective foundation of L2 learning and teaching. *Language Learning* has also played an important role in publishing primarily empirical studies, and this was the forum where Crookes and Schmidt's (1991) influential position paper on the need for more education-friendly motivation research has come out. Because motivation is a key factor in determining the rate and success of second language acquisition, *Studies in Second Language Acquisition* has also considered contributions on the topic despite its predominantly linguistic orientation. Recently, the newly founded journal *Language Teaching Research* has published several motivation papers, which reflects the significance of the subject for classroom practitioners.

Because of the importance of motivation research in Canada, the *Canadian Modern Language Review* has always been a natural forum for research conducted in that context. *System* and *Foreign Language Annals* have published several related papers (e.g. on learner autonomy, classroom dynamics and learner strategies). Articles highlighting the social dimension of L2 motivation have been welcome in the *Journal of Multilingual and Multicultural Development*. Finally, two journals geared at practising teachers as their main audience, *Language Learning Journal* and *ELT Journal*, have also published some motivation articles which had practical classroom implications. In order to provide a quantitative summary, below I have tabulated the frequency of L2 motivation articles referred to in this book, broken down by the L2 journals in which they appeared. Only journals with at least two relevant articles are listed. The figures given reflect the trends described above.

- *Modern Language Journal* (16)
- *Language Learning* (10)
- *Studies in Second Language Acquisition* (4)
- *Language Teaching Research* (3)
- *Canadian Modern Language Review* (3)
- *System* (3)
- *Foreign Language Annals* (3)
- *Journal of Multilingual and Multicultural Development* (3)
- *Language Learning Journal* (3)
- *TESOL Quarterly* (2)

12.2 Databases, abstracting journals and discussion groups

A central issue in any scientific domain is to find ways of keeping abreast of the professional literature. One way of knowing what has been written on the topic is by looking at the references of published articles or books. However, these references are obviously selective, and because of the time lapse between the completion and the publication of a work the references will not be completely up-to-date. How can we learn about the most recent materials coming out in the field? In the following I will list the various methods that I have used in the past.

12.2.1   Information about books

Obtaining up-to-date information about books is easier than finding out about articles. There are several sources that contain relevant data on published books:

- '*Books in Print*': various versions of such collections (under somewhat different titles) exist both in a book format and on CD-ROM. These can be accessed in libraries and they allow searches by the author, the title and (sometimes) the main subject area.

- The *catalogues of most major libraries* are accessible on the Internet (e.g. the British Library: http://www.bl.uk or the Library of Congress: http://catalog.loc.gov), offering various search possibilities. A full list of on-line catalogues and other on-line reference materials and services is available on the web sites of the British Library and the Library of Congress.

- A very useful information source is the '*Amazon*' *bookstore*, which is a 'virtual' shop on the Internet (http://www.amazon.com or http://www.amazon.co.uk), storing literally millions of titles. It has excellent search facilities that you can use even if you do not want to buy anything, and it even provides a free service of sending one an e-mail message if a book on a given topic has been published!

12.2.2   Information about articles

Finding information about articles is less straightforward than finding out about books, and it is easier to do so through a library. However the variety of on-line resources is rapidly growing, making it increasingly convenient to conduct searches from home. In the following I will summarise some methods of information gathering that have worked for me; however, I am certain that many other options exist.

1. The richest information sources are *computer databases* that are available either on CD-ROMs or on-line on the Internet (often with a password that you can either subscribe to or obtain from your subject librarian). For a comprehensive overview of 250 leading databases (including subscription information on Internet access to over 200

of these), see SilverPlatter's web site: http://www.silverplatter.com/catalog.htm. In my past research I have used four databases:

- *The MLA International Bibliography*. Produced by the Modern Language Association of America, this database covers academic articles (from over 3,000 journals) and (some) chapters of edited volumes in the areas of literature, languages, linguistics and folklore. Further information: http://www.silverplatter.com/catalog/mlab.htm.

- *ERIC* and *the British Education Index*. These databases cover a great number of educational and educational psychological journal articles, book chapters and ERIC Documents. ERIC, which is presently the largest education database in the world (containing over 700,000 citations), is produced by the Educational Resources Information Center of the US Department of Education. Further information: http://www.silverplatter.com/catalog/eric.htm and http://www.bids.ac.uk.

- *PsycLIT*. 'Psychological Abstracts' is the main bibliographic information source in psychology and the electronic version is called *PsycLIT*, which contains over 1.3 million records. It allows various search modes and full abstracts are available for all the articles included. I have found this to be the most comprehensive database for motivation studies outside the L2 field. Further information: http://www.silverplatter.com/catalog/psyc.htm.

- *Linguistics and Language Behavior Abstracts*. This is the major database on the nature and use of language, containing over 250,000 records (books, book chapters, dissertations, and reviews of books and other media). Further information: http://www.silverplatter.com/catalog/llba.htm.

2. There are also two *citation indexes* that can be used to find relevant information about articles (including any references that are cited in an article and the list of articles that have cited your own work!):

- *Social Sciences Citation Index*

- *Arts and Humanities Citation Index*.

Because of the interdisciplinary nature of L2 motivation research, both indices cover this area, although I have found the former to be considerably more exhaustive. Both indices exist in book format, on CD-ROM and also on-line on the Internet, but access to the Internet indices requires special authorisation, usually from a library. Further information: http://www.bids.ac.uk or http://wos.mimas.ac.uk.

3. There are some further, *commercially maintained databases* that contain information about academic journals; it is usually free to look at the content pages of the journals and to conduct thematic searches, and if you have made certain arrangements (e.g. financial subscription or through your library) it is also possible to download the full text of the articles. I am aware of three such databases (but I suspect that more exist):

   - *'ingentaJournals'* in 'BIDS' (http://www.bids.ac.uk via 'guest access'), covering over 800 journals published by 18 publishers, offering full abstracts for the articles;

   - *Catchword* (http://www.catchword.com), covering 662 academic journals, offering a range of search facilities;

   - *International Digital Electronic Access Library (IDEAL)*, covering 174 Academic Press journals (http://www.idealibrary.com or http://www.europe.idealibrary.com).

4. Several *international publishers* (e.g. Cambridge University Press) also offer article search facilities of their own journals on their web sites.

5. Finally, there is an *abstracting journal* specialising in the field of language education published by Cambridge University Press:

   - *Language Teaching*. Each quarterly issue contains about 160 abstracts of articles and some reviews of new books, as well as one lead offering a state-of-the-art overview of a specific sub-domain, written by one of the international authorities in the field.

12.2.3   Internet discussion group

I am aware of one Internet discussion group that specialises in student motivation and is maintained by the 'Motivation in Education' Special Interest Group of the American Educational Research Association. Information about how to subscribe to it can be found on the web site of the Special Interest Group:

http://ccwf.cc.utexas.edu/~tgarcia/motivhome.html

This web site also contains other useful information, for example, an on-line newsletter.

12.3 Sample tests and measurement instruments

In 8.2.3, I argued that because of the great diversity of language-learning environments and because of the social sensitivity of attitude/motivation questionnaires, no battery can be used mechanically (i.e. without making considerable adjustments) in contexts other than where it was developed. This does not mean, however, that we cannot benefit from drawing on existing item pools as long as we realise that the items may not have the same psychometric properties in our sample as in the population they were originally devised for. In the following I will:

• list a number of publications whose appendices contain the motivation scales or interview guides used in the particular study;

• present three sets of motivation items that I have used with Hungarian learners of English in the past.

There are two things I would like to note at the outset concerning the questionnaire items used in Hungary:

1. The items will be listed without clustering them into multi-item scales; this is because they may form different clusters when used in other samples.

2. When the original Hungarian items were developed, we were drawing on published motivation questionnaires from Clément and Kruidenier (1983), Gardner (1985), Lukmani (1972), Pierson et al. (1980) and Roger et al. (1981), as well as on the instrument used by Clément (1986). The Hungarian questionnaires therefore owe much to the work of these authors.

12.3.1 Publications containing questionnaires and interview guides

Bourhis et al. (1981): Subjective Vitality Questionnaire
Burstall et al. (1974)
Christophel (1990)
Clément and Kruidenier (1983)
Colletta et al. (1983)
Dörnyei (1990) → reproduced, next pp.
Ehrman (1996)
Ely (1986)
Gardner (1985): the Attitude/Motivation Test Battery
Gardner et al. (1997)

Genesee et al. (1983)

Green (1993)

Horwitz (1988): Beliefs About Language Learning Inventory (BALLI)
(reprinted in Young, 1999)

Horwitz et al. (1986): Foreign Language Classroom Anxiety Scale
(reprinted in Young, 1999)

Julkunen (1989)

Julkunen and Borzova (1997)

Kruidenier and Clément (1986)

Lukmani (1972)

✕ Noels et al. (2000)

Pierson et al. (1980)

Roger et al. (1981)

✓ Schmidt et al. (1996) (also contains the Arabic version)

Sparks and Ganshow (1999)

Speiller (1988)

Wen (1997)

✓ Williams and Burden (1999)

Young (1999): this edited volume contains several anxiety scales

12.3.2 The motivation questionnaire used by Dörnyei (1990)

The original language of the following items was Hungarian. The
items are thematically grouped, but they were presented in a random
order to the students. Background questions are not included.

*Section 1 (six-point Likert scales; for the format of the questionnaire,
see the 'Likert Scale Format' in 9.2.3)*

1. If I had to spend a longer period – say one or one and a half years
   – abroad, I would make a great effort to learn the local language
   even if I could get along with English.

2. I would like to learn as many languages as possible.

3. After finishing English I'd like to start learning another language.

4. For me language learning is a hobby.

5. Sometimes language learning is a burden for me.

6. Language learning is an exciting activity.

7. I don't particularly like the process of language learning and I do it
   only because I need the language.

8. Language learning often gives me a feeling of success.

9. Language learning often makes me happy.

10. Studying English is important to me because it provides an interesting intellectual activity.

11. English proficiency is a part of the general culture.

12. I am learning English to become more educated.

13. English proficiency is important to me because it allows me to learn about the current intellectual trends of the world, and thus to broaden my view.

14. English proficiency is indispensable for a Hungarian person to be able to live a valuable and colourful life.

15. Everybody in Hungary should learn English to at least an intermediate level.

16. The more I learn about the British/Americans, the more I like them.

17. Most of my favourite artists (e.g. actors, musicians) are either British or American.

18. Britain and America are among the most exciting countries of the world.

19. British/American culture is of vital importance in the world nowadays.

20. If I spoke English I could do a more interesting job.

21. If I spoke English I could travel more for official purposes.

22. English proficiency would have financial benefits for me.

23. I don't think it is very important to speak elaborately in a foreign language; the point is only to be able to express my thoughts.

24. Pronunciation in a foreign language is important only insofar as one can make himself/herself understood.

25. It doesn't matter if I make mistakes in a foreign language; the point is only to be fluent.

26. I think I have a good sense for languages.

27. I think language learning is more difficult for me than for the average learner.

28. I have had some bad experiences with learning languages.

29. I think I belong to the class of learners who can completely lose their interest in learning if they have a bad teacher.

30. My colleagues usually speak a foreign language on at least an intermediate level.

31. My bosses expect me to learn English.

32. Without English proficiency I cannot expect a promotion.

33. The prominent members of my profession speak English on at least an intermediate level.

34. English proficiency is important to me because it is indispensable for establishing an international reputation.

35. I would like to take the intermediate level State Language Examination.

36. Taking the State Language Examination does not play an important role in my learning English.

37. There would be a serious gap in my life if I couldn't learn English.

38. I believe that I'll be able to learn English to an extent that satisfies me.

39. At present learning English is one of the most important things to me.

40. English proficiency is important to me because it will allow me to get to know various cultures and peoples.

41. Studying English is important to me because it offers a new challenge in my life, which has otherwise become a bit monotonous.

42. I am learning English because I would like to spend a longer period abroad.

43. It is indispensable for me to take the State Language Examination in order to achieve a specific goal (e.g. to get a degree or scholarship).

44. I'd like to take the advanced level State Language Examination in English.

Section 2 (six-point rating scales indicating the extent to which the lack of English has affected the respondents in each of the listed fields: 'I haven't felt the lack of English' → 'the lack of English has really hindered me')

1. doing my job/profession
2. reading English literature
3. reading English newspapers, magazines

4. reading English technical literature
5. writing English articles and lectures
6. travelling abroad as a tourist
7. business or study trips abroad
8. working abroad
9. making friends with foreigners
10. keeping in touch with foreign friends, acquaintances
11. professional contact with foreign colleagues
12. understanding English films, videos
13. understanding English broadcasting
14. understanding English pop music
15. learning about what's happening in the world.

12.3.3   The motivation questionnaire used by Clément et al. (1994)

The original language of the following items was Hungarian. The items are thematically grouped, but they were presented in a random order to the students. Background questions are not included.

Section 1 (six-point Likert scales)

Studying English is important to me . . . (this sentence beginning was added to all the following statements and it is left out here only for the sake of space economy):

1. because I would like to meet foreigners with whom I can speak English.
2. because I would like to make friends with foreigners.
3. because it will enable me to get to know new people from different parts of the world.
4. so that I can keep in touch with foreign friends and acquaintances.
5. because I would like to learn as many foreign languages as possible.
6. because it will help me when travelling.
7. because it will enable me to get to know various cultures and peoples.
8. because it will enable me to learn more about the English world.

9. because it will enable me to learn more about what is happening in the world.

10. because an educated person is supposed to be able to speak English.

11. so that I can be a more knowledgeable person.

12. because without it one cannot be successful in any field.

13. so that I can broaden my outlook.

14. because I may need it later (for job, studies).

15. because without English I won't be able to travel a lot.

16. so that I can understand English-speaking films, videos, TV or radio.

17. so that I can understand English pop music.

18. so that I can read English books, newspapers or magazines.

19. because I would like to travel to countries where English is used.

20. because I would like to spend some time abroad.

It is important for me to know English . . . (this sentence beginning was added to all the following statements and it is left out here only for the sake of space economy):

21. in order to think and behave like the English/Americans do.

22. in order to be similar to the British/Americans.

23. in order to know the life of the English-speaking nations.

24. in order to better understand the English-speaking nations' behaviour and problems.

Further items in this section

25. I do not particularly like the process of learning English and I do it only because I may need the language.

26. I would rather spend my time on subjects other than English.

27. I really like learning English.

28. The British are open-minded and modern people.

29. The more I learn about the British, the more I like them.

30. The British are usually reliable and honest.

31. The British are kind and friendly.

32. I would like to know more British people.

33. The Americans are sociable and hospitable.

34. I like the way the Americans behave.

35. I would like to know more American people.

36. The Americans are friendly people.

37. The Americans are kind and cheerful.

38. I enjoy hard work.

39. I easily give up goals which prove hard to reach.

40. I hate to do a job with less than my best effort.

41. In my work I seldom do more than is necessary.

42. If my teacher wanted someone to do an extra English assignment, I would certainly volunteer.

43. I frequently think over what we have learnt in my English class.

44. To be honest, I very often skimp on my English homework.

45. I get nervous and confused when I am speaking in my English class.

46. I always feel that the other students speak English better than I do.

47. It embarrasses me to volunteer answers in our English class.

48. I never feel quite sure of myself when I am speaking English in our English class.

49. I am afraid that other students will laugh at me when I speak English.

50. I usually get uneasy when I have to speak in English.

51. I feel calm and confident in the company of English-speaking people.

52. I do not find it embarrassing at all if I have to give directions in English to English-speaking tourists.

53. When I have to speak English on the phone I easily become confused.

54. Compared to other groups like mine, I feel my group is better than most.

55. There are some cliques in this group.

56. If I were to participate in another group like this one, I would want it to include people who are very similar to the ones in this group.

57. This group is composed of people who fit together.

58. There are some people in this group who do not really like each other.
59. I am dissatisfied with my group.

Section 2 (six-point rating scales ranging from 'absolutely not' to 'definitely yes')

60. Are you satisfied with your work in the English course?
61. Are you satisfied with your English proficiency?

Section 3 (five-point rating scales ranging from 'elementary' to 'advanced')

62. Please indicate on the following scale the level of English that would already satisfy you.

Section 4 (seven-point semantic differential scales)

Appraisal of the English teacher

63. imaginative–unimaginative
64. interesting–boring
65. suited–unsuited
66. consistent–inconsistent
67. conscientious–slapdash
68. enthusiastic–unenthusiastic
69. hardworking–lazy
70. helpful–unhelpful
71. fair–unfair
72. sympathetic–unsympathetic

Appraisal of the English classes

73. varied–uniform
74. good atmosphere–bad atmosphere
75. interesting–boring
76. easy–difficult
77. useful–useless
78. meaningful–meaningless

12.3.4   The motivation questionnaire used by Dörnyei et al. (1996)

The original language of the following items was Hungarian. The items appear in the random order they were presented in the questionnaire. Background questions are not included.

Section 1 (five-point rating scales ranging from 5 = very much to 1 = not at all). All the questions concerned five languages: German, French, Russian, English and Italian (for the format of the questionnaire, see the 'Rating Scale Format' in 9.2.3)

1. How much do you like these languages?
2. How much do you think knowing these languages would help you to become a more knowledgeable person?
3. How important do you think these languages are in the world these days?
4. How important do you think learning these languages is in order to learn more about the culture and art of its speakers?
5. How much effort are you prepared to expend in learning these languages?
6. How much do you think knowing these languages would help you when travelling abroad in the future?
7. How much do you think knowing these languages would help your future career?
8. How well does your mother speak these languages?
9. How well does your father speak these languages?
10. How much would you like to become similar to the people who speak these languages?

Section 2 (five-point rating scales ranging from 5 = very much to 1 = not at all; all the questions concerned six countries: France, Britain, Russia, Germany, USA, Italy)

11. How much would you like to travel to these countries?
12. How rich and developed do you think these countries are?
13. How important a role do you think these countries play in the world?
14. How much do you like meeting foreigners from these countries?
15. How much do you like the films made in these countries? (Write 0 if you don't know them.)

16. How much do you like the TV programmes made in these countries? (Write 0 if you don't know them.)

17. How much do you like the people who live in these countries?

18. How often do you see films/TV programmes made in these countries?

19. How much do you like the magazines made in these countries? (Write 0 if you don't know them.)

20. How often do you meet foreigners (e.g. in the street, restaurants, public places) coming from these countries?

21. How much do you like the pop music of these countries? (Write 0 if you don't know it.)

Section 3 (five-point Likert scales ranging from 'not at all true' to 'absolutely true')

22. I am sure I will be able to learn a foreign language well.

23. I think I am the type who would feel anxious and ill at ease if I had to speak to someone in a foreign language.

24. People around me tend to think that it is a good thing to know foreign languages.

25. I don't think that foreign languages are important school subjects.

26. I often watch satellite programmes on TV.

27. My parents do not consider foreign languages important school subjects.

28. Learning foreign languages makes me fear that I will feel less Hungarian because of it.

29. Learning a foreign language is a difficult task.

Section 4

30. If you could choose, which foreign languages would you choose to learn next year at school (or work)? Please mark three languages in order of importance.

1) ....

2) ....

3) ....

References

Abrams D and Hogg M A (eds) 1999 *Social identity and social cognition*. Blackwell, Oxford

Ajzen I 1988 *Attitudes, personality and behavior*. Dorsey Press, Chicago

Ajzen I 1996 The directive influence of attitudes on behaviour. In Gollwitzer P M and Bargh J A (eds) *The psychology of action: Linking cognition and motivation to behaviour*. Guilford Press, New York pp 385–403

Ajzen I and Fishbein M 1980 *Understanding attitudes and predicting social behaviour*. Prentice-Hall, Englewood Cliffs, NJ

Alison J 1993 *Not bothered? Motivating reluctant language learners in Key Stage 4*. CILT, London

Allard R and Landry R 1994 Subjective ethnolinguistic vitality: A comparison of two measures. *International Journal of the Sociology of Language* **108**: 117–44

Ames C 1992 Classrooms, goals, structures and student motivation. *Journal of Educational Psychology* **84**: 267–71

Anderman E M and Maehr M L 1994 Motivation and schooling. *Review of Educational Research* **64**: 287–309

Anderson L W 1985 Attitudes and their measurement. In Husén T and Postlethwaite T N (eds) *The international encyclopedia of education. Vol. 1*. Pergamon, Oxford pp 352–8

Arnold J (ed.) 1999 *Affective language learning*. New York, Cambridge University Press

Ashton P 1985 Motivation and the teacher's sense of efficacy. In Ames C and Ames R (eds) *Research on motivation in education: The classroom milieu*. Academic Press, Orlando, FL pp 141–71

Atkinson J W and Birch D 1974 The dynamics of achievement-oriented activity. In Atkinson J W and Raynor J O (eds) *Motivation and Achievement*. Winston & Sons, Washington, DC pp 271–325

Atkinson J W and Raynor J O (eds) 1974 *Motivation and achievement*. Winston & Sons, Washington, DC

Ausubel D, Novak J D and Hanesian H 1978 *Educational Psychology: A Cognitive View. 2nd edition*. Holt & Rinehart, New York

Bachman L F 1990 *Fundamental considerations in language testing*. Oxford University Press, Oxford

Bachman L F and Palmer A S 1996 *Language testing in practice*. Oxford University Press, Oxford

Bandura A 1991 Self-regulation of motivation through anticipatory and self-reactive mechanisms. *Nebraska Symposium on Motivation 1990* **39**: 69–164

Bandura A 1993 Perceived self-efficacy in cognitive development and functioning. *Educational Psychologist* **28**: 117–48

Bandura A and Schunk D 1981 Cultivating competence, self-efficacy and intrinsic interest through proximal self-motivation. *Journal of Personality and Social Psychology* **41**: 586–98

Baumeister R F 1996 Self-regulation and ego threat: Motivated cognition, self-deception and destructive goal setting. In Gollwitzer P M and Bargh J A (eds) *The psychology of action: Linking cognition and motivation to behaviour*. Guilford Press, New York pp 27–47

Berliner D C 1989 Furthering our understanding of motivation and environments. In Ames C and Ames R (eds) *Research on motivation in education, Vol. 3: Goals and cognitions*. Academic Press, New York pp 317–43

Benson P 2000 *Teaching and researching autonomy in language learning*. Longman, London

Bess J L 1997 The motivation to teach: Perennial conundrums. In Bess J L (ed.) *Teaching well and liking it: Motivating faculty to teach effectively*. Johns Hopkins University Press, Baltimore pp 424–39

Blackburn R T 1997 Career phases and their effect on faculty motivation. In Bess J L (ed.) *Teaching well and liking it: Motivating faculty to teach effectively*. Johns Hopkins University Press, Baltimore pp 314–36

Blackburn R T and Lawrence J H 1995 *Faculty at work: Motivation, expectation, satisfaction*. Johns Hopkins University Press, Baltimore

Boekaerts M 1988 Motivated learning: Bias in appraisals. *International Journal of Educational Research* **12**: 267–80

Boekaerts M 1994 Action control: How relevant is it for classroom learning? In Kuhl J and Beckmann J (eds) *Volition and personality: Action versus state orientation*. Hogrefe & Huber, Seattle, WA pp 427–35

Boekaerts M 1998 Boosting students' capacity to promote their own learning: A goal theory perspective. *Research Dialogue in Learning and Instruction* **1**: 13–22

Bourhis R Y, Giles H and Rosenthal D 1981 Notes on the construction of a 'subjective vitality questionnaire' for ethnolinguistic groups. *Journal of Multilingual and Multicultural Development* **2**: 144–55

Bronfenbrenner U 1993 The ecology of cognitive development: Research models and fugitive findings. In Wozniak R H and Fischer K W (eds) *Development in context: Acting and thinking in specific environments*. Lawrence Erlbaum, Hillsdale, NJ pp 3–44

Brophy J E 1985 Teachers' expectations, motives and goals for working with problem students. In Ames C and Ames R (eds) *Research on motivation in education: The classroom milieu*. Academic Press, Orlando, FL pp 175–214

Brophy J E 1987 Synthesis of research on strategies for motivating students to learn. *Educational Leadership* **45**: 40–8

Brophy J E 1998 *Motivating students to learn*. McGraw-Hill, Boston, MA

Brophy J E 1999 Toward a model of the value aspects of motivation in education: Developing appreciation for particular learning domains and activities. *Educational Psychologist* **34**: 75–85

Brophy J E and Good T L 1986 Teacher behaviour and student achievement. In Wittrock M C (ed.) *Handbook of research on teaching. 3rd edition.* Macmillan, New York pp 328–75

Brophy J E and Kher N 1986 Teacher socialization as a mechanism for developing student motivation to learn. In Feldman R S (ed.) *The social psychology of education: current research and theory.* Cambridge University Press, Cambridge pp 257–88

Brown H D 1981 Affective factors in second language learning. In Alatis J E, Altman H B and Alatis P M (eds) *The second language classroom: Directions for the eighties.* Oxford University Press, New York pp 111–29

Brown H D 1990 MandMs for language classrooms? Another look at motivation. In Alatis J E (ed.) *Georgetown University round table on language and linguistics 1990.* Georgetown University Press, Washington, DC pp 383–93

Brown H D 1994 *Teaching by principles.* Prentice Hall, Englewood Cliffs, NJ

Brown J D 1988 *Understanding research in second language learning.* Cambridge University Press, Cambridge

Burden P R 1995 *Classroom management and discipline.* Longman, New York

Burden R and Williams M 1998 Language learners' perceptions of supportive classroom environments. *Language Learning Journal* **17**: 29–32

Burstall C, Jamieson M, Cohen S and Hargreaves M 1974 *Primary French in the balance.* NFER, Windsor

Bygate M 1999 Task as context for the framing, reframing and unframing of language. *System* **27**: 33–48

Bygate M 2000 Effects of task repetition on the structure and control of oral language. In Bygate M, Skehan P and Swain M (eds) *Researching Pedagogic Tasks: Second Language Learning, Teaching and Testing.* Longman, London

Carroll J B 1993 *Human cognitive abilities: A survey of factor-analytic studies.* Cambridge University Press, Cambridge

Cattell R B 1966 The scree test for the number of factors. *Multivariate Behavioral Research* **1**: 245–76

Cattell R B and Kline P 1977 *The scientific analysis of personality and motivation.* Academic Press, London

Chambers G N 1993 Talking the 'de' out of demotivation. *Language Learning Journal* **7**: 13–16

Chambers G N 1999 *Motivating language learners.* Multilingual Matters, Clevedon

Chen C and Stevenson H W 1995 Culture and academic achievement: Ethnic and cross-national differences. *Advances in Motivation and Achievement* **9**: 119–51

Christophel D M 1990 The relationships among teacher immediacy behaviors, student motivation and learning. *Communication Education* **39**: 323–39

Christophel D M and Gorham J 1995 A test–retest analysis of student motivation, teacher immediacy and perceived sources of motivation and demotivation in college classes. *Communication Education* **44**: 292–306

Clark A and Trafford J 1995 Boys into modern languages: An investigation of the discrepancy in attitudes and performance between boys and girls in modern languages. *Gender and Education* **7**: 315–25

Clemans W V 1971 Test administration. In Thorndike R L (ed.) *Educational measurement. 2nd edition.* American Council on Education, Washington, DC pp 188–201

Clément R 1980 Ethnicity, contact and communicative competence in a second language. In Giles H, Robinson W P and Smith P M (eds) *Language: Social psychological perspectives.* Pergamon, Oxford pp 147–54

Clément R 1986 Second language proficiency and acculturation: An investigation of the effects of language status and individual characteristics. *Journal of Language and Social Psychology* **5**: 271–90

Clément R, Dörnyei Z and Noels K A 1994 Motivation, self-confidence and group cohesion in the foreign language classroom. *Language Learning* **44**: 417–48

Clément R, Gardner R C and Smythe P C 1977 Motivational variables in second language acquisition: A study of francophones learning English. *Canadian Journal of Behavioural Science* **9**: 123–33

Clément R and Kruidenier B 1983 Orientations on second language acquisition: 1. The effects of ethnicity, milieu and their target language on their emergence. *Language Learning* **33**: 273–91

Clément R and Kruidenier B G 1985 Aptitude, attitude and motivation in second language proficiency: A test of Clément's model. *Journal of Language and Social Psychology* **4**: 21–37

Clément R and Noels K A 1992 Towards a situated approach to ethnolinguistic identity: The effects of status on individuals and groups. *Journal of Language and Social Psychology* **11**: 203–32

Cohen A D 1998 *Strategies in learning and using a second language.* Longman, London

Coleman J A 1995 *Progress, proficiency and motivation among British university language learners.* CLCS Occasional Paper No. 40. Trinity College, Centre for Language and Communication Studies, Dublin

Coleman J A 1996 *Studying languages: A survey of British and European students.* CILT, London

Colletta S P, Clément R and Edwards H P 1983 *Community and parental influence: Effects on student motivation and French second language proficiency.* International Center for Research on Bilingualism, Québec

Cook T D and Campbell D T 1979 *Quasi-experimentation: Design and analysis issues for field settings.* Houghton Mifflin, Boston, MA

Corno L 1993 The best-laid plans: Modern conceptions of volition and educational research. *Educational Researcher* **22**: 14–22

Corno L 1994 Student volition and education: Outcomes, influences, and practices. In Schunk D H and Zimmerman B J (eds) *Self-regulation of learning and performance: Issues and educational applications.* Lawrence Erlbaum, Hillsdale, NJ pp 229–51

Corno L and Kanfer R 1993 The role of volition in learning and performance. *Review of Research in Education* **19**: 301–41

Côté P and Clément R 1994 Language attitudes: An interactive situated approach. *Language and Communication* **14**: 237–51

Covington M 1992 *Making the grade: A self-worth perspective on motivation and school reform.* Cambridge University Press, Cambridge

Covington M 1999 Caring about learning: The nature and nurturing of subject-matter appreciation. *Educational Psychologist* **34**: 127–36

Cranmer D 1996 *Motivating high level learners.* Longman, London

Creswell J W 1994 *Research design: Qualitative and quantitative approaches.* Sage, Thousand Oaks, CA

Crookes G 1997 What influences what and how second and foreign language teachers teach? *Modern Language Journal* **81**: 67–79

Crookes G and Schmidt R W 1991 Motivation: Reopening the research agenda. *Language Learning* **41**: 469–512

Crookes G and Gass S M (eds) 1993a *Tasks in a pedagogical context: Integrating theory and practice.* Multilingual Matters, Clevedon

Crookes G and Gass S M (eds) 1993b *Tasks and language learning: Integrating theory and practice.* Multilingual Matters, Clevedon

Csikszentmihalyi M 1997 Intrinsic motivation and effective teaching: A flow analysis. In Bess J L (ed.) *Teaching well and liking it: Motivating faculty to teach effectively.* Johns Hopkins University Press, Baltimore pp 72–89

Daniels R 1994 Motivational mediators of cooperative learning. *Psychological Reports* **74**: 1011–22

Davies K A 1995 Qualitative theory and methods in applied linguistics research. *TESOL Quarterly* **29**: 427–53

Deci E L, Kasser T and Ryan R M 1997 Self-determined teaching: Opportunities and obstacles. In Bess J L (ed.) *Teaching well and liking it: Motivating faculty to teach effectively.* Johns Hopkins University Press, Baltimore pp 57–71

Deci E L and Ryan R M 1985 *Intrinsic motivation and self-determination in human behavior.* Plenum, New York

Deci E L, Vallerand R J, Pelletier L G and Ryan R M 1991 Motivation and education: The self-determination perspective. *Educational Psychologist* **26**: 325–46

Dickinson L 1995 Autonomy and motivation: A literature review. *System* **23**: 165–74

Dinham S and Scott C 1998 A three domain model of teacher and school executive career satisfaction. *Journal of Educational Administration* **36**: 362–78

Dinham S and Scott C (forthcoming) Moving into the third, outer domain of teacher satisfaction. *Journal of Educational Administration*

Djigunoviç M J 1994 Variations in learner effort: Effects of the teaching setting. *Studia Romanica et Anglica Zagrabiensia* **39**: 53–7

Dörnyei Z 1990 Conceptualizing motivation in foreign language learning. *Language Learning* **40**: 46–78

Dörnyei Z 1994a Motivation and motivating in the foreign language classroom. *Modern Language Journal* **78**: 273–84

Dörnyei Z 1994b Understanding L2 motivation: On with the challenge! *Modern Language Journal* **78**: 515–23

Dörnyei Z 1995a On the teachability of communication strategies. *TESOL Quarterly* **29**: 55–85

Dörnyei Z 1995b Student participation in different types of classroom interaction tasks: A longitudinal investigation. In Roth S (ed.) *Studies in English and American.* Vol. 7. Eötvös Loránd University, Budapest, Hungary pp 213–18

Dörnyei Z 1996 Moving language learning motivation to a larger platform for theory and practice. In Oxford R L (ed.) *Language learning motivation: Pathways to the new century.* University of Hawaii Press, Honolulu, HI pp 89–101

Dörnyei Z 1997 Psychological processes in cooperative language learning: Group dynamics and motivation. *Modern Language Journal* **81**: 482–93

Dörnyei Z 1998a Motivation in second and foreign language learning. *Language Teaching* **31**: 117–35

Dörnyei Z 1998b Demotivation in foreign language learning. Paper presented at the TESOL '98 Congress, Seattle, WA, March

Dörnyei Z 2000 Motivation. In Verschueren J, Östmann J-O, Blommaert J and Bulcaen C (eds) *Handbook of pragmatics*. John Benjamins, Amsterdam

Dörnyei Z In press Motivation in action: Towards a process-oriented conceptualisation of student motivation. *British Journal of Educational Psychology* **70**

Dörnyei Z and Clément R 2000 Motivational characteristics of learning different target languages: Results of a nationwide survey. Paper presented at the AAAL Convention, Vancouver, Canada, March

Dörnyei Z and Csizér K 1998 Ten commandments for motivating language learners: Results of an empirical study. *Language Teaching Research* **2**: 203–29

Dörnyei Z and Kormos J 1998 Problem-solving mechanisms in L2 communication: A psycholinguistic perspective. *Studies in Second Language Acquisition* **20**: 349–85

Dörnyei Z and Kormos J 2000 The role of individual and social variables in oral task performance. *Language Teaching Research* **4**

Dörnyei Z and Malderez A 1997 Group dynamics and foreign language teaching. *System* **25**: 65–81

Dörnyei Z and Malderez A 1999 Group dynamics in foreign language learning and teaching. In Arnold J (ed.) *Affective language learning*. Cambridge University Press, Cambridge pp 155–69

Dörnyei Z, Nyilasi E and Clément R 1996 Hungarian school children's motivation to learn foreign languages: A comparison of five target languages. *Novelty* **3**: 6–16

Dörnyei Z and Ottó I 1998 Motivation in action: A process model of L2 motivation. *Working Papers in Applied Linguistics (Thames Valley University, London)* **4**: 43–69

Dörnyei Z and Scott M L 1997 Communication strategies in a second language: Definitions and taxonomies. *Language Learning* **47**: 173–210

Dörnyei Z and Thurrell S 1992 *Conversation and dialogues in action*. Prentice Hall, Hemel Hempstead

Doyle T and Kim Y M 1999 teacher motivation and satisfaction in the United States and Korea. *MEXTESOL Journal* **23** (2): 35–48

Eagly A H and Chaiken S 1993 *The psychology of attitudes*. Harcourt Brace, New York

Eccles J S and Wigfield A 1995 In the mind of the actor: The structure of adolescents' achievement task values and expectancy-related beliefs. *Personality and Social Psychology Bulletin* **21**: 215–25

Eccles J S, Wigfield A and Schiefele A 1998 Motivation to succeed. In Damon W and Eisenberg N (eds) *Handbook of child psychology. 5th Edition, Vol. 3: Social, emotional, and personality development*. John Wiley & Sons, New York pp 1017–95

Ehrman M E 1996 An exploration of adult language learning motivation, self-efficacy and anxiety. In Oxford R L (ed.) *Language learning motivation: Pathways to the new century*. University of Hawaii Press, Honolulu, HI pp 103–31

Ehrman M E and Dörnyei Z 1998 *Interpersonal dynamics in second language education: The visible and invisible classroom*. Sage, Thousand Oaks, CA

Ellis R 1994 *The study of second language acquisition*. Oxford University Press, Oxford

Ellis N 1996 Sequencing in SLA: Phonological memory, chunking, and points of order. *Studies in Second Language Acquisition* **18**: 91–126

Ely C M 1986 Language learning motivation: A descriptive causal analysis. *Modern Language Journal* **70**: 28–35

Erickson F 1986 Qualitative methods in research on teaching. In Wittrock M C (ed.) *Handbook of research on teaching*. Macmillan, New York pp 119–61

Evans C R and Dion K L 1991 Group cohesion and performance: A meta-analysis. *Small Group Research* **22**: 175–86

Færch C and Kasper G (eds) 1987 *Introspection in second language research*. Multilingual Matters, Clevedon

Ford M 1992 *Motivating humans: Goals, emotions and personal agency beliefs*. Sage, Newbury Park, CA

Forsyth D R 1998 *Group dynamics. 3rd edition*. Brooks/Cole, Pacific Grove, CA

Fotos S S 1994 Motivation in second language learning pedagogy: A critical review. *Senshu University Annual Bulletin of the Humanities* **24**: 29–54

Fraser B J and Walberg H J (eds) 1991 *Educational environments: Evaluation, antecedents and consequences*. Pergamon, Oxford

Freud S 1966 *The complete introductory lectures on psychoanalysis*. Norton, New York

Galloway D, Rogers C, Armstrong D and Leo E 1998 *Motivating the difficult to teach*. Longman, London

Gardner R C 1979 Social psychological aspects of second language acquisition. In Giles H and St. Clair R (eds) *Language and social psychology*. Blackwell, Oxford pp 193–220

Gardner R C 1985 *Social psychology and second language learning: The role of attitudes and motivation*. Edward Arnold, London

Gardner R C 1995 Interview with Jelena Mihaljeviç Djigunoviç. *Strani Jezici* **24**: 94–103

Gardner R C 1996 Motivation and second language acquisition: Perspectives. *Journal of the CAAL* **18**: 19–42

Gardner R C and Lambert W E 1959 Motivational variables in second language acquisition. *Canadian Journal of Psychology* **13**: 266–72

Gardner R C, Lambert W E 1972 *Attitudes and motivation in second language learning*. Newbury House, Rowley, MA

Gardner R C and MacIntyre P D 1991 An instrumental motivation in language study: Who says it isn't effective? *Studies in Second Language Acquisition* **13**: 57–72

Gardner R C and MacIntyre P D 1993a A student's contributions to second-language learning. Part II: Affective variables. *Language Teaching* **26**: 1–11

Gardner R C and MacIntyre P D 1993b On the measurement of affective variables in second language learning. *Language Learning* **43**: 157–94

Gardner R C, Masgoret A-M and Tremblay P F 1999 Home background characteristics and second language learning. *Journal of Language and Social Psychology* **18**: 419–37

Gardner R C and Smythe P C 1981 On the development of the Attitude/Motivation Test Battery. *Canadian Modern Language Review* **37**: 510–25

Gardner R C and Tremblay P F 1994a On motivation, research agendas and theoretical frameworks. *Modern Language Journal* **78**: 359–68

Gardner R C and Tremblay P F 1994b On motivation: Measurement and conceptual considerations. *Modern Language Journal* **78**: 524–7

Gardner R C, Tremblay P F and Masgoret, A-M 1997 Towards a full model of second language learning: An empirical investigation. *Modern Language Journal* **81**: 344–62

Gass S M and Selinker L 1994 *Second language acquisition: An introductory course*. Lawrence Erlbaum, Hillsdale, NJ

Gass S M and Varonis E 1994 Input, interaction and second language production. *Studies in Second Language Acquisition* **16**: 283–302

Geen R G 1995 *Human motivation: A social psychological approach*. Brooks/Cole, Pacific Grove, CA

Genesee F, Rogers P and Holobow N 1983 The social psychology of second language learning: Another point of view. *Language Learning* **33**: 209–24

Giles H and Byrne J L 1982 An intergroup approach to second language acquisition. *Journal of Multilingual and Multicultural Development* **3**: 17–40

Gollwitzer P M 1990 Action phases and mind-sets. In Higgins E T and Sorrentino R M (eds) *Handbook of motivation and cognition: Foundations of social behaviour. Vol. 2*. Guilford Press, New York pp 53–92

Good T L 1994 Teacher's expectations. In Husén T and Postlethwaite T N (eds) *The international encyclopedia of education. Vol. 10*. Pergamon, Oxford pp 6106–12

Good T L and Brophy J E 1994 *Looking in classrooms. 6th edition*. HarperCollins, New York

Gorham J and Christophel D M 1992 Students' perceptions of teacher behaviors as motivating and demotivating factors in college classes. *Communication Quarterly* **40**: 239–52

Gottfried A E, Fleming J S and Gottfried A W 1994 Role of parental motivational practices in children's academic intrinsic motivation and achievement. *Journal of Educational Psychology* **86**: 104–13

Graham S 1994 Classroom motivation from an attributional perspective. In O'Neil H F Jr and Drillings M (eds) *Motivation: Theory and research*. Lawrence Erlbaum, Hillsdale, NJ pp 31–48

Graham S and Weiner B 1996 Theories and principles of motivation. In Berliner D C and Calfee R C (eds) *Handbook of educational psychology*. Macmillan, New York pp 63–84

Green J M 1993 Student attitudes toward communicative and non-communicative activities: Do enjoyment and effectiveness go together? *Modern Language Journal* **77**: 1–10

Grotjahn R 1987 On the methodological basis of introspective methods. In Færch C and Kasper G (eds) *Introspection in second language research*. Multilingual Matters, Clevedon pp 54–81

Gully S M, Devine D J and Whitney D J 1995 A meta-analysis of cohesion and performance: Effects on level of analysis and task interdependence. *Small Group Research* **26**: 497–520

Hackman J R 1991 Work design. In Steers R M and Porter L W (eds) *Motivation and work behavior*. McGraw-Hill, New York pp 418–44

Hadfield J 1992 *Classroom Dynamics*. Oxford University Press, Oxford

Halmos B 1997 *Demotivation in foreign language learning: The learner level*. Unpublished MA thesis, Department of English Applied Linguistics, Eötvös University, Budapest, Hungary

Harwood J, Giles H and Bourhis R Y 1994 The genesis of vitality theory: Historical patterns and discoursal dimensions. *International Journal of the Sociology of Language* **108**: 167–206

Hatch E and Lazaraton A 1991 *The research manual*. Newbury House, New York

Heckhausen H 1991 *Motivation and action.* Springer, New York

Heckhausen H and Kuhl J 1985 From wishes to action: The dead ends and short cuts on the long way to action. In Frese M and Sabini J (eds) *Goal-directed behaviour: The concept of action in psychology.* Lawrence Erlbaum, Hillsdale, NJ

Hersey P and Blanchard K H 1988 *Management of organizational behavior. 5th edition.* Prentice Hall, Englewood Cliffs, NJ

Hersey P, Blanchard K H and Johnson D E 1996 *Management and organizational behavior: Utilizing human resources. 7th edition.* Prentice Hall, Englewood Cliffs, NJ

Hickey D T 1997 Motivation and contemporary socio-constructivist instructional perspectives. *Educational Psychologist* **32**: 175–193

Hogg M A and Abrams D (eds) 1993 *Group motivation: Social psychological perspectives.* Harvester Wheatsheaf, Hemel Hempstead

Horwitz E K 1988 The beliefs about language learning of beginning university foreign language students. *Modern Language Journal* **72**: 283–94

Horwitz E K, Horwitz M B and Cope J 1996 Foreign language classroom anxiety. *Modern Language Journal* **70**: 125–32

Hotho-Jackson S 1995 Motivation and group context: Tackling the drop-out factor. *Language Learning Journal* **11**: 20–3

Husband C and Saifullah Khan V 1982 The viability of ethnolinguistic vitality: Some creative doubts. *Journal of Multilingual and Multicultural development* **3**: 193–205

Husman J and Lens W 1999 The role of the future in student motivation. *Educational Psychologist* **34**: 113–25

Inbar O, Shohamy E and Donitsa-Schmidt S 1999 The effect of teaching spoken Arabic on students' attitudes, motivation and achievements. Paper presented at the AAAL '99 Convention, Stamford, March

Jesuíno J C 1996 Leadership: Micro-macro links. In Witte E H and Davis J H (eds) *Understanding group behaviour: Small group processes and interpersonal relations. Vol. 2.* Lawrence Erlbaum, Mahwah, NJ pp 93–125

Johnson P, Giles H and Bourhis R Y 1983 The viability of ethnolinguistic vitality: A reply. *Journal of Multilingual and Multicultural development* **4**: 255–69

Johnson D M 1992 *Approaches to research in second language learning.* Longman, New York

Johnston B 1997 Do EFL teachers have careers? *TESOL Quarterly* **31**: 681–712

Jones V F and Jones L S 1995 *Comprehensive classroom management: Creating positive learning environments for all students. 4th edition.* Allyn & Bacon, Needham Heights, MA

Julkunen K 1989 *Situation- and task-specific motivation in foreign-language learning and teaching.* University of Joensuu, Joensuu

Julkunen K 1993 On foreign language learning motivation in the classroom. In Tella S (ed.) *Kielestä mieltä – Mielekästä kieltä.* University of Helsinki, Teacher Education Department, Helsinki pp 70–8

Julkunen K and Borzova H 1997 *English language learning motivation in Joensuu and Petrozavodsk.* University of Joensuu, Joensuu

Juvonen J and Nishina A 1997 Social motivation in the classroom: Attributional accounts and developmental analysis. *Advances in Motivation and Achievement* **10**: 181–211

Juvonen Y and Wentzel K R (eds) 1996 *Social motivation: Understanding children's school adjustment.* Cambridge University Press, New York

Kanfer R 1996 Self-regulatory and other non-ability determinants of skill acquisition. In Gollwitzer P M and Bargh J A (eds) *The psychology of action: Linking cognition and motivation to behaviour*. Guilford Press, New York pp 404–23

Karniol R and Ross M 1996 The motivational impact of temporal focus: Thinking about the future and the past. *Annual Review of Psychology* **47**: 593–620

Kasper G 1998 Analysing verbal protocols. *TESOL Quarterly* **32**: 358–62

Kasper G and Kellerman E 1997 *Communication strategies: Psycholinguistic and sociolinguistic perspectives*. Longman, London

Keeves J P 1994 Longitudinal research methods. In Husén T and Postlethwaite T N (eds) *The international encyclopedia of education. 2nd edition. Vol. 6*. Pergamon, Oxford pp 3512–24

Keller J M 1983 Motivational design of instruction. In Reigelruth C M (ed.) *Instructional design theories and models: An overview of their current status*. Lawrence Erlbaum, Hillsdale, NJ pp 383–434

Keller J M 1994 Motivation in instructional design. In Husén T and Postlethwaite T N (eds) *The international encyclopedia of education. 2nd edition. Vol. 7*. Pergamon, Oxford pp 3943–7

Kelly C, Sachdev I, Kottsieper P and Ingram M 1993 The role of social identity in second-language proficiency and use: Testing the intergroup model. *Journal of Language and Social Psychology* **12**: 288–301

Kim Y M and Doyle T 1998 Factors affecting teacher motivation. Paper presented at the AAAL '98 Convention, Seattle, WA, March

Kohlmann K 1996 *Demotivating factors in learning English*. Unpublished MA thesis, Department of English Applied Linguistics, Eötvös University, Budapest, Hungary

Kormos J 1998 Verbal reports in L2 speech production research. *TESOL Quarterly* **32**: 353–8

Kormos J 1999 Monitoring and self-repair in L2. *Language Learning* **49**: 303–42

Kraemer R 1993 Social psychological factors related to the study of Arabic among Israeli high school students. *Studies in Second Language Acquisition* **15**: 83–105

Kruidenier B and Clément R 1986 *The effect of context on the composition and role of orientations in second language learning*. International Center for Research on Bilingualism, Québec

Kuhl J 1985 Volitional mediators of cognition-behaviour consistency: Self-regulatory processes and action versus state orientation. In Kuhl J and Beckmann J (eds) *Action control: From cognition to behaviour*. Springer, New York pp 101–28

Kuhl J 1986 Motivation and information processing: A new look at decision making, dynamic change, and action control. In Sorrentino R M and Higgins E T (eds) *Handbook of motivation and cognition: Foundations of social behaviour*. Guilford Press, New York pp 404–34

Kuhl J 1987 Action control: The maintenance of motivational states. In Halish F and Kuhl J (eds) *Motivation, intention and volition*. Springer, Berlin pp 279–91

Kuhl J 1992 A theory of self-regulation: Action versus state orientation, self-discrimination and some applications. *Applied Psychology: An International Review* **41**: 97–129

Kuhl J 1994 A theory of action and state orientations. In Kuhl J and Beckmann J (eds) *Volition and personality: Action versus state orientation*. Hogrefe & Huber, Seattle, WA pp 9–45

Kuhl J and Beckmann J (eds) 1994 *Volition and personality: Action versus state orientation.* Hogrefe & Huber, Seattle, WA

Kuhl J and Goschke T 1994 A theory of action control: Mental subsystems, modes of control and volitional conflict-resolution strategies. In Kuhl J and Beckmann J (eds) *Volition and personality: Action versus state orientation.* Hogrefe & Huber, Seattle, WA pp 93–124

Labrie N and Clément R 1986 Ethnolinguistic vitality, self-confidence and second language proficiency: An investigation. *Journal of Multilingual and Multicultural Development* **7**: 269–82

Laine E J 1995 *Learning second national languages: A research report.* Peter Lang, Frankfurt

Lalonde R N and Gardner R C 1993 Statistics as a second language? A model for predicting performance in psychology students. *Canadian Journal of Behavioural Science* **25**: 108–25

Lambert W E 1980 The social psychology of language: A perspective for the 1980s. In Giles H, Robinson W P and Smith P M (eds) *Language: Social psychological perspectives.* Pergamon, Oxford pp 415–24

Latham G P, Daghinghi S and Locke E A 1997 Implications of goal-setting theory for faculty motivation. In Bess J L (ed.) *Teaching well and liking it: Motivating faculty to teach effectively.* Johns Hopkins University Press, Baltimore pp 125–42

Lazaraton A 1995 Qualitative research in applied linguistics: A progress report. *TESOL Quarterly* **29**: 455–72

Levelt W J M 1989 *Speaking: From intention to articulation.* MIT Press, Cambridge, MA

Lewin K, Lippitt R and White R 1939 Patterns of aggressive behavior in experimentally created 'social climate'. *Journal of Psychology* **10**: 271–99

Little B L and Madigan R M 1997 The relationship between collective efficacy and performance in manufacturing work groups. *Small Group Research* **28**: 517–34

Little D 1991 *Learner autonomy 1: Definitions, issues and problems.* Authentik, Dublin

Littlewood W 1999 Defining and developing autonomy in East Asian contexts. *Applied Linguistics* **20**: 71–94

Locke E A 1996 Motivation through conscious goal setting. *Applied & Preventive Psychology* **5**: 117–24

Locke E A and Latham G P 1990 *A theory of goal setting and task performance.* Prentice Hall, Englewood Cliffs, NJ

Lortie D C 1975 *Schoolteacher: A sociological study.* University of Chicago Press, Chicago

Ludwig J 1983 Attitudes and expectations: A profile of female and male students of college French, German and Spanish. *Modern Language Journal* **67**: 216–27

Lukmani Y M 1972 Motivation to learn and language proficiency. *Language Learning* **22**: 261–73

MacFarlane A and Wesche M B 1995 Immersion outcomes: Beyond language proficiency. *Canadian Modern Language Review* **51**: 250–74

MacIntyre P D 1999 Language anxiety: A review of the research for language teachers. In Young D J (ed.) *Affect in foreign language and second language learning.* McGraw-Hill, Boston, MA pp 24–45

MacIntyre P D, Clément R, Dörnyei Z and Noels K A 1998 Conceptualizing willingness to communicate in a L2: A situated model of confidence and affiliation. *Modern Language Journal* **82**: 545–62

MacIntyre P D and Noels K A 1996 Using social-psychological variables to predict the use of language learning strategies. *Foreign Language Annals* **29**: 373–86

Maehr M L 1976 Continuing motivation. *Review of Educational Research* **46**: 443–62

Maehr M L and Braskamp L A 1986 *The motivation factor: A theory of personal investment*. Lexington Books, Lexington, MA

Maehr M L and Midgley C 1991 Enhancing student motivation: A schoolwide approach. *Educational Psychologist* **26**: 399–427

Maslow A H 1970 *Motivation and personality. 2nd edition*. Harper & Row, New York

McCaslin M and Good T L 1996 The informal curriculum. In Berliner D C and Calfee R C (eds) *Handbook of educational psychology*. Macmillan, New York pp 622–70

McCombs B L 1994 Strategies for assessing and enhancing motivation: Keys to promoting self-regulated learning and performance. In O'Neil H F Jr and Drillings M (eds) *Motivation: Theory and research*. Lawrence Erlbaum, Hillsdale, NJ pp 49–69

McCombs B L and Pope J E 1994 *Motivating hard to reach students*. American Psychological Association, Washington, DC

McCormick F G Jr 1994 *The power of positive teaching*. Krieger, Malabar, FL

McCracken G 1988 *The long interview*. Sage, Newbury Park, CA

McCroskey J C and Richmond V P 1991 Willingness to communicate: A cognitive view. In Booth-Butterfield M (ed.) *Communication, cognition and anxiety*. Sage, Newbury Park, CA pp 19–37

McGroarty M 1998 Constructive and constructivist challenges for applied linguistics. *Language Learning* **48**: 591–622

McInerney D M, Roche L A, McInerney V and Marsh H W 1997 Cultural perspectives on school motivation: The relevance and application of goal theory. *American Educational Research Journal* **34**: 207–36

McKeachie W J 1997 Wanting to be a good teacher: What have we learned to date? In Bess J L (ed.) *Teaching well and liking it: Motivating faculty to teach effectively*. Johns Hopkins University Press, Baltimore pp 19–36

McNamara T F 1996 *Measuring second language performance*. Longman, London

McNamara T F 1997 Theorizing social identity: What do we mean by social identity? Competing frameworks, competing discourses. *TESOL Quarterly* **31**: 561–67

Menard S 1991 *Longitudinal research*. Sage, Newbury Park, CA

Menzies I L 1959 The functioning of social systems as a defence against anxiety: A report on a study of the nursing service of a general hospital. *Human Relations* **13**: 95–121

Mihaljeviç J 1992 Attitudes towards the teacher as a factor in foreign language learning. *Studia Romanica et Anglica Zagrabiensia* **36–37**: 143–52

Morgan C 1993 Attitude change and foreign language culture learning. *Language Teaching* **26**: 63–75

Mowday R T and Nam S H 1997 Expectancy theory approaches to faculty motivation. In Bess J L (ed.) *Teaching well and liking it: Motivating faculty to teach effectively*. Johns Hopkins University Press, Baltimore pp 110–24

Mullen B and Copper C 1994 The relationship between group cohesiveness and performance: An integration. *Psychological Bulletin* **115**: 210–27

Nikolov M 1999 'Why do you learn English?' 'Because the teacher is short.' A study of Hungarian children's foreign language learning motivation. *Language Teaching Research* **3**: 33–56

Noels K A and Clément R 1996 Communication across cultures: Social determinants and acculturative consequences. *Canadian Journal of Behavioural Science* **28**: 214–28

Noels K A, Clément R and Pelletier L G 1999 Perceptions of teachers' communicative style and students' intrinsic and extrinsic motivation. *Modern Language Journal* **83**: 23–34

Noels K A, Pelletier L G, Clément R and Vallerand R J 2000 Why are you learning a second language? Motivational orientations and self-determination theory. *Language Learning* **50**: 57–85

Noels K A, Pon G and Clément R 1996 Language, identity and adjustment: The role of linguistic self-confidence in the acculturation process. *Journal of Language and Social Psychology* **15**: 246–64

Norton Pierce B 1995 Social identity, investment and language learning. *TESOL Quarterly* **29**: 9–31

Norton B 2000 *Identity and language learning: Social processes and educational practice.* Longman, London

Nunnally J C 1978 *Psychometric theory.* McGraw-Hill, New York

Oller J W Jr and Perkins K 1978a Intelligence and language proficiency as sources of variance in self-reported affective variables. *Language Learning* **28**: 85–97

Oller J W Jr and Perkins K 1978b A further comment on language proficiency as a source of variance in self-reported affective variables. *Language Learning* **28**: 417–23

O'Malley J M and Chamot A U 1990 *Learning strategies in second language acquisition.* CUP, New York and Cambridge

Operario D and Fiske S T 1999 Integrating social identity and social cognition: A framework for bridging diverse perspectives. In Abrams D and Hogg M A (eds) *Social identity and social cognition.* Blackwell, Oxford pp 26–54

Oppenheim A N 1992 *Questionnaire design, interviewing and attitude measurement. New edition.* Pinter, London

Oxford R L 1990 *Language learning strategies: What every teacher should know.* Heinle & Heinle, Boston, MA

Oxford R L 1994 Where are we with language learning motivation? *Modern Language Journal* **78**: 512–14

Oxford R L (ed.) 1996 *Language learning motivation: Pathways to the new century.* University of Hawaii Press, Honolulu

Oxford R L 1998 The unravelling tapestry: Teacher and course characteristics associated with demotivation in the language classroom. Demotivation in foreign language learning. Paper presented at the TESOL '98 Congress, Seattle, WA, March

Oxford R L and Shearin J 1994 Language learning motivation: Expanding the theoretical framework. *Modern Language Journal* **78**: 12–28

Oxford R L and Shearin J 1996 Language learning motivation in a new key. In Oxford R L (ed.) 1996 *Language learning motivation: Pathways to the new century.* University of Hawaii Press, Honolulu pp 155–87

Paris S G and Turner J C 1994 Situated motivation. In Pintrich P R, Brown D R and Weinstein C E (eds) *Student motivation, cognition and learning.* Lawrence Erlbaum, Hillsdale, NJ pp 213–37

Pedhazur E J and Schmelkin L P 1991 *Measurement, design and analysis: An integrated approach*. Lawrence Erlbaum, Hillsdale, NJ

Pennington M C 1995 *Work satisfaction, motivation and commitment in teaching English as a second language*. ERIC Document ED 404850

Pennycook A 1989 The concept of method, interested knowledge and the politics of language teaching. *TESOL Quarterly* **23**: 589–618

Phalet K and Lens W 1995 Achievement motivation and group loyalty among Turkish and Belgian youngsters. *Advances in Motivation and Achievement* **9**: 31–72

Pica T 1994 Research on negotiation: What does it reveal about second-language learning conditions, processes and outcomes? *Language Learning* **44**: 493–527

Pierson H D, Fu G S and Lee S 1980 An analysis of the relationship between language attitudes and English attainment of secondary students in Hong Kong. *Language Learning* **30**: 289–316

Pimsleur P 1966 *The Pimsleur Language Aptitude battery*. Harcourt, Brace, Jovanovitch, New York

Pinder C C 1997 *Work motivation in organizational behavior*. Prentice Hall, Englewood Cliffs, NJ

Pintrich P R and Maehr M L 1995 Culture, motivation and achievement: Foreword. *Advances in Motivation and Achievement* **9**: ix–xi

Pintrich P R and Schunk D H 1996 *Motivation in education: Theory, research and applications*. Prentice Hall, Englewood Cliffs, NJ

Pressley M and Harris K R 1994a Increasing the quality of educational intervention research. *Educational Psychology Review* **6**: 191–208

Pressley M and Harris K R 1994b More about increasing the quality of educational intervention research: A synthesis. *Educational Psychology Review* **6**: 271–89

Raffini J P 1993 *Winners without losers: Structures and strategies for increasing student motivation to learn*. Allyn & Bacon, Needham Heights, MA

Raffini J P 1996 *150 ways to increase intrinsic motivation in the classroom*. Allyn & Bacon, Needham Heights, MA

Rampton B 1995 *Crossing: Language and ethnicity among adolescents*. Longman, London

Raynor J O 1974a Future orientation in the study of achievement motivation. In Atkinson J W and Raynor J O (eds) *Motivation and achievement*. Winston & Sons, Washington, DC pp 121–54

Raynor J O 1974b Motivation and career striving. In Atkinson J W and Raynor J O (eds) *Motivation and achievement*. Winston & Sons, Washington, DC pp 369–87

Raynor J O and Entin E E 1983 The function of future orientation as a determinant of human behaviour in step-path theory of action. *International Journal of Psychology* **18**: 464–87

Raynor J O and Roeder G P 1987 Motivation and future orientation: Task and time effects for achievement motivation. In Halish F and Kuhl J (eds) *Motivation, intention and volition*. Springer, Berlin pp 61–71

Reid J 1997 *Centering on the learner*. Prentice Hall Regents, Englewood Cliffs, NJ

Reilly P J 1994 *The effect of teacher strategies on students' motivation levels in English language classrooms*. Unpublished MA thesis. Department of Education, The University of the Americas, Mexico City

Richmond V P 1990 Communication in the classroom: Power and motivation. *Communication Education* **39**: 181–95

Roger D, Bull P and Fletcher Y 1981 The construction and validation of a questionnaire for measuring attitudes towards learning foreign languages. *Educational Review* **33**: 223–30

Rogers C 1961 *On becoming a person.* Houghton Mifflin, Boston, MA

Rosenthal R and Jacobson L 1968 *Pygmalion in the classroom.* Holt, Rinehart & Winston, New York

Rubin H J and Rubin I S 1995 *Qualitative interviewing: The art of hearing data.* Sage, Thousand Oaks, CA

Rubin E B and Rubin A M 1992 Antecedents of interpersonal communication motivation. *Communication Quarterly* **40**: 305–17

Rudnai Z 1996 *Demotivation in learning English among secondary school students in Budapest.* Unpublished MA thesis, Department of English Applied Linguistics, Eötvös University, Budapest, Hungary

Rueda R and Dembo M H 1995 Motivational processes in learning: A comparative analysis of cognitive and sociocultural frameworks. *Advances in Motivation and Achievement* **9**: 255–89

Schmidt R 1992 Psychological mechanisms underlying second language fluency. *Studies in Second Language Acquisition* **14**: 357–85

Schmidt R (ed.) 1995 *Attention and awareness in foreign language learning.* University of Hawaii Press, Honolulu, HI

Schmidt R, Boraie D and Kassabgy O 1996 Foreign language motivation: Internal structure and external connections. In Oxford R (ed.) *Language learning motivation: Pathways to the new century.* University of Hawaii Press, Honolulu, HI pp 9–70

Schmitt N 1997 Vocabulary learning strategies. In Schmitt N and McCarthy M (eds) *Vocabulary: Decription, acquisition and pedagogy.* Cambridge University Press, Cambridge pp 199–227

Schmuck R A and Schmuck P A 1997 *Group processes in the classroom. 7th edition.* Brown & Benchmark, Dubuque, IA

Schneider B, Csikszentmihalyi M and Knauth S 1995 Academic challenge, motivation and self-esteem: The daily experience of students in high school. In Hallinan M T (ed.) *Restructuring schools: Promising practices and policies.* Plenum, New York pp 175–95

Schrank W 1968 The labelling effect of ability grouping. *Journal of Educational Research* **62**: 51–2

Schumann J H 1978 The acculturation model for second language acquisition. In Gingras R (ed.) *Second language acquisition and foreign language teaching.* Center for Applied Linguistics, Arlington, VA pp 27–107

Schumann J H 1986 Research on the acculturation model for second language acquisition. *Journal of Multilingual and Multicultural Development* **7**: 379–92

Schumann J H 1998 *The neurobiology of affect in language.* Blackwell, Oxford

Schumann J H 2000 Learning as mental foraging. Paper presented at the AAAL Convention, Vancouver, Canada, March

Seliger H W and Shohamy E 1989 *Second language research methods.* Oxford University Press, Oxford

Sharan S and Shaulov A 1990 Cooperative learning, motivation to learn and academic achievement. In Sharan S (ed.) *Cooperative learning: Theory and research.* Praeger, New York pp 173–202

Silver W S and Bufanio K M 1996 The impact of group efficacy and group goals on group task performance. *Small Group Research* **27**: 347–59

Skehan P 1989 *Individual differences in second-language learning*. Edward Arnold, London

Skehan P 1991 Individual differences in second-language learning. *Studies in Second Language Acquisition* **13**: 275–98

Skehan P 1998a *A cognitive approach to language learning*. Oxford University Press, Oxford

Skehan P 1998b Task-based instruction. *Annual Review of Applied Linguistics* **18**: 268–86

Skehan P 1998c Processing perspectives to second language development, instruction, performance and assessment. *Working Papers in Applied Linguistics (Thames Valley University, London)* **4**: 70–88

Skehan P and Foster P 1997 Task type and task processing conditions as influences on foreign language performance. *Language Teaching Research* **1**: 185–211

Skehan P and Foster P 1999 The influence of task structure and processing conditions on narrative retellings. *Language Learning* **49**: 93–120

Slavin R E 1996 Research on cooperative learning and achievement: What we know, what we need to know. *Contemporary Educational Psychology* **21**: 43–69

Snow R E, Corno L and Jackson D N 1996 Individual differences in affective and conative functions. In Berliner D C and Calfee R C (eds) *Handbook of educational psychology*. Macmillan, New York pp 243–310

Snow R E and Jackson D N 1994 Individual differences in conation: Selected constructs and measures. In O'Neil H F Jr and Drillings M (eds) *Motivation: Theory and research*. Lawrence Erlbaum, Hillsdale, NJ pp 71–99

Sorrentino R M 1996 The role of conscious thought in a theory of motivation and cognition: The uncertainty orientation paradigm. In Gollwitzer P M and Bargh J A (eds) *The psychology of action: Linking cognition and motivation to behaviour*. Guilford Press, New York pp 619–44

Sparks R L and Ganshow L 1999 Native language skills, foreign language aptitude and anxiety about foreign language learning. In Young D J (ed.) 1999 *Affect in foreign language and second language learning*. McGraw-Hill, Boston, MA pp 169–90

Sparks R L, Ganshow L and Patton J 1995 Prediction of performance in first-year foreign language courses: Connections between native and foreign language learning. *Journal of Educational Psychology* **87**: 638–55

Speiller J 1988 Factors that influence high school students' decisions to continue or discontinue the study of French and Spanish after Levels II, III and IV. *Foreign Language Annals* **21**: 535–44

Stake R E 1995 *The art of case study research*. Sage, Thousand Oaks, CA

Steers R M and Porter L W 1991 *Motivation and work behavior*. McGraw-Hill, New York

Stipek D J 1996 Motivation and instruction. In: Berliner D C and Calfee R C (eds) *Handbook of educational psychology*. Macmillan, New York pp 85–113

Stroebe, W, Diehl M and Abakoumkin G 1996 Social compensation and the Köhler effect: Toward a theoretical explanation of motivation gains in group productivity. In Witte E H and Davies J H (eds) *Understanding group behaviour: Small group processes and interpersonal relations. Vol. 2*. Lawrence Erlbaum, Mahwah, NJ pp 37–65

Swezey R W, Meltzer A L and Salas E 1994 Some issues involved in motivating teams. In O'Neil H F Jr and Drillings M (eds) *Motivation: Theory and research.* Lawrence Erlbaum, Hillsdale, NJ pp 141–69

Tajfel H 1978 Intergroup behaviour II: Group perspectives. In Tajfel H and Fraser C (eds) *Introducing social psychology: An analysis of individual reaction and response.* Penguin, Harmondsworth pp 423–46

Terry D J, Hogg M A and Duck J M 1999 Group membership, social identity and attitudes. In Abrams D and Hogg M A (eds) *Social identity and social cognition.* Blackwell, Oxford pp 280–314

Tremblay P F and Gardner R C 1995 Expanding the motivation construct in language learning. *Modern Language Journal* 79: 505–20

Triandis H C 1995 Motivation and achievement in collectivist and individualist cultures. *Advances in Motivation and Achievement* 9: 1–30

Uguroglu M E and Walberg H J 1986 Predicting achievement and motivation. *Journal of Research and Development in Education* 19: 1–12

Urdan T C and Maehr M L 1995 Beyond a two-goal theory of motivation and achievement: A case for social goals. *Review of Educational Research* 65: 213–43

Ushioda E 1994 L2 motivation as a qualitative construct. *Teanga* 14: 76–84

Ushioda E 1996a *Learner autonomy 5: The role of motivation.* Authentik, Dublin

Ushioda E 1996b Developing a dynamic concept of motivation. In Hickey T and Williams J (eds) *Language, education and society in a changing world.* Multilingual Matters, Clevedon pp 239–45

Ushioda E 1997 The role of motivational thinking in autonomous language learning. In Little D and Voss B (eds) *Language centres: Planning for the new millennium.* CERCLES, Centre for Modern Languages, University of Plymouth, Plymouth pp 39–50

Ushioda E 1998 Effective motivational thinking: A cognitive theoretical approach to the study of language learning motivation. In Soler E A and Espurz V C (eds) *Current issues in English language methodology.* Universitat Jaume I, Castelló de la Plana, Spain pp 77–89

Vallerand R J 1997 Toward a hierarchical model of intrinsic and extrinsic motivation. *Advances in Experimental Social Psychology* 29: 271–360

Veenman S 1984 Perceived problems of beginning teachers. *Review of Educational Research* 54: 143–78

Walker C J and Symons C 1997 The meaning of human motivation. In Bess J L (ed.) *Teaching well and liking it: Motivating faculty to teach effectively.* Johns Hopkins University Press, Baltimore pp 3–18

Wallace M J 1998 *Action research for language teachers.* Cambridge University Press, Cambridge

Webb N M and Palincsar A S 1996 Group processes in the classroom. In D C Berliner and R C Calfee (eds) *Handbook of Educational Psychology.* Macmillan, New York pp 841–73

Weiner B 1984 Principles for a theory of student motivation and their application within an attributional framework. In Ames R and Ames C (eds) *Research on motivation in Education: Student motivation. Vol.1.* Academic Press, San Diego, CA pp 15–38

Weiner B 1986 Attribution, emotion and action. In Sorrentino R M and Higgins E T (eds) *Handbook of motivation and cognition: Foundations of social behaviour.* The Guilford Press, New York pp 281–312

Weiner B 1992 *Human motivation: Metaphors, theories and research*. Sage, Newbury Park, CA

Weiner B 1994 Integrating social and personal theories of achievement motivation. *Review of Educational research* **64**: 557–73

Weldon E and Weingart L R 1993 Group goals and group performance. *British Journal of Social Psychology* **32**: 307–34

Wen X 1997 Motivation and language learning with students of Chinese. *Foreign Language Annals* **30**: 235–51

Wenden A 1991 *Learner strategies for learner autonomy*. Prentice Hall, Hemel Hempstead

Wentzel K R 1999 Social-motivational processes and interpersonal relationships: Implications for understanding motivation at school. *Journal of Educational Psychology* **91**: 76–97

Wigfield A 1994 Expectancy-value theory of achievement motivation: A developmental perspective. *Educational Psychology Review* **6**: 49–78

Wigfield A, Eccles J S and Rodriguez D 1998 The development of children's motivation in school contexts. *Review of Research in Education* **23**: 73–118

Wild T C, Enzle M E and Hawkins W L 1992 Effects of perceived extrinsic versus intrinsic teacher motivation on student reactions to skill acquisition. *Personality and Social Psychology Bulletin* **19**: 245–51

Williams G 1992 *Sociolinguistics: A sociological critique*. Routledge, London

Williams M 1994 Motivation in foreign and second language learning: An interactive perspective. *Educational and Child Psychology* **11**: 77–84

Williams, M and Burden R 1997 *Psychology for language teachers*. Cambridge University Press, Cambridge

Williams M and Burden R 1999 Students' developing conceptions of themselves as language learners. *Modern Language Journal* **83**: 193–201

Winne P H and Marx R W 1989 A cognitive-processing analysis of motivation within classroom tasks. In Ames C and Ames, R, editors, *Research on motivation in education. Vol. 3: Goals and cognitions*. Academic Press, New York pp 223–57

Wittrock M C (ed.) 1996 *Handbook of research on teaching. 3rd edition*. Macmillan, New York pp 328–375

Wlodkowski R J 1986 *Enhancing adult motivation to learn*. Jossey-Bass, San Francisco, CA

Wolters C A 1998 Self-regulated learning and college students' regulation of motivation. *Journal of Educational Psychology* **90**: 224–35

Wong M M and Csikszentmihalyi M 1991 Motivation and academic achievement: The effects of personality traits and the quality of experience. *Journal of Personality* **59**: 539–74

Young D J (ed.) 1999 *Affect in foreign language and second language learning*. McGraw-Hill, Boston, MA

Zimmerman B J 1994 Dimensions of academic self-regulation: A conceptual framework for education. In Schunk D H and Zimmerman B J (eds) *Self-regulation of learning and performance: Issues and educational applications*. Lawrence Erlbaum, Hillsdale, NJ pp 3–21

Author Index

Subject Index

Page numbers in bold refer to definitions or key discussions of the particular concept.